20th Century

Original Edition edited by

A J P Taylor MA FBA (Editor-in-Chief)

Fellow of Magdalen College, University of Oxford

J M Roberts MA DPhil (General Editor)

Fellow and Tutor at Merton College, University of Oxford

1979 Edition revised by
Editor
R. W. Cross
Assistant Editors
Lesley Toll, John Moore
Designer
John Clement

PURNELL REFERENCE BOOKS

Milwaukee · Toronto · Melbourne · London

Volume 5

Reference edition copyright © 1979
Purnell Reference Books, a division of
MacDonald Raintree, Inc. Last previous
edition copyright © 1973 Phoebus Publishing
Company.

Library of Congress Cataloging in Publication Data

Main entry under title:

20th century.

   Edition for 1971 published under title: Purnell's
history of the 20th century.
   Bibliography: p.
   1. History, Modern — 20th century. I. Taylor,
Alan John Percivale, 1906–   II. Roberts, James
Morris, 1928–   III. Cross, R. W.   IV. Purnell's
history of the 20th century.
D421.P87   1979   909.82   78-27424
ISBN 0-8393-6079-7 lib. bdg.
ISBN 0-8393-6080-0 trade

Authors in this Volume

Corelli Barnett	Military historian
Hugh Brogan	Lecturer in History, University of Essex
Colin Cross	Education Correspondent, *The Observer* newspaper, London
Christopher Falkus	Publishing Director and Deputy Chairman, Weidenfeld and Nicolson Publishers, London
Robert H. Ferrell	Author specializing in the history of American diplomacy
Constantine FitzGibbon	Author and biographer
David Floyd	Special Correspondent on Communist Affairs, *The Daily Telegraph* newspaper, London
Alexander Grunt	Senior member of the History Staff, Moscow State University
Alistair Horne	Author and journalist; Founder of the A. Horne Resident Fellowship in Modern History, St. Antony's College, Oxford
Geoffrey A. Hosking	Lecturer in History, University of Essex
George Katkov	Former Fellow and Lecturer in Soviet Institutions, St. Antony's College, University of Oxford
K.H. Janssen	Journalist with *Die Zeit* newspaper, Hamburg
Arthur S. Link	George Henry Davis Professor of American History, University of Princeton
Michael Llewellyn Smith	Author of *The Great Island—A Study of Crete* and contributor to *The Spectator* magazine, London
Major-General James Lunt	Domestic Bursar and Fellow, Wadham College, University of Oxford
Kenneth Morgan	Fellow in Modern History and Politics, The Queen's College, University of Oxford
C.L. Mowat	Former Professor of History, University College of North Wales
Antony Polonsky	Formerly Lecturer in Politics, University of Strathclyde
J.M. Roberts	Fellow and Tutor, Merton College, University of Oxford
T.G. Rosenthal	Managing Director, Secker and Warburg Publishing Company, London
Wolfgang Steglich	Lecturer in Modern and Contemporary History, University of Freiburg
David Thornley	Fellow and Associate Professor of Political Science, University of Dublin
J.N. Westwood	Senior Lecturer in History, University of Sydney
Elizabeth Wiskemann	Author; formerly Tutor in Modern European History, University of Sussex

Contents

Chapter 21
562 Verdun and the Somme/Alistair Horne
577 The Brusilov Offensive/J.N. Westwood
581 Britain Organizes for Total War/C.L. Mowat
586 The New Leaders:
Lloyd George/Kenneth Morgan
Clemenceau/J.M. Roberts
Ludendorff/K.H. Janssen

Chapter 22
590 The Arabs and Lawrence/Major-General James Lunt
596 The Easter Rising/Constantine FitzGibbon
609 Four Nationalist Leaders:
de Valera/David Thornley
Venizelos/Michael Llewellyn Smith
Masaryk/Elizabeth Wiskemann
Pilsudski/Antony Polonsky
615 India at War/Christopher Falkus

Chapter 23
618 The Meaning of Total War/Colin Cross
623 Women at Work and War/Louise Black
628 War and the Artist/T.G. Rosenthal
634 The Dominions at War/Christopher Falkus
641 The War Poets/Michael Llewellyn Smith

Chapter 24
646 The Fatal Decision/Wolfgang Steglich
652 Wilson and the Ordeal of Neutrality/Arthur S. Link
657 The American People and the War/Hugh Brogan
663 Declaration of War/Robert H. Ferrell
667 The New Military Balance/Correlli Barnett

Chapter 25
674 Russia at War/Alexander Grunt
689 Rasputin and the 'Dark Forces'/Geoffrey A. Hosking
692 Overthrow of the Tsar/David Floyd
695 Kerensky's Summer/George Katkov

Chapter 21

Introduction by J.M.Roberts

In 1916, each of the main combatant nations made great efforts to achieve a decisive victory. Each failed, with huge losses, although the Russians had the greatest partial success. But the effort exhausted the Tsarist army. The Russian soldier was already bowing under the strain of two and a half years' warfare with inadequate supplies, bad planning, a depleted officer corps, a shattered transport system, and a chronic shortage of weapons and ammunition. After their last great success under Brusilov, the exhausted Russian armies were suddenly called to cover a new front extending to the Black Sea. It was to be too much. The battles on the Eastern Front in 1916 are analysed by J.N.Westwood in **The Brusilov Offensive**.

The Russian effort, though followed by disappointment, had probably saved the French army. Alistair Horne, in **Verdun and the Somme**, describes the terrible fighting of the summer in the west. The German strategy of deliberately destroying the French will to fight in a great battle of attrition at Verdun came near to success. The diversion of troops to face Brusilov was one factor thwarting it. Another was the persistence of the British army in sustaining its offensive on the Somme in the teeth of enormous losses. Both these battles were to leave scars for decades to come. The memory of the forts of Verdun inspired the faith in the passive strategy of the Maginot line, and Great Britain's generals in the Second World War were determined that the British army should never again squander its blood as it had done in 1916.

By the autumn the war was beginning to wear out men and institutions under which it had opened. The implications for Great Britain are described by C.L.Mowat in **Britain Organizes for Total War**; the old, unchallenged assumptions about government and the economy were one by one found inadequate to maintain the struggle. New leaders were needed, too. In this Chapter there are the profiles of the three under whom Great Britain, France, and Germany were to fight out the rest of the war. **Ludendorff** was the first to take power, though his virtual dictatorship came to an end just before the end of the war, because he preferred to resign before he was associated with defeat. His opponents, **Lloyd George** and **Clemenceau**, were both veteran politicians, not soldiers. Both had radical backgrounds and both inspired much distrust. Yet both also succeeded in inspiring their countrymen as others had failed to do, and in convincing them that after terrible suffering they could still win the war. With warfare no longer a matter of professional armies, but demanding the physical and psychological mobilization of whole populations, theirs was a decisive contribution.

Ambulance at German field hospital is wrecked during a British bombardment,

German cartoon derides Brusilov's offensive. He examines tree of victory with neutrals

Girl munition workers parading for Lloyd George when he visited Wales, August 1918

Great Britain

1914 8th August: Defence of the Realm Act gives government wide measure of control over persons and property; government takes control of the railways.
November: employers and unions sign the Crayford Agreement on 'dilution' of labour.

1915 March: Treasury Agreement clears up union opposition to 'dilution' by providing safeguards.
25th May: Asquith government reorganized as a coalition; the War Committee takes over the conduct of the war; Lloyd George becomes minister in the new ministry of munitions.
July: coal miners in South Wales go on strike.
June: legislation controls licensing hours of public houses.
During the year seventy-three 'national factories' are built, and the government takes control of the meat exports of Australia and New Zealand.

1916 January: conscription of unmarried men introduced.
March: industrial troubles on the Clyde lead to the arrest and deportation of the leaders of the Clyde Workers' Committee.
May: Conscription extended to married men.
1st December: South Wales coalfield put under government control.
7th December: Lloyd George becomes prime minister; he forms the War Cabinet and creates the ministries of labour, food, and shipping.

1917 1st January: food production ministry created to encourage agriculture.
March: all coal mines put under control of the Coal Controller.
March: prime ministers of the Dominions assemble as the Imperial War Cabinet.

1918 April: government takes over flour mills.

Western Front

1915 2nd December: Joffre appointed supreme commander of the French forces.
6th December: Joffre holds conference of Allied commanders; plans are formed to co-ordinate a summer offensive.

1916 21st February: Germans begin bombardment of Verdun and first assault troops move forward.
22nd February: main German infantry attacks Verdun.
24th February: second line of the French defences falls.
25th February: Radtke takes fort of Douaumont just outside Verdun.
May: the Germans finish clearing the left bank of the Meuse.
2nd June: Germans take Fort Vaux.
5th June: Kitchener lost in *HMS Hampshire*.
26th June: Haig's preliminary bombardment of the Somme begins.
1st July: British attack on the Somme begins.
11th July: Germans make last assault on Verdun.
14th July: Rawlinson attacks by night.
30th August: after Falkenhayn's resignation, Hindenburg appointed German chief of staff.
15th September: Haig decides to use tanks in third major Somme offensive; they are all scattered or destroyed.
2nd November: French recapture Douaumont and Vaux.
13th November: British take Beaumont-Hamel.
18th November: battle of the Somme ends.
12th December: Nivelle replaces Joffre.
18th December: battle of Verdun ends.

Eastern Front

1916 19th March-30th April: after battle of Lake Naroch Russians withdraw with heavy losses.
14th April: Tsar replaces Ivanov with Brusilov; Brusilov proposes an attack on all fronts.
15th May-3rd June: Austrians make successful offensive against the Italians in the Trentino.
4th June: Brusilov's Offensive is launched.
8th June: Brusilov takes Lutsk.
9th June: Evert informs Brusilov that he will postpone his attack until 18th June.
18th June: instead of attacking towards Wilno, Evert moves south towards Baranowicze; he is then sent to join Brusilov.
10th August: Brusilov Offensive comes to an end.
17th August: Rumania signs alliance with Russia.
27th August: Rumanian troops strike north towards Transylvania, and in early September take Hermannstadt and Kronstadt.
7th-9th October: Austro-German forces retake Kronstadt.
23rd October: Mackensen takes Constanta.
6th December: Germans take Bucharest; Rumanians hemmed in area around Jassy.

Verdun and the Somme

Few before the First World War could have visualized the atrocious slaughter that was to take place at Verdun and the Somme. The total of British, French, and German dead, wounded, and missing in these battles was well over 1,500,000. Other casualties were the French and German commanders, the British and French prime ministers —and most of the idealism left in the war

The year 1916 was the watershed of the First World War. Beyond it all rivers ran in changed directions. It was the year that saw German hopes of outright victory vanish, and the Allied prospects of winning the war with their existing tactics and resources—without the United States— disappear. It was the last year in which Russia would be a powerful military force, and by the end of it Great Britain would have assumed the principal burden on the Western Front. It was also the last year in which the 'Old World' of pre-1914 still had a chance of surviving by means of a negotiated, 'stalemate' peace; it would have been as good a year as any to have ended the war. Finally, 1916 was the year of heavy guns, and—with the exception of the cataclysm of 1918—the year that brought the highest casualty lists.

On land in 1916 there were two battles which more than any others came to symbolize the First World War for the post-war generation: Verdun and the Somme. Verdun was the occasion of Germany's only deviation—between 1915 and 1918— from her profitable strategy of standing on the defensive in the west and letting the Allies waste themselves against an almost impregnable line at unimaginable cost.

By the end of 1915 deadlock had been reached along a static front stretching from Switzerland to the Channel. The Germans had failed, at the Marne (Vol. 4, p. 456), to win the war by one hammer blow against their numerically superior enemies, while suffering three-quarters of a million casualties. In attempting to repulse them from her soil, France had lost 300,000 killed and another 600,000 wounded, captured, and missing. Great Britain's naval might had proved impotent to wrest the Dardanelles from Turkey. Isolated Russia staggered on from defeat to defeat, yet still the Central powers could not bring the war to a decision in the limitless spaces of the east.

But on neither side had these early losses and disillusions impaired the will to fight on. Civilian resolution matched military morale. The opposing troops of France and Germany were no longer the green enthusiasts of 1914, nor yet the battle-weary veterans of 1917-18; they represented the best the war was to produce. In the munitions industries of both sides, artillery programmes had also reached a peak. In Great Britain Kitchener's army of conscripts was about to replace the lost 'First Hundred Thousand'. On 2nd December, 1915, Joffre, the 'vic-

tor of the Marne', was appointed supreme commander of French military forces throughout the world. A sixty-three year-old engineer with little experience of handling infantry, he was now incomparably the most powerful figure on the Allied side and his new ascendancy enabled him to concentrate everything on the Western Front. Four days later Joffre held an historic conference of the Allied commanders at his HQ in Chantilly. From it sprang plans for a co-ordinated offensive by all the allies the following summer. By then, for the first time, there would be an abundance of men, heavy guns, and ammunition. The principal component of this offensive would be a Franco-British 'push' astride the river Somme. Forty French and twenty-five British divisions would be involved. There were no strategic objectives behind this sector of the front; Joffre's principal reason for selecting it was his instinct that he could be most assured of full British participation if they went over the top arm in arm with the French— 'bras dessus bras dessous'.

Sir Douglas Haig, who had also just taken over command of the British forces in France from General French, would have preferred to attack in Flanders (a preference which was to reassert itself with disastrous consequences a year later). However, after a meeting with Joffre on 29th December, he allowed himself to be won over to the Somme strategy. But on the other side of the lines, the chief of the German general staff, General Erich von Falkenhayn—a strange compound of ruthlessness and indecision—had his own plans. The Germans were to beat the Allies to the draw.

To bleed France white

Prospects would never again seem so bright for German arms as at the close of 1915. In mid-December Falkenhayn prepared a lengthy memorandum for the Kaiser in which he argued that the only way to achieve victory was to cripple the Allies' main instrument, the French army, by luring it into the defence of an indefensible position. Verdun, perched precariously at the tip of a long salient, about 130 air miles south-east of where Joffre intended to attack on the Somme and just 150 miles due east of Paris, fulfilled all of Falkenhayn's requirements.

Verdun's history as a fortified camp stretched back to Roman times, when Attila had found it worth burning. In the 17th century Louis XIV's great ▷ **565**

Opposite page: Verdun burning, 26th March 1916. A painting by François Flameng. Below: French soldier wearing gas mask mounts guard at an entrance to Fort Souville, Verdun. The fort, part of the main French defence line on the east bank of the Meuse, consistently defied capture

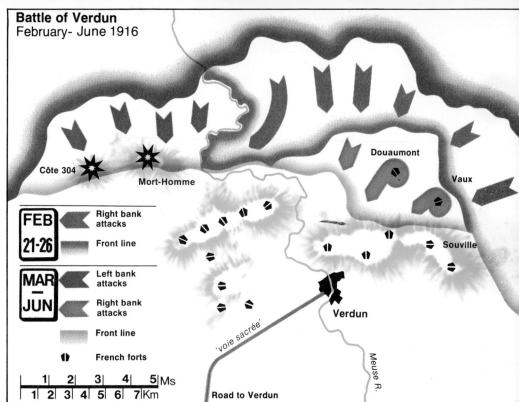

Battle of Verdun
February– June 1916

Côte 304
Mort-Homme
Douaumont
Vaux
Souville
Verdun
'voie sacrée'
Meuse R.
Road to Verdun

FEB 21-26	Right bank attacks
	Front line
MAR – JUN	Left bank attacks
	Right bank attacks
	Front line
	French forts

| 1 | 2 | 3 | 4 | 5 | Ms |
| 1 | 2 | 3 | 4 | 5 | 6 | 7 | Km |

1 Raemaekers cartoon. Crown Prince Wilhelm tells his father: 'We must have a higher pile to see Verdun.' 2 The battle-ground. 3 German soldier using a flame-thrower at Verdun. By Max Rabes

engineer, Vauban, had made Verdun the most powerful fortress in his cordon protecting France; in the Franco-Prussian War of 1870 it had been the last of the great French strongholds to fall, surviving Sedan, Metz, and Strasbourg. After 1870 it had become the key bastion in the chain of fortresses guarding France's frontier with Germany. In 1914, Verdun had provided an unshakable pivot for the French line, and without it Joffre might not have been able to stand on the Marne and save Paris.

From his knowledge both of her history and character, Falkenhayn calculated that France would be forced to defend this semi-sacred citadel to the last man. By menacing Verdun with a modest outlay of only nine divisions, he expected to draw the main weight of the French army into the salient, where German heavy artillery would grind it to pieces from three sides.

In Falkenhayn's own words, France was thus to be 'bled white'. It was a conception totally novel to the history of war and one that, in its very imagery, was symptomatic of that Great War where, in their callousness, leaders could regard human lives as mere corpuscles.

The V Army, commanded by the Kaiser's heir, the Crown Prince, was appointed to conduct the victorious operation. Day and night the great cannon and their copious munition trains now began to flow toward the V Army from all other German fronts. Aided by the railways behind their front and the national genius for organization, preparations moved with astonishing speed and secrecy. By the beginning of February 1916 more than 1,200 guns were in position—for an assault frontage of barely eight miles. More than 500 were 'heavies', including 13 of the 420mm 'Big Bertha mortars', the 'secret weapon' of 1914 which had shattered the supposedly impregnable Belgian forts. Never before had such a concentration of artillery been seen.

Verdun lay less than ten miles up the tortuous Meuse from the German lines. Most of its 15,000 inhabitants had departed when the war reached its gates in 1914, and its streets were now filled with troops, but this was nothing new for a city which had long been a garrison town.

In notable contrast to the featureless open country of Flanders and the Somme, Verdun was surrounded by interlocking patterns of steep hills and ridges which provided immensely strong natural lines of defence. The key heights were studded with three concentric rings of mighty underground forts, totalling no less than twenty major and forty intermediary works. Each was superbly sited so that its guns could dislodge any enemy infantry appearing on the superstructure of its neighbour. With concrete carapaces eight feet thick,

staunch enough to resist even the German 'Big Berthas', some of the major forts—such as Douaumont—were equipped with heavy artillery and machine-guns firing from retractable steel turrets. Outlying blockhouses linked by subterranean passages made them able to repel an attack from whatever direction it might come, and in their shell-proof cellars each could house as much as a battalion of infantry.

These forts lay between five and ten miles from Verdun itself. Between them and no man's land stretched a protective network of trenches, redoubts, and barbed wire such as was to be found throughout the whole length of the Western Front. Verdun deserved its reputation as the world's most powerful fortress. In theory.

In fact—despite, or perhaps because of, its reputation—by February 1916, Verdun's defences were in a lamentable state. The fate of the Belgian forts had persuaded Joffre to evacuate the infantry garrisons from the Verdun forts, and remove many of their guns. The troops themselves had become slack, lulled by many months spent in so quiet and 'safe' a sector, whose deceptive calm was deepened by the influence of one of the nastiest, rainiest, foggiest, and most enervating climates in France. The French soldier has never been renowned for his ardour for digging in, and the forward lines of trenches at Verdun compared poorly with the immensely deep earthworks the Germans had constructed at their key points on the Western Front. And, in contrast to the seventy-two battalions of elite storm troops, the Crown Prince held ready for the attack, the French trenches were manned by only thirty-four battalions, some of which were second-class units.

One outstanding French officer, Lieutenant Colonel Emile Driant, who commanded two battalions of *chasseurs* in the very tip of the salient, actually warned the French high command of the impending attack and the bad state of the Verdun defences. For this impertinence, his knuckles were severely rapped; the imperturbable Joffre paid little attention.

'Sauve qui peut!'

After a nine-day delay caused by bad weather (the first serious setback to German plans), the bombardment began at dawn on 21st February. For nine appalling hours it continued. Even on the shell-saturated Western Front nothing like it had ever been experienced. The poorly prepared French trenches were obliterated, many of their defenders buried alive. Among the units to bear the brunt of the shelling were Driant's *chasseurs*.

At 4 that afternoon the bombardment lifted and the first German assault troops

moved forward out of their concealed positions. This was, in fact, but a strong patrol action, testing like a dentist's probe for the weakest areas of the French front. In most places it held. The next morning, the brutal bombardment began again. It seemed impossible that any human being could have survived in that methodically worked-over soil. Yet some had, and, with a heroic tenacity that was to immortalize the French defence during the long months ahead, they continued to face the unseen enemy from what remained of their trenches.

On the afternoon of 22nd February the Germans' first main infantry wave went in. The defenders' front line buckled.

General Philippe Pétain in 1916. From warrior-hero he later turned defeatist

Driant was shot through the head while withdrawing the remnants of his *chasseurs*. Of these two battalions, 1,200 strong, a handful of officers and about 500 men, many of them wounded, were all that eventually straggled back to the rear. But the French resistance once again caused the German storm troops to be pulled back, to await a third softening-up bombardment the following morning.

On 23rd February, there were signs of mounting confusion and alarm at the various HQs before Verdun. Telephone lines were cut by the shelling; runners were not getting through; whole units were disappearing from the sight of their commanders. Order and counter-order were followed by the inevitable consequence. One by one the French batteries were falling silent, while others shelled their own positions, in the belief that these had already been abandoned to the enemy.

24th February was the day the dam burst. A fresh division, flung in piecemeal, broke under the bombardment, and the whole of the second line of the French defences fell within a matter of hours. ▷ **566**

*Below: German troops at Verdun
scramble up the soft earth of a devastated
trench to launch a grenade attack*

During that disastrous day, German gains equalled those of the first three days put together. By the evening it looked as if the war had again become one of movement—for the first time since the Marne.

Between the attackers and Verdun, however, there still lay the lines of the forts—above all, Douaumont, the strongest of them all, a solid bulwark of comfort behind the backs of the retreating *poilus*. Then, on 25th February, the Germans pulled off—almost in a fit of absent-mindedness—one of their greatest coups of the entire war. Acting on their own initiative, several small packets of the 24th Brandenburg Regiment, headed by a twenty-four-year-old lieutenant, Eugen Radtke (who, though seriously wounded later on, still lives in Berlin today), worked their way into Douaumont without losing a man. To their astonishment, they discovered the world's most powerful fort to be virtually undefended.

In Germany church bells rang throughout the country to acclaim the capture of Douaumont. In France its surrender was rightly regarded as a national disaster of the first magnitude (later reckoned to have cost France the equivalent of 100,000 men). Through the streets of Verdun itself survivors of broken units ran shouting, *'Sauve qui peut!'*

At his headquarters in Chantilly even Joffre had at last become impressed by the urgency of events. To take over the imminently threatened sector, he dispatched Henri Philippe Pétain, France's outstanding expert in the art of the defensive. No general possessed the confidence of the *poilu* more than Pétain. Now—in tragic irony—this uniquely humanitarian leader was called upon to subject his men to what was becoming the most inhuman conflict of the whole war. Pétain's orders were to hold Verdun, 'whatever the cost'.

But the German attack was beginning to bog down. Losses had already been far heavier than Falkenhayn had anticipated, many of them inflicted by flanking fire from French guns across the Meuse. The German lines looped across the river to the north of Verdun, and, from the very first, the Crown Prince had urged that his V Army be allowed to attack along both banks simultaneously. But Falkenhayn—determined to keep his own outlay of infantry in the 'bleeding white' strategy down to the barest minimum—had refused, restricting operations to the right bank. Now, to clear the menace of the French artillery, Falkenhayn reluctantly agreed to extend the offensive across to the left bank, releasing for this purpose another army corps from his tightly hoarded reserves. The deadly escalation of Verdun was under way.

Mission of sacrifice

The lull before the next phase of the German offensive enabled Pétain to stabilize the front to an almost miraculous extent. He established a road artery to Verdun, later known as the Voie Sacrée, along which the whole lifeblood of France was to pour, to reinforce the threatened city; during the critical first week of March alone 190,000 men marched up it.

The Crown Prince now launched a new all-out attack along the left bank toward a small ridge called the Mort-Homme, which, with its sinister name, acquired from some long-forgotten tragedy of another age, was to be the centre of the most bitter, see-saw fighting for the better part of the next three months. On this one tiny sector a monotonous, deadly pattern was establishing that continued almost without let-up. It typified the whole battle of Verdun. After hours of saturating bombardment, the German assault troops would surge forward to carry what remained of the French front line. There were no longer any trenches; what the Germans occupied were for the most part clusters of shell holes, where isolated groups of men lived and slept and died defending their 'position' with grenade and pick helve.

'You have a mission of sacrifice,' ran the typical orders that one French colonel gave to his men. 'Here is a post of honour

where they want to attack. Every day you will have casualties . . . On the day they want to, they will massacre you to the last man, and it is your duty to fall.'

At Verdun most fell without ever having seen the enemy, under the murderous non-stop artillery bombardment, which came to characterize this battle perhaps more than any other. 'Verdun is terrible,' wrote French Sergeant-Major César Méléra, who was killed a fortnight before the armistice, 'because man is fighting against material, with the sensation of striking out at empty air . . .' Describing the effects of a bombardment, Paul Dubrulle, a thirty-four-year-old Jesuit serving as an infantry sergeant (also later killed), said: 'The most solid nerves cannot resist for long; the moment arrives where the blood mounts to the head; where fever burns the body and where the nerves, exhausted, become incapable of reacting . . . finally one abandons oneself to it, one has no longer even the strength to cover oneself with one's pack as protection against splinters, and one scarcely still has left the strength to pray to God.'

Despite the heroic sacrifices of Pétain's men, each day brought the sea of *Feldgrau* a few yards closer to Verdun. By the end of March, French losses totalled 89,000; but the attackers had also lost nearly 82,000 men. Even once they had taken the Mort-Homme, the Germans found themselves hamstrung by French guns on the Côte 304, another ridge still farther out on the flank. Like a surgeon treating galloping cancer, Falkenhayn's knife was enticed ever farther from the original point of application. More fresh German divisions were hurled into the battle—this time to seize Côte 304.

Not until May was the German 'clearing' operation on the left bank of the Meuse at last completed. The final push towards Verdun could begin. But the Crown Prince was now for calling off the offensive, and even Falkenhayn's enthusiasm was waning. The strategic significance of Verdun had long since passed out of sight; yet the battle had somehow achieved a demonic existence of its own, far beyond the control of generals of either nation. Honour had become involved to an extent which made disengagement impossible. On the French side, Pétain—affected (too deeply, according to Joffre) by the horrors he had witnessed—was promoted and replaced by two more ferocious figures: General Robert Nivelle and General Charles Mangin, nicknamed 'The Butcher'.

By now men had become almost conditioned to death at Verdun. 'One eats, one drinks beside the dead, one sleeps in the midst of the dying, one laughs and sings in the company of corpses,' wrote Georges Duhamel, the poet and dramatist,

who was serving as a French army doctor. The highly compressed area of the battlefield itself had become a reeking open cemetery where 'you found the dead embedded in the walls of the trenches; heads, legs and half-bodies, just as they had been shovelled out of the way by the picks and shovels of the working party'. Conditions were no longer much better for the attacking Germans; as one soldier wrote home in April under the French counter-bombardment: 'Many would rather endure starvation than make dangerous expeditions for food.'

On 26th May a 'very excited' Joffre visited Haig at his HQ and appealed to him to advance the date of the Somme offensive. When Haig spoke of 15th August, Joffre shouted that 'The French Army would cease to exist if we did nothing by then.' Haig finally agreed to help by attacking on 1st July instead. Although Haig entertained vague hopes of a breakthrough to be exploited by cavalry, neither he nor Rawlinson—whose 4th Army were to fight the battle—had yet arrived at any higher strategic purpose than that of relieving Verdun and 'to kill as many Germans as possible' (Rawlinson).

Meanwhile, at Verdun the beginning of a torrid June brought the deadliest phase in the three-and-a-half-month battle, with the Germans throwing in a weight of attack comparable to that of February—but this time concentrated along a front only three, instead of eight, miles wide. The fighting reached Vaux, the second of the great forts, where 600 men under Major Sylvain Eugène Raynal in an epic defence held up the main thrust of the German V Army for a whole week until thirst forced them to surrender.

The Suicide Club

Then, just as Vaux was falling, the first of the Allied summer offensives was unleashed. In the east, General Brusilov struck at the Austro-Hungarians with forty divisions, achieving a spectacular initial success. Falkenhayn was forced to transfer troops badly needed at Verdun to bolster up his sagging ally. Verdun was reprieved; although in fact it was not until 23rd June that the actual crisis was reached. On that day, using a deadly new gas called phosgene, the Crown Prince (reluctantly) attacked towards Fort Souville, astride the last ridge before Verdun. At one moment, machine-gun bullets were striking the city streets. Still the French held but there were ominous signs that morale was cracking. Just how much could a nation stand?

Two days later, however, the rumble of heavy British guns was heard in Verdun. Haig's five-day preliminary bombardment on the Somme had begun.

Because of her crippling losses at Verdun, the French contribution on the Somme had shrunk from forty to sixteen divisions, of which only five actually attacked on 1st July, compared with fourteen British divisions. Thus, for the first time, Great Britain was shouldering the main weight in a Western Front offensive. Of the British first-wave divisions, eleven were either Territorials or from Kitchener's 'New Armies'. Typical of the latter force was one battalion which had only three 'trained officers', including one who was stone deaf, another who suffered from a badly broken leg, and a sixty-three-year-old commanding officer who had retired before the Boer War. These new amateur units of 'civvies' had been trained to advance in rigid parade-ground formations that would have served well at Dettingen—straight lines two to three paces between each man, one hundred yards between each rank in the assault waves. In their rawness, their leaders did not trust them to attempt any of the more sophisticated tactics of infiltration such as the Germans and French had evolved at Verdun—despite a recommendation by Haig himself. French farmers were reluctant to allow their fields to be used for badly needed extra infantry training. But what 'K's' men

French troops attempt to take up position under fire in the Helby defile at Verdun

lacked in expertise, they more than made up for in zeal and courage.

The Somme meanders through a flat, wide, and marshy valley. In the areas where the battle was to be fought, there are few geographical features of any note, except the high ground running south-east from Thiepval to Guillemont. This lay in German hands, and was the principal tactical objective for Rawlinson's 4th Army. The British, therefore, would everywhere be fighting uphill; whereas opposite General Fayolle's 6th Army, the French faced more or less level ground. The Germans had superb observation points gazing down on the British lines, their excellence matched only by the depth of their fortifications.

In the nearly two years that they had sat on the Somme, they had excavated dugouts and vast dormitories out of the chalk

Verdun landscape: bombardments left shattered woods and pockmarked hillsides

as deep as forty feet below ground, comfortably safe from all but the heaviest British shell. Ironically, the British, by their policy of continual 'strafing' (in contrast to the prevalent German and French philosophy of 'live and let live'), had provoked the defenders to dig even deeper. When captured, the German dugouts astonished everybody by their depth and complexity. The German line on the Somme was, claims Churchill, 'undoubtedly the strongest and most perfectly defended position in the world'.

British security surrounding the Somme offensive was by no means perfect. Among other indiscretions, the press reported a speech made by a member of the government, Arthur Henderson, requesting workers in a munitions factory not to

question why the Whitsun Bank Holiday was being suspended. In his diary for 10th June, Crown Prince Rupprecht, the German army group commander, wrote: '. . . This fact should speak volumes. It certainly does so speak, it contains the surest proof that there will be a great British offensive before long. . . .' Abundantly aware of just where the 'Big Push' was coming, for several weeks previously the German defenders had industriously practised rushing their machine-guns up from the dugouts. This had been perfected to a three-minute drill, which would give the Germans an ample margin on 'Z-day' between the lifting of the British barrage and the arrival of the attacking infantry.

For five days Rawlinson's artillery preparation blasted away without let-up (Haig would have preferred a short preliminary bombardment) – thereby dissipating what little element of surprise there still remained. By British standards of the day, it was a bombardment of unprecedented weight. Yet on their much wider front they could mount not nearly half as many heavy guns as the French; and they had nothing to compare with the French 240mm mortars and 400 'super-heavies' with which Foch (French northern army group commander) had equipped Fayolle. A depressing quantity of the British shells turned out to be dud; while defective American ammunition caused so many premature explosions that some of the 4.5 howitzer gun crews nicknamed themselves 'the Suicide Club'. The fire-plan also suffered from the same inflexibility which characterized the training of the new infantry. Through sheer weight of metal, large sections of the German front-line trenches were indeed obliterated, their skeleton outposts killed. But down below in the secure depths of the dugouts, the main body of the German defenders sat playing *Skat* while the shelling raged above.

The worst shortcoming of the five-day bombardment, however, was that it failed in its essential task of breaking up the barbed wire through which the British assault waves were to advance. Divisional commanders appear to have known this, but to have kept the knowledge to themselves. On the eve of the 'Big Push', Haig wrote in his diary with the misguided optimism that was to be found at almost every level prior to 1st July: 'The wire has never been so well cut, nor the Artillery preparation so thorough. I have seen personally all the Corps commanders and one and all are full of confidence. . . .'

At 0245 hours on 1st July a German listening post picked up a message from Rawlinson wishing his 4th Army 'Good Luck'. A little less than five hours later there was suddenly a strange silence as the British bombardment ended. Some-

where near a hundred thousand men left their trenches at this moment and moved forward at a steady walk. On their backs they carried their personal kit – including a spare pair of socks – water bottles, a day's rations, two gas masks, mess tins and field dressings, as well as rifle, bayonet, 220 rounds of ammunition, and an entrenching tool. Some also carried hand grenades or bombs for a trench mortar. The minimum load was 66lb; some men were laden with as much as 85 to 90lb. It was about to become a broiling hot day.

'. . . They got going without delay,' wrote the commanding officer of a battalion of the Royal Inniskilling Fusiliers;

'No fuss, no shouting, no running, everything solid and thorough – just like the men themselves. Here and there a boy would wave his hand to me as I shouted good luck to them through my megaphone. And all had a cheery face . . . Fancy advancing against heavy fire with a big roll of barbed wire on your shoulders! . . .'

Seen from the defenders' point of view, a German recorded that the moment the bombardment lifted:

'. . . Our men at once clambered up the steep shafts leading from the dug-outs to daylight and ran for the nearest shell craters. The machine-guns were pulled out of the dug-outs and hurriedly placed into position, their crews dragging the heavy ammunition boxes up the steps and out to the guns. A rough firing line was thus rapidly established. As soon as in position, a series of extended lines of British infantry were seen moving forward from the British trenches. The first line appeared to continue without end to right and left. It was quickly followed by a second line, then a third and fourth. They came on at a steady easy pace as if expecting to find nothing alive in our front trenches. . . .'

Reading from left to right along the line, the British forces involved in the principal offensive were the 8th, 10th, 3rd, 15th, and 13th Corps, while below them on the river Somme itself came the French 20th and 35th Corps. General Hunter-Weston's 8th Corps had the most difficult task of all – the terrain was particularly difficult – and, because of its inexperience, it was the corps about which Haig had entertained the most doubts. With the 31st Division holding its left flank, the Yorks and Lancs were encouraged to see ahead of them numerous gaps in the wire opened up by the shelling. But at the moment of reaching them, they were scythed down by devastating machine-gun fire from the weapons which the Germans had rushed up from their dug-outs. It was an experience that was to be repeated innumerable times that day. By early afternoon the 31st Division had lost 3,600 officers and men, of whom only eight were prisoners. ▷ **571**

1 Aerial view of Fort Moulainville, Verdun, after months of bombardment. 2 Laughter at the top. From left: Joffre, President Poincaré of France, King George V, Foch, and Haig

3 & 4 Fort Douaumont, the world's most powerful fortress. 5 The terrible toll on the Western Front. 6 Losses at Verdun, Feb-Aug 1916. 7 Losses in the battle of the Somme

5

Losses on the Western Front

1915 1916 1917

German
British
French

296,583
873,248
876,000
643,246
569,000
817,790
958,467
1,192,451
1,624,000

6

Battle of Verdun — February-August 1916

French losses		German losses
24,000	**feb**	25,363
65,000	**mar**	56,244
42,000	**apr**	38,299
59,000	**may**	54,309
67,000	**jun**	51,567
31,000	**jul**	25,969
27,000	**aug**	30,572

total French losses 315,000 total German losses 282,323

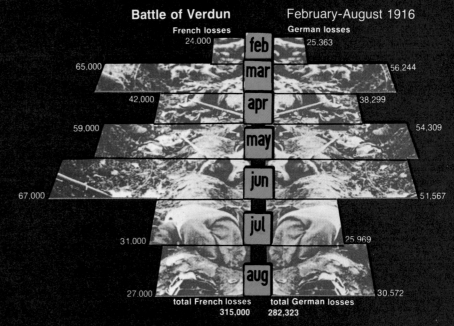

7

Battle of the Somme — July-November 1916

British losses	French losses		German losses
158,736	49,859	**jul**	103,000
58,085	18,806	**aug**	68,000
76,147		**sep**	140,000
101,313	37,626		
57,722		**oct**	78,500
39,784	20,129*	**nov**	45,000

total British losses 419,654   total French losses 204,253 *incomplete   total German losses 500,000

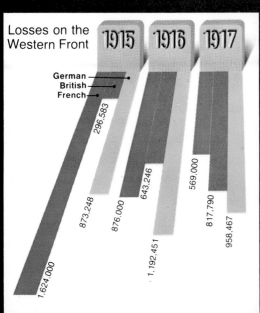

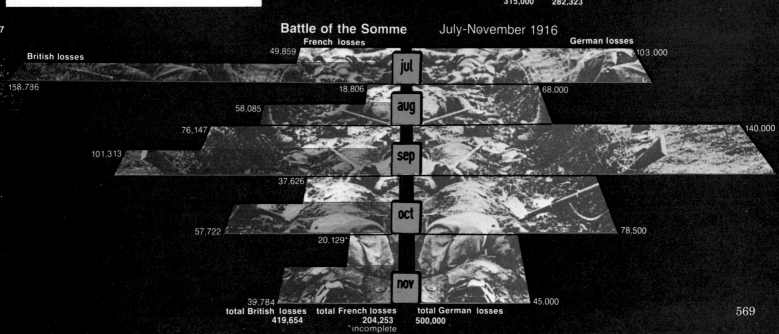

569

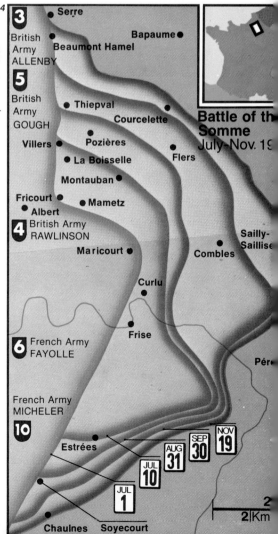

1 *Painting of the Somme battlefield, Colincamps to Fouquevillers, from a German balloon.*
2 *A British military policeman escorts a German prisoner captured in November, 1916*

Bayer. Armeemuseum, Munich

Imperial War Museum

3 *A British heavy howitzer battery in action on the Somme. 4 The farthest extent of the Allied advances in the battle of the Somme. The offensive lost impetus amid rain and mud, capturing nothing of strategic importance. 5 Abandoned British trench in the Fricourt salient, September 1916. Flints and chalk are spilling out of the rotting sandbags*

Imperial War Museum

Battle of the Somme
July–Nov. 19

3 Serre
British Army ALLENBY
Bapaume
Beaumont Hamel
5 British Army GOUGH
Thiepval
Courcelette
Villers
Pozières
Flers
La Boissele
Montauban
Fricourt
Mametz
Albert
4 British Army RAWLINSON
Maricourt
Combles
Sailly-Saillise
Curlu
Frise
6 French Army FAYOLLE
French Army MICHELER
10
Péro
Estrées
JUL 10
AUG 31
SEP 30
NOV 19
JUL 1
Chaulnes
Soyecourt
2 Km

Imperial War Museum

Next to it, the 29th Division, recently returned from Gallipoli, had the task of rushing the 'Hawthorn Redoubt' after an immense mine had been detonated under it. But the mine had been timed to go off ten minutes before zero hour; giving the German machine-gunners plenty of time to reoccupy the crater. Moving across no man's land the Royal Fusiliers could see ahead of them the bodies of their first waves festooning the uncut wire; all that came back from this one battalion was 120 men. The divisional commander, in a supreme understatement, noted that his men had been 'temporarily held up by some machine-guns', and pushed up another brigade; one battalion found itself so obstructed by the dead and the endless lines of wounded that it physically could not get forward. Attacking unsuccessfully but with fantastic courage at Beaumont-Hamel, the Newfoundlanders won their greatest battle honour: in a matter of minutes 710 men fell.

Also at Beaumont-Hamel, troops that had captured the Heidenkopf position were tragically shot down by the second wave, unaware that the German strong-point was already in British hands.

By nightfall, the 8th Corps alone had lost 14,000 officers and men without even broaching the main objective. It had taken only twenty-two prisoners. For the 10th, the 3rd, and part of 15th Corps the story of bloody failure was much the same:

'I get up from the ground and whistle,' recalled an officer commanding an Irish battalion in the second wave. 'The others rise. We move off with steady pace. I see rows upon rows of British soldiers lying dead, dying or wounded in no man's land. Here and there I see the hands thrown up and then a body flops on the ground. The bursting shells and smoke make visibility poor. We proceed. Again I look southward from a different angle and perceive heaped up masses of British corpses suspended on the German wire, while live men rush forward in orderly procession to swell the weight of numbers in the spider's web. . . .'

The Highland Light Infantry went into battle behind their pipers. Swiftly their leading companies invested the German trenches, but while they were still exulting at their success, hidden German machine-guns opened fire. Within little more than an hour of the beginning of the attack, half the HLI were killed or wounded, bringing the assault to a sudden halt.

Opposite Thiepval, the 36th (Ulster) Division came tantalizingly, tragically close to achieving success. Better trained than most of Rawlinson's units, the Inniskillings managed to advance a mile in the first hour of the attack, attaining the top of the ridge and capturing the Schwaben Redoubt, an important strongpoint in the

German first-line. But, following the experiences of 1915 when so many field officers had been killed off, it was Haig's orders that no battalion commanding officers or second-in-commands should go in with their men in the first wave. Thus there was no one senior enough to consolidate the Ulstermen's fine success. Communications with the rear were appalling. Runners sent back for fresh orders never returned. Precious time was thrown away, while the Germans recovered their balance. When finally a reserve brigade was sent up to reinforce the Inniskillings, it too had no senior officers with it; with the result it advanced too fast, running into its own artillery barrage, where it lost something like two-thirds of its soldiers. That evening, of the 10th Corps' 9,000 losses, over half came from the Ulster Division—a fact which was long to cause bitterness against the neighbouring English units. The division was left clinging precariously to the German front line.

On the 3rd Corps' front, the 8th Division was another unit to suffer appalling casualties in return for very little progress. It lost a shocking total of 1,927 officers and men killed; one of its battalions, the 2nd Middlesex, lost 22 officers and 601 men, another—the 8th Yorks and Lancs—21 and 576 respectively, out of an average of 27-30 officers and roughly 700 men to a battalion.

Over the whole British front, only Congreve's 13th Corps, next door to the French, registered any notable success that day. Attacking through Montauban, it captured the entire HQ of the German 62nd Regiment; making a total bag of 1,882 prisoners (compared with the 8th Corps' 22). At Montauban, the cellars were found to be filled with German dead; apparently killed by the French heavy mortars.

Fighting in hell

Indeed, for all the incredible fortitude of Kitchener's men, it was the French who won the laurels on 1st July. The terrain opposite them was admittedly much more favourable, the defences weaker; they had more and heavier guns, which had smashed up even some of the deepest enemy dugouts; their infantry moved with greater skill and flexibility; and they had the advantage of a certain degree of surprise. After the losses inflicted at Verdun, German intelligence could not believe that the French were capable of making a serious contribution on the Somme. To reinforce this belief, Foch cleverly delayed the French attack until several hours after the British.

By early afternoon, Fayolle's troops had taken 6,000 prisoners, destroyed the whole of the German 121st Division's artillery, and come close to making a breakthrough. Péronne itself was threatened. General

Balfourier, commanding the 'Iron' (20th) Corps which had saved Verdun in February, urged Congreve on his left to join him in continuing the advance. But Congreve would budge no farther. Above him, Rawlinson was bent more on consolidation than exploitation. Thus Balfourier, with his left flank hanging in the air, was unable to advance either. It was not until 10 o'clock that night that Rawlinson made any attempt to push reserves up to the areas of least resistance. What prospect there had been of capitalizing on any success gained during the 1st July was swiftly lost; the Germans were soon replacing the machine-guns destroyed that day.

When the casualties were counted, the British figures came to 60,000, of which the dead numbered 20,000. Most of the slaughter had been accomplished by perhaps a hundred German machine-gun teams. 1st July was one of the blackest days in British history. Even at Verdun, the total French casualty list for the worst month barely exceeded what Great Britain had lost on that one day. Fayolle lost fewer men than the defending Germans.

Haig had no idea of the full extent of the British losses until 3rd July and neither he nor Rawlinson quite knew why some efforts had succeeded and others failed. On the 3rd Haig ordered Rawlinson to attack again; this time rightly trying to follow up the good results achieved on his southern sector. But the guns were now short of ammunition, and the losses on 1st July greatly reduced the strength of the new blows. That night it rained, and the next day 'walking, let alone fighting, became hellish'.

On 14th July, Rawlinson—chastened by the terrible casualties his army had suffered—decided to try something new. He would attack by night. Describing it caustically as 'an attack organized for amateurs by amateurs', the French predicted disaster. Haig, equally dubious, caused the attack to be postponed twenty-four hours—a delay that diminished the chances of success. Nevertheless, throwing in six brigades which totalled some 22,000 men, Rawlinson after a short hurricane bombardment punched out a salient four miles wide and a thousand yards deep, breaching the Germans' second line—and thereby briefly restoring the element of surprise to the Western Front. A French liaison officer telephoned the sceptical Balfourier: 'Ils ont osé. Ils ont réussi!'

Once again, however, the fruits of victory were thrown away by poor communications and the painful slowness to react of the British command. As at Gallipoli, there was a horrifying absence of any sense of urgency. The cavalry were waiting in the wings, but too far back to be available to exploit any gains, and not until mid-after-

Snark International

British go over the top in the Somme battle. Their dead bodies were to festoon the wire

noon that day was it decided to push up the already battle-weary 7th Infantry Division. Thus nine valuable hours were wasted, and darkness was falling when at last the British cavalry and infantry reserves attacked. By then the shaken Germans had rallied.

Deeply disappointed, Haig now settled for a long-protracted 'battle of attrition'. Writing to the government, he declared his intention 'to maintain a steady pressure on Somme battle'... proceeding thus, I expect to be able to maintain the offensive well into the Autumn....' All through August and into September the bloody slogging match continued. As seen by the Australian official history, Haig's new technique 'merely appeared to be that of applying a battering-ram ten or fifteen times against the same part of the enemy's battle-front with the intention of penetrating for a mile, or possibly two ... the claim that it was economic is entirely unjustified'. By the end of the summer, one level-headed Australian officer was writing '... we have just come out of a place so terrible that ... a raving lunatic could never imagine the horror the last thirteen days....'

Meanwhile, however, Verdun had been finally and definitively relieved by the dreadful British sacrifices on the Somme. On 11th July, one last desperate effort was mounted against Verdun, and a handful of Germans momentarily reached a height whence they could actually gaze down on Verdun's citadel. It was the high-water mark of the battle, and—though not apparent at the time—was perhaps the turning point, the Gettysburg of the First World War. Rapidly the tide now receded at Verdun, with Falkenhayn ordering the German army to assume the defensive all along the Western Front.

At the end of August Falkenhayn was replaced by the formidable combination of Hindenburg and Ludendorff.

Visiting the Somme, Ludendorff criticized the inflexibility of the defence there; '... Without doubt they fought too dog-gedly, clinging too resolutely to the mere holding of ground, with the result that the losses were heavy.... The Field Marshal and I could for the moment only ask that the front line should be held more lightly....' It was a prelude to the strategic withdrawal to the 'Hindenburg Line' in the following spring.

'A pretty mechanical toy'

On the Somme, 15th September was to become a red-letter day in the history of warfare. Haig decided to throw into a third major attack the first fifty newly invented tanks. Rejected by Kitchener as 'a pretty mechanical toy but of very limited military value', the tank had been developed under the greatest secrecy and crews trained with similar security behind a vast secret enclosure near Thetford in Norfolk. Even the name 'tank' was intended to deceive the enemy. Its inventors begged the army not to employ the first machines, however, until they were technically more reliable; while even Asquith visiting the front on 6th September thought it: '... a mistake to put them into the battle of the Somme. They were built for the purpose of breaking an ordinary trench system with a normal artillery fire only, whereas on the Somme they will have to penetrate a terrific artillery barrage, and will have to operate in a broken country full of shell-craters...'

But Haig was determined. Historians will long continue to argue whether he was right or not; on Haig's side, the Cambrai raid the following year tends to prove that the surprise value of the tank had not entirely been thrown away, and undoubtedly, sooner or later, it would have had to be tried out under battle conditions.

On the day of the attack, only thirty-two of the original fifty tanks reached the assembly area in working order; twenty-four actually went into battle, and most of these broke down, became bogged, or were knocked out. At Flers the tank showed what it could do, and the infantry advanced cheering down the main street of the village behind four solitary machines. But once again poor communications between front and rear gave the Germans a chance to reorganize before success could be exploited. By the evening of the 15th all the tanks were either scattered or destroyed. With them vanished the last of Haig's three opportunities on the Somme; Montauban on 1st July, Rawlinson's night attack on the 14th, and Flers on 15th September.

Now the equinoctial rains turned the battlefield into a slippery bog. But, pressed by Joffre, Haig stuck out his Celtic jaw and soldiered on, in the mystic belief that—somehow, somewhere—an exhausted foe might suddenly break. The British army was equally exhausted. Conditions became even more appalling. In November, a soldier wrote: '... Whoever it is we are relieving, they have already gone. The trench is empty ... Corpses lie along the parados, rotting in the wet; every now and then a booted foot appears jutting over the trench. The mud makes it all but impassable, and now, sunk in it up to the knees, I have the momentary terror of never being able to pull myself out ... This is the very limit of endurance....'

In a last attack on 13th November, shattered Beaumont-Hamel was finally captured. Having won the bloodily disputed high ground, the British were now fighting their way down into the valley beyond—condemning themselves to spend a winter in flooded trenches. Nothing of any strategic value had been attained. The 'Big Push' was over.

At Verdun in the autumn, Nivelle and Mangin recaptured forts Douaumont and Vaux in a series of brilliant counter-strokes—plus much of the territory gained so painfully by the Crown Prince's men. By Christmas 1916 both battles were finished. After ten terrible months Verdun had been saved. But at what a cost! Half the houses in the city itself had been destroyed by the long-range German guns, and nine of its neighbouring villages had vanished off the face of the earth. When the human casualties came to be added up, the French admitted to having lost 377,231 men, of whom 162,308 were listed as dead or missing. German losses amounted to no less than 337,000. But, in fact, combined casualties may easily have totalled much more than 800,000.

What caused this imprecision about the slaughter at Verdun, as well as giving the battle its particularly atrocious character, was the fact that it all took place in so concentrated an area—little larger than the London parks. Many of the dead were never found, or are still being discovered to this day. One combatant recalled how 'the shells disinterred the bodies, then reinterred them, chopped them to pieces, played with them as a cat plays ▷**576**

1 Australian Royal Field Artillery pass
by 4.7 gun during the Somme battle.
2 Germans captured in the battle of Morval.
3 Somme: Dead German with live grenades

4 British troops supporting the first
assault wave near Morval on the Somme.
5 French troops marching to positions in
the battle. 6 A guide awaiting a patrol

Previous page: Under lowering night skies French military traffic winds along the Voie Sacrée at Verdun. The whole life-blood of France poured along this artery to reinforce the threatened city. Painting by Georges Scott (Musée de la Guerre, Paris)

*Painters capture the meaning of these sacrificial battles. **Left:** 'Paths of Glory' by C. Nevinson. **Bottom left:** 'Gassed and Wounded' painted by Eric Kennington*

with a mouse'. Inside the great sombre *Ossuaire* at Verdun lie the bones of more than 100,000 unknown warriors.

On the Somme, the British had lost some 420,000 men; the French about 200,000 and the Germans probably about 450,000 – although a miasma of mendacity and error still surrounds the exact figures. On the battlefields of Verdun and the Somme, there also expired the last flickers of idealism; yet the war would go on.

The casualties of the two battles included among them the highest warlords on both sides. Falkenhayn had fallen; then Joffre, to be replaced (disastrously) by Nivelle, and Asquith by Lloyd George; a few months later Premier Briand's head would also topple. Because of the appalling extent to which Verdun had 'bled white' his own army, Falkenhayn's grim experiment had failed. Yet, in its longer-range effects, it contained an element of success. As Raymond Jubert, a young French ensign, wrote in prophetic despair before he was killed at Verdun: 'They will not be able to make us do it again another day; that would be to misconstrue the price of our effort. . . .' The excessive sacrifices of the French army at Verdun germinated the seeds of the mutinies that were to sprout in the summer of 1917, thereby making it finally plain that the war could no longer be won without American troops.

In many ways Verdun and Somme were the First World War in microcosm, with all its heroism and futility, its glorious and unspeakable horrors. They were indecisive battles in an indecisive war. Of the two, Verdun undoubtedly had the greater historical significance. Years after the 1918 Armistice this Pyrrhic victory of the 20th century continued to haunt the French nation. From the role the forts at Verdun had played, France's military leaders (headed by Pétain) drew the wrong conclusions, and the Maginot Line – with all its disastrous strategic consequences in 1940 – was born.

Spiritually, perhaps, the damage was even greater. More than three-quarters of the whole French army passed through the hell of Verdun – almost an entire generation of Frenchmen. Nobody knew this better than Pétain who, years after the war, remarked that at Verdun 'the constant vision of death had penetrated him (the French soldier) with a resignation which bordered on fatalism'.

For a symbol of what Verdun did to France, one need hardly search beyond the tragic figure of Pétain, the warrior-hero of 1916, the resigned defeatist of 1940.

The Brusilov Offensive

One of the most successful of the Allied campaigns took place on the Eastern Front in 1916 when Brusilov's armies smashed through the Austrians. It was the only victory of the war to be named after a commander. But, unfortunately for the Russians, the victory was probably too successful . . .

After its great retreat of autumn 1915 the Russian army, which had withdrawn in good order though with great losses, settled down on a new line. This ran from north to south for over 500 miles, from Riga on the Baltic through the Pinsk marshes to the Rumanian frontier. In the north it faced the Germans under Ludendorff, in the south the Austrians under Archduke Frederick. The line was divided into three fronts (army groups). The northernmost of these was the North-West Front, commanded by the same Kuropatkin who in the Russo-Japanese War had specialized in the tactic of the mis-timed retreat (Vol. 1, p. 96). The next sector was the West Front under General Evert, who was also to manifest a dislike for offensive actions. Finally there was the South-West Front commanded by another master of timidity, General Ivanov.

Major-General Alekseyev who, as chief of staff to the commander-in-chief (Tsar Nicholas), was responsible for the Russian operations, was one of the better generals of the First World War – but his front commanders certainly were not. That men of their outlook held such responsible positions was, on the one hand, an indictment of the Russian political situation: with the Tsar, weak-willed in any case, out of touch at the front, the conduct of affairs at Petrograd (as St Petersburg was now called) was dependent more and more on the intrigues of the Tsarina and her favourites, and this circle tended to oppose the appointment of men of strong character and intellectual energy. On the other hand, there was another reason why so many Russian officers were unaggressive: the victory of 1812 over Napoleon had by now, aided by Tolstoy's dramatic and erroneous interpretation in *War and Peace,* entered the Russian tradition as a victory won by a great general called Kutuzov who had deliberately retreated in order to win the war. Thus there existed a concept – conscious and subconscious – of victory through retreat, which is why so many Russian generals seemed reluctant and over-anxious in attack.

During the winter of 1915-16 the Russian army was slowly restored to fighting condition. The deficiencies in 1915, the lack of rifles, of ammunition, of boots, and of properly-trained soldiers, would not be repeated in 1916. In early 1916 rifles were being produced at the rate of 10,000 per month; most front-line units had their full complement of field and machine-guns; ammunition, except perhaps for the heaviest guns, was being delivered fast

enough to build up stocks for a full summer campaign; the quiet winter months had given time for proper training of recruits – although the shortage of good experienced officers could not be remedied so easily. The Red Cross detachments organized by local civilians were doing much to maintain front-line morale, not least because they made it their business to provide for many of the physical and recreational needs which the war ministry had so obviously neglected.

The last battle of 1915 had been a minor Russian offensive in the south, aimed at helping the Serbian army, which had been driven into retreat when Bulgaria declared war. In the winter an inter-Allied military conference held at Chantilly in France laid plans for the 1916 summer campaign. Russia was to play a relatively small part in these plans, because of the heavy losses she had sustained in 1915: the main Allied offensive was to be on the Somme, and was to be preceded by a small diversionary attack made by the Russian army. However, the Germans disturbed this scheme by their massive attack on Verdun in February: not for the first time – nor the last – Russia was called upon to save her western allies by mounting a hastily-planned offensive to draw German divisions from the west to the east. In March and April a Russian army of the West Front, with artillery support whose intensity surprised the Germans, attacked through the mud of the spring thaw and overcame the German advanced lines. Ludendorff brought up reinforcements, for some reason the Russian GHQ withdrew its heavy artillery and aircraft from the sector, and the Russian soldiers were left almost defenceless in shallow marsh trenches, without gas masks. Unable to withstand the prolonged barrage of gas and high-explosive shells, and sustaining great losses, the Russians, still singing their hymns, were driven back to their start line in one day.

This disaster – the battle of Lake Naroch – was a relatively minor action, and the Russians were already planning bigger things, both to honour their pledge to the Allies (for the Somme operation was still scheduled) and to take pressure off the French, who were bearing heavy losses and in a desperate situation at Verdun. On 14th April the Tsar had presided at a meeting of the front commanders at GHQ. By this time the pessimistic Ivanov had been replaced by General Alexey Brusilov, who as an army commander had distinguished himself in the 1915 retreat even

General Alexey Brusilov. He later claimed that if his fantastically successful offensive had been properly exploited, Russia could have won the war for the Allies. Even if he had not won the war he probably prevented the Allies losing it

Novosti

though he was a champion of an offensive strategy.

Brusilov risks his reputation

At the 14th April meeting the idea of attacking on the West (Evert's) Front was discussed. Both Evert and Kuropatkin declared that they preferred to stay on the defensive, alleging that there was not enough heavy artillery and shells to start an offensive. Brusilov disagreed, and recommended attacks on all fronts. This latter proposal was made in view of the superior rail communications on the German side of the line. By quickly shifting troops from a quiet sector the German command could easily reinforce that part of its line under threat: if the Russian attack came not at one point but at several this would be more difficult, especially as it would be hard to divine which of the attacks was intended to develop into the main thrust.

It was finally agreed that an offensive would be launched at the end of May, and that Brusilov's South-West Front would make the first move but that the main thrust would in fact start soon afterwards on Evert's West Front and be directed towards Wilno.

As he left this meeting Brusilov was told by a colleague that he had been unwise to risk his reputation by offering to launch an offensive. Unperturbed by this pessimism, he returned to his South-West Front to make the most of his six-week preparation time. He decided not to concentrate his forces but to ask each of the generals commanding his four armies to prepare an attack; with preparations being made at four places on his 200-mile sector of the line the enemy would be unable to anticipate where the main blow would fall. In previous actions, as Brusilov was well aware, both the place and the time of an attack had seemed to produce no surprise, so, in addition to avoiding troop concentrations, he took the precaution of dismissing newspaper correspondents. Also, since he suspected that the Tsarina was a careless talker, he avoided telling her the details of his plan.

The Austro-Hungarian line which Brusilov was preparing to break through was strongly fortified, consisting in most parts of three defensive belts one behind the other at intervals of one or two miles. Each belt had at least three lines of full-depth trenches, with fifty to sixty yards between each trench. There were well-built dugouts, machine-gun nests, sniper hideouts, and as many communication trenches as were needed. Before each belt there was a barbed wire barrier, consisting of about twenty rows of posts to which were attached swathes of barbed wire, some of which was very thick and some electrified or

mined. Brusilov's aircraft had made good photographs of these defences and the information was transferred to large-scale maps so that, as was shown later, the Russian officers had as good maps of the opposing line as had the Austrians. Moreover, although during the preparation period most of the soldiers were kept well behind the line, the officers spent much time in advanced positions studying the terrain over which they would fight. Meanwhile, with odd sighting shots the gunners were able to get the range of their prescribed targets, and shell stocks were building up. Trenches to serve as assembly and jumping-off points were dug near to the front-line Austrian trenches, in some places getting as close as one hundred or even seventy-five yards. Because this was to be a widely dispersed effort and not a conventional hammer-blow attack, no reserves were assembled.

While his four army commanders were each planning the details of their respective attacks, Brusilov was in touch – frequently acrimonious touch – with GHQ on the question of timing. On the one hand, Evert was declaring that his West Front attack, for which Brusilov's was only a preliminary diversion, needed more preparation time. On the other hand, to the urgent situation at Verdun was now added the rout of the Italian army by the Austrians at Trentino: unless Russia could do something to relieve the pressure Italy would be driven out of the war and the Central powers would be able to bring even greater strength against Verdun. In the end, 'Brusilov's Offensive', as it was later called (it was the only victory during the First World War named after a commander) was launched on 4th June.

The Archduke's birthday party

Three of Brusilov's four armies broke through at once, aided by thorough artillery preparation, surprise, and the alacrity with which the Czech elements of the Austro-Hungarian army offered themselves as grateful prisoners of war. Brusilov's main thrust was towards Lutsk and Kovel. The former was taken on the 8th: the Archduke Josef Ferdinand was forced by Russian shells to abandon his birthday party which he was celebrating there. With three deep and wide gaps in their line the Austrians were soon in full and fast retreat. However, the ever-reluctant Evert was still unwilling to start his own attack and on 9th June Brusilov learned that this attack would be postponed until the 18th. By this time Ludendorff was desperately trying to organize a counter-attack, and scraping together German units which he sent south to stiffen the demoralized Austrians. Fortunately for Austria, Brusilov's main thrust, confused by unclear instruc-

tions from GHQ, advanced in two directions at once, and thus lost the chance of capturing Kovel.

On 18th June Evert's promised attack towards Wilno did not materialize. Instead, that general made a minor, ill-prepared, and unsuccessful advance farther south at Baranowicze. By now it was clear that GHQ would do what Brusilov had always opposed: instead of attacking on the West Front it would send Evert's troops to Brusilov, believing that the latter with these reinforcements would be able to exploit his success fully. As Brusilov expected, as soon as the Germans noticed these Russian troop movements they felt able to transfer their own troops southwards and, because they had better railways, got there first. In this way the German command was able to make the best possible use of its scanty resources. Despite a renewed push at the end of July, Brusilov made less and less headway as he found more and more German units opposing him. In general, the Brusilov Offensive came to an end about 10th August, by which time the Austrians had lost not only vast areas of territory but also 375,000 prisoners of war, not to speak of killed and wounded. But Russian casualties already exceeded half a million.

Brusilov later claimed that if his wildly successful offensive had been properly exploited, Russia could have won the war for the Allies. It does seem very possible that if Evert had carried out the main attack as planned (thus occupying those German troops which in fact were sent to help the Austrians) Brusilov would have been able to drive Austria out of the war – which almost certainly would have entailed the surrender of Germany before the end of 1916. In any case, Brusilov's Offensive achieved all the aims which it had been set, and more: Austrian troops in Italy had to abandon their victories and rush north to fight the Russians, and the Germans were forced to end the Verdun operation and transfer no less than thirty-five divisions from France to the Eastern Front. Even if Brusilov had not won the war, he probably stopped the Allies losing it.

Persuading Rumania

In mid-August, just as Brusilov's Offensive was slowing down, it was brought to a definite end by the decision of Rumania to abandon her neutrality and join the Allies, her first step in this direction being to sign a military alliance.

Right from the beginning of the war Allied diplomacy had been busy in Rumania. The Russian effort in this respect was two-pronged and, in view of the Tsar's habit of acting independently of his ministers, it is possible that neither prong knew what the other was doing. ▷ **580**

3 *Russian troops on the Galician Front, 1916. 4 Austrian field gun in the Rumanian mountains.*
5 *Russian troops in helmets of French design sight a machine-gun during the Brusilov Offensive*

1 *The Brusilov Offensive. The main thrust towards Lutsk and Kovel sent the Austrians reeling, but Evert failed to attack on the West Front.*
2 *Painting of Austrian soldiers on the South-west Front, by Karl Sterrer*

The conventional weapon in this diplomatic campaign was the Russian ambassador in Bucharest, who enjoyed a certain influence in Rumanian political circles. But his talents were well matched by the Rumanian statesman Bratianu, who was long able to postpone a decision. Rumania at this time had well-balanced ties with both Russia and the Central powers, and public opinion was more or less equally

Below: Fund raising for Rumania. British poster depicts a serene King Ferdinand of Rumania warding off the sinister outline of the Kaiser in pickelhaube. *Rumania declared war on Austria on 27th August 1916*

split between those who favoured the Allies and those who supported Germany and Austria. It seems likely that most Rumanians were behind Bratianu in his efforts to delay a decision until the bandwagon of ultimate victory had moved unmistakably in one direction or another.

Russia's second agent in Bucharest was less correct than the ambassador, but may have been more effective in the long run. This was Rear-Admiral Veselkin, who from his miniature flagship *Rus* commanded the Danube Flotilla of the Russian Imperial Navy. This flotilla, directly controlled by GHQ, had been formed in 1914 by arming Danubian steamers and adding a few gunboats from the Black Sea Fleet. Its purpose had been to keep Serbia supplied, but after that nation was overrun it had little to do, apart from engaging in intrigues to push Rumania into war on Russia's side.

Veselkin was a witty, open-hearted, and eloquent officer, popular with his colleagues and, more important, a favourite of the Tsar. Whether he dabbled in genuine cloak-and-dagger activities is doubtful: the mysterious packages which he entrusted to transient Russians for strictly personal delivery to the Tsar contained not secret documents but merely Nicholas's favourite kind of Rumanian smoked sausage. But certainly he devoted all his spare time to the persuasion of the Rumanians. He had been entrusted with two million roubles' worth of jewellery which he distributed as 'gifts' to influential Rumanians and their wives. However, this was little compared to the wealth at the disposal of the German agents (who admittedly needed large sums to bribe railwaymen to turn a blind eye on the thinly-disguised war materials passing through on their way from Germany to Turkey). In mid-1916 it seemed that the pro-German party in Rumania was still strong enough to thwart Russian efforts.

In any case, some influential Russians believed that a neutral Rumania was more advantageous than an allied Rumania. Both the Russian naval and military attachés were sending mournful accounts of Rumania's unpreparedness for any serious war, and other Russian officials had the foresight to realize that an Allied Rumania would ask for help which Russia could not spare. However, a change of Russian foreign ministers was followed by what was virtually an ultimatum setting Rumania a time limit in which to make up her mind: the success of Brusilov's Offensive – then in progress – had encouraged this Russian move while at the same time providing an extra inducement for Rumania to choose the side of the Allies.

Rumania at war

Thus it came about that on 17th August Rumania signed the military alliance which had been pressed upon her, and then immediately began to disprove the belief – still current among the great powers fifty years later – that an ally is inevitably better than a neutral. The Allies had hoped that the more than half-a-million-strong Rumanian army would be sent south against Bulgaria, and then perhaps join up with their own forces at Salonika. However, Rumanian appetites in the direction of Bulgaria had already been satisfied by the Treaty of Bucharest of 1913 which had ended the Balkan War. On the other hand, Rumania still had desires (termed 'national aspirations') for Austrian Transylvania. So, on 27th August, to the consternation of friends and enemies alike, Rumania struck north.

Germany, which had been hoping that the Rumanian government would procrastinate just a little longer, was ill-placed to meet this new threat: help had already been sent to Austria to stop Brusilov, the western Allies were starting their Somme offensive at the same time as their forces at Salonika were becoming more active. So at first the Rumanian army carried all before it, capturing the capital of Transylvania in early September. However, by tight organization and by taking great risks in scraping together reinforcements from quiet sectors of other fronts, the German high command did just manage to master the situation. Falkenhayn attacked the Rumanians in Transylvania, while Mackensen went through Bulgaria and attacked the new enemy from the south, forcing the Rumanians to relinquish their Dobrudja territory. It now became evident that the Rumanian army was even worse trained and worse equipped than the pessimists had claimed, and in any case the easy-going Rumanian officers were ill-adapted to modern warfare. The Rumanians called for Russian help, and it was Russian troops which inflicted a temporary check on Mackensen in mid-September. Before the end of the month, despite Russian diversionary pressure farther north, the two German armies were threatening the heart of Rumania. In the south Mackensen drove his enemy over the Danube, while the Rumanian forces which had so cheerfully invaded Transylvania a month previously, were now in full retreat. On 23rd October Mackensen captured the key Black Sea port of Constanta, and in early December Bucharest fell. The Rumanian army was now finished for the time being: it occupied a small part of Rumanian territory around Jassy and was being reorganized by a French general in the hope of better days to come.

By this time two Russian armies were involved in Rumania, and it was not long before a quarter of the Russian army was devoted to this area. The Russian front had now, in effect, been extended to the Black Sea: no longer was there a safely neutral Russo-Rumanian frontier, so that for Petrograd at least the Rumanian alliance had proved to be of negative value. For Germany, once the immediate crisis was over, the entry of Rumania was a blessing: she now occupied the wheatlands and oilfields of that country and had better communications with her ally Turkey. Moreover, rightly or wrongly, the German high command had been anticipating the entry into the war of Holland and Denmark on the Allied side, and the rout of Rumania convinced it that these two countries were now unlikely to risk the same fate.

The Rumanian opportunists did the best they could to retrieve their country's fortunes: they declared peace in May 1918 but rejoined the Allies on the eve of their final victory.

Britain Organizes for Total War

*New men at the top, new powers for the government, new organizations—
all were needed to gear the nation for an all-out effort*

'We are going to lose this war', Lloyd George told Colonel Maurice Hankey, the all-important but unobtrusive secretary of the cabinet's War Committee, some time in November 1916. And indeed 'this war' was going very badly, and no end, let alone victory, seemed in sight after more than two years of fighting.

Herbert Asquith, the Liberal prime minister, seemed to many to be unsuited for his task. His virtues, equanimity, patience, a certain lack of imagination, a readiness to wait for the right moment to decide and to act, had served well in the 'constitutional crisis' of 1909-11, less well during the Ulster rebellion of 1912-14 (Vol. 3, p. 412). Now they seemed irrelevant: '. . . with the war going badly, the Prime Minister appeared positively wooden . . . the passive spectator of events, fundamentally unwilling . . . to alter the course of the juggernaut he had helped set in motion,' a later commentator wrote. Asquith had retained the cabinet of twenty-one members and had resorted to improvised bodies, a war council, then the Dardanelles Committee, then a War Committee, to deal with wartime administration and policy; but he had not given these committees the necessary authority.

The final decisions, after another round of argument, still rested with the cabinet. There was no one to direct and co-ordinate the general management of the war. Kitchener, 'an ageing ignorant man armed only with a giant's reputation', was put in as secretary of war and left both to direct strategy and to organize his voluntary armies without informed criticism from outside; and Asquith's failure to demand information and to co-ordinate the plans of the War Office and Admiralty had added to the Dardanelles disaster (Vol. 4, p. 506). The system of 'business as usual', applied to munitions and supplies, helped to bring about the 'shell scandal' of May 1915. The coalition government which Asquith had formed at that time had brought in Conservatives and Labour MPs to share responsibility; and in fact problems of war production and administration were tackled much more effectively when this had been done. There remained, or seemed to remain (and in war, psychology is a vital factor), a lack of drive and grasp of purpose.

With the main parties already within the government, change could come only from within. Lloyd George alone 'had a passion to win the war', and as minister

A queue forming outside Southwark Town Hall after Lord Derby's recruiting campaign 1915

The King's Royal Rifle Corps on a recruiting march in 1915   *Young Britons entering a No-Conscription Fellowship meeting*

of munitions (May 1915-June 1916), and then, after Kitchener's death, as war secretary, he had grappled with the production of arms and the transport services, and was ready, indeed desperately anxious, to have a wider scope for initiative. But as Asquith wrote to Bonar Law, the Conservative leader, 'he lacks the one thing needful—he does not inspire trust'. No change of direction could be made without the support of the Conservatives and they, in particular, distrusted Lloyd George. But there were notable exceptions: Bonar Law, the cautious, melancholy leader, aware of his precarious authority within his own party, and adventurers like Carson, the Ulster leader, Milner, the rabid imperialist, and Northcliffe, the overweening press lord, who saw in Lloyd George a kindred spirit. What was needed was a go-between, to bring together those who, acting together, could produce a change of direction. And one was at hand: Max Aitken (later Lord Beaverbrook). It was at Aitken's country house, Cherkley (near Leatherhead), that Bonar Law and Lloyd George met after Kitchener's death; Bonar Law's support persuaded Asquith to appoint Lloyd George to the War Office—a portent for the future.

Lloyd George takes over

The political crisis which brought Lloyd George to the premiership on 7th December 1916 occurred inside a week—or rather a week-end—but it had really begun early in November when Carson quarrelled with Bonar Law over some trivial matter and was followed by almost half the Conservatives. Aitken went into action to save his friend Bonar Law: a series of meetings, calls, dinners followed. Lloyd George had his own reasons for wanting a change (and had been in touch with Carson and Milner): his authority at the War Office was limited by the independent position of the chief of the general staff, Sir William Robertson, who worked against Lloyd George and leaked information to the press. Lloyd George wanted a small and effective war cabinet for the direction of the war, with himself as the working chairman, though Asquith as prime minister would be the formal head. On 25th November Bonar Law, Lloyd George, Carson, and Aitken met at Bonar Law's London house,

Pembroke Lodge, and agreed to put forward to Asquith the plan for a war cabinet. Asquith's reply on the 27th was a polite rejection.

Lloyd George, confident of Bonar Law's support, though of little else, now acted. On 1st December he wrote to Asquith, again proposing a war cabinet. Asquith declined. Bonar Law, dining with Aitken at the Hyde Park Hotel, decided that he must see Lloyd George that evening. 'I had the means of finding Lloyd George at that time at any hour of the day or night, and I knew he was dining at the Berkeley Hotel,' wrote Aitken in his long and fascinating story of the crisis. They hauled Lloyd George out of his dinner party. Bonar Law decided that night to hold firm in supporting Lloyd George. Next day the *Daily Express* and the *Daily Chronicle* came out in criticism of the government and called for a 'war council': for this Aitken was responsible, though not for other newspaper comment favourable to Lloyd George. Similar comment in the Sunday papers increased the annoyance of Bonar Law's Conservative colleagues, and they came to a meeting at Pembroke Lodge, on Sunday 3rd December, in an angry mood. They believed that Asquith was indispensable as prime minister and preserver of national unity, and wanted to turn Lloyd George out. They passed a resolution calling on Asquith to resign because 'in our opinion the publicity given to Mr Lloyd George's intentions makes reconstruction from within no longer possible', and declared that they would themselves resign if Asquith refused. The intention was to enable him to form a new government with or without Lloyd George. However, when Bonar Law told him of the resolution that afternoon, Asquith took fright at the word 'resignation'. He decided to compromise with Lloyd George over his plans and that night published a notice that the government was being reconstructed.

On Monday 4th December, Asquith changed his mind. Several Liberal ministers advised him to stand firm, and Lord Curzon and other Conservative ministers promised him support, Curzon pledging himself not to take office under either Lloyd George or Bonar Law. Asquith was also annoyed by an editorial in that morning's *Times,* which he wrongly attributed

to Lloyd George. He sent Lloyd George a note that evening again rejecting his plan. Lloyd George resigned. After discouraging advice from both Liberal and Conservative ministers, Asquith also resigned. Bonar Law saw Lloyd George a little later; again, they agreed to act together, each to support the other in forming a government.

At the Palace that night (5th December) the King asked Bonar Law to form a government. For this Asquith's support was essential. Asquith refused, and Bonar Law resigned the commission. Lloyd George was given the task next day, and succeeded. He had the support of Bonar Law, of course, and the other Conservatives (Curzon forgot his pledge). Balfour, the ex-prime minister, who had been ill during the crisis, agreed at once to join. So did many Liberals, whose support was canvassed by Dr Christopher Addison. And Lloyd George won round the Labour leaders, promising the party a larger share in the government.

These events had important consequences, and not only in the direction of the war. The Liberals were split, a large number following Asquith into opposition. The decline of the Liberal Party has been attributed to this division and blamed on Lloyd George's conspiracy and seizure of power. Four points must be made. There is such a thing as legitimate ambition. Lloyd George was convinced that he could save his country and win the war; stalemate, the reckless, hopeless outpouring of life, seemed the alternative. If he split with Asquith, Asquith equally split with him; by refusing to join a new government Asquith perpetuated the split—whether because, as he said, he could serve the country more effectively in opposition, or because he believed that Lloyd George would fail and he would be recalled to office untrammelled, makes no difference. There are many reasons, besides those of personalities, which underlie the Liberal decline. And, lastly, Lloyd George would never have gained office without the support of the Conservatives, and particularly of Bonar Law—but equally, he could not have succeeded without the support of the press and the public—which believed, without necessarily liking or admiring him, that he had the vision and power which the country needed.

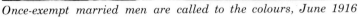
Once-exempt married men are called to the colours, June 1916 *Shells pile up. Shortages resulted in a munitions ministry*

The War Cabinet

Lloyd George at once formed his proposed War Cabinet. Carson (who became first lord of the Admiralty) was not a member; instead, Lloyd George chose Curzon and Milner, men of great ability who represented important sides of the Conservative party, Bonar Law and Arthur Henderson (Labour). None of these except Bonar Law, who was chancellor of the exchequer, had departmental responsibilities. The War Cabinet met almost daily (200 days in the first 235), devoting itself to over-all problems of strategy and administration. For three periods in 1917 and 1918 it was reinforced by the prime ministers of the Dominions, becoming the Imperial War Cabinet. This was a large and imaginative development, though it did not survive the war.

Lloyd George's reorganization of the government for total war was a combination of drive, information, and co-ordination. At the top was the War Cabinet, with its own secretary (Hankey) and secretariat, its agenda and minutes; hitherto, the cabinet had had no secretariat, no official records (the system survived the war and peacetime cabinets continued to keep minutes). Much of the work of the War Cabinet was done by committees of which one or other of its members was in charge. At the other end came the regular government departments, reinforced by new ministries (Labour, Food, Shipping, Pensions) and innumerable departments and committees. The essential link between the two ends was provided partly by committees, partly by the prime minister's enlarged number of secretaries. These bright young men, often called the 'garden suburb' (because of the huts they were housed in) and disliked as interfering and superior persons, were Lloyd George's 'leg men', co-ordinating the work of the War Cabinet with the other layers of government. Many of them came from Milner's old 'Kindergarten' which had helped to reorganize South Africa after the Boer War: Lionel Curtis, Philip Kerr (later Lord Lothian), Leopold Amery, Waldorf Astor. Among their many functions was the gathering of precise information and statistics, information either lacking altogether or buried in departments isolated from each other. Thus one secretary was Joseph

Davies, a statistician from the South Wales coal trade, whose work on the statistics of ship sinkings and farm production was of the highest value. Only in the co-ordination of political and military strategy did the system fail to achieve full success, largely because of the mutual distrust of Lloyd George and the generals – a difficulty Churchill overcame in the Second World War.

War and welfare

Before looking at the effects of these new arrangements we should notice that much had already been done, piecemeal, to gear the nation for total war. By the Defence of the Realm Act ('Dora'), passed on 8th August 1914, the government had taken powers to make regulations of the widest scope over persons and property. Almost everything was subject to government regulations from the internment of aliens and the taking over of factories to street lighting or the whistling for cabs. An early problem was trade union opposition to the replacement ('dilution') of skilled labour in engineering works and shipyards by the employment of less skilled men and of women. An agreement was made between the employers and the unions in November 1914 (the Crayford Agreement), but difficulties continued until the 'Treasury Agreement' was made at a conference in March 1915 presided over by Lloyd George (then chancellor of the exchequer). Dilution was accepted but with certain safeguards, and on condition that after the war working conditions would return to normal; disputes were to be arbitrated, strikes outlawed. Plenty of room remained for friction, and the unions, by supporting government measures, were accused of deserting the workers and were challenged by a shop stewards' movement. The worst troubles were in the engineering works and shipyards on the Clyde, and culminated in the arrest and deportation (to Edinburgh) of David Kirkwood and other leaders of the Clyde Workers' Committee in March 1916. Industrial conscription, though talked of, was never introduced; but there were regulations controlling the employment and discharge of workmen – in particular a system of leaving certificates by which, if withheld, his employer could prevent a worker from moving to another job. Wage

increases and bonuses averted many disputes, but there were some strikes – for example, a coal strike in South Wales in July 1915. The railways were taken under government control at the start of the war and put under an executive committee of the leading managers. Shipping and the ports were progressively controlled under a system of requisitions and licensing. The South Wales coalfield was put under government control on 1st December 1916. Government purchases built up stocks of sugar, wheat, meat, and hides; for example, the government took over the entire meat exports of Australia and New Zealand in 1915. Drunkenness and absenteeism led the government into controlling licensing hours through the Central Control Board (Liquor Traffic) created in June 1915; early in 1916 the board took over all licensed premises in three districts, Enfield Lock, Carlisle and Gretna, and Invergordon. Government control of the public's drinking habits, through licensing laws, is one of the so far permanent legacies of the First World War.

The most spectacular advance was in munitions manufacture. The War Office and Admiralty were slow to expand the channels through which they traditionally procured equipment. Lloyd George early took up the question, and Asquith appointed a special committee in October 1914, but its work was thwarted by Kitchener. The 'shell scandal' of May 1915 followed newspaper reports from the front of the shortage of ammunition. When, soon afterwards, Asquith formed his Coalition government, Lloyd George took over a new Ministry of Munitions. Within a year he had built up a department whose headquarters staff alone numbered 25,000. Businessmen, engineers, and economists were drawn in, a network of local committees created; huge orders were placed at home and abroad, often in anticipation of far greater demands than the service chiefs recognized; firms were persuaded to change over to munitions production. New 'national factories' were built, 73 in 1915, 218 by the end of the war.

Three inter-related consequences followed. In munitions work, as in industry and transport generally, women were employed in place of men; the status of women was raised, and their emancipation advanced by the war. Equally, the new field of industrial welfare developed. Building factories in new areas and transferring workers, particularly women, to them brought the need for amenities hitherto thought unnecessary: canteens, nurseries, rest rooms, hostels, billeting arrangements. Lloyd George created a welfare section of the ministry of munitions and put in charge of it Seebohm Rowntree, a pioneer in new methods of management. And to protect war workers in the future, unemployment insurance which had been started in a small way in the National Insurance Act of 1911 was extended in 1916 to all workers in munitions and a wide range of related industries. War and the welfare state were as closely linked between 1914 and 1918 as they were between 1939 and 1945.

Conscription for military service was the other side of the coin. The pre-war army and the Territorials were recruited from volunteers. Kitchener continued to raise volunteer armies, and enlisting became a patriotic duty. War production suffered when skilled men joined the colours, though a system of badges encouraged many to stay at work without stigma to their patriotism. The toll of life in the campaigns of 1915 soon made it clear that volunteering, besides being wasteful and undiscriminating, would fail to keep up the strength of the army. Kitchener resisted conscription, however, and so did many Liberals, so that the demand for it, pushed by the Conservatives, nearly split Asquith's government. Asquith first bought time by getting Lord Derby to head a recruiting scheme (October 1915) under

which men would 'attest' their willingness to serve, and if rejected on personal grounds, or because they were needed on the Home Front, would be issued with khaki armbands. No married men were to be called up until the unmarried had been taken. When it was clear that many unmarried men had not attested, a conscription bill was introduced in January 1916, imposing service on unmarried men not subject to exemption. This, too, proved inadequate, and a second act in May 1916 applied conscription to all men between the ages of eighteen and forty-one. As an afterthought some provisions were added for conscientious objectors; many were allowed to do civilian work of national importance, many others served prison sentences, including a hard core of 985 'absolutists'.

Leviathan

All this organization for war, widely ramified by the end of 1915, was extended and knit together under Lloyd George's government in 1917. Industrialists like Lord Inverforth, Lord Leverhulme, Lord Rhondda, Albert Stanley (Lord Ashfield), and Sir Joseph Maclay were brought in to head new ministries or offices. Rationing of meat, sugar, butter, eggs was introduced in 1918, more because of queues and hoarding than because of actual shortages of supply. Flour mills were taken over in April 1918. Agricultural production was encouraged by the new Food Production Department (created 1st January 1917) under the Board of Agriculture. The government empowered itself to seize and

cultivate unoccupied or badly farmed land. Guaranteed prices were offered, and agricultural wages raised under local wages boards. Some two million acres of grassland were ploughed up for grain crops. All coal mines were put under the Coal Controller in March 1917 (sequel to control in South Wales). By the end of the war the nation was at full stretch, and no sphere of life was outside the rule of war.

The wartime controls and organization were swept away within three years. Other effects remained. Lack of price control, rising prices, matched more or less by increased wages, produced inflation: in December 1918 the index of retail food prices stood at 229 (1913=100). Many new fortunes had been made, but there were also the 'new poor' who lived on fixed incomes or slowly rising salaries; working men, and particularly unskilled and semi-skilled workers, were better off unless unemployment overtook them. At the same time taxation took a much larger share of the national income, eighteen per cent after the war compared to seven and a half per cent before. The budget, which in 1913 was under £200 millions, allowed for expenditure of £2,579 millions in 1918. Income tax had been raised from 1s. 8d. in the £ to 6s.; surtax had been raised, and the exemption limit lowered from £5,000 to £2,000; and excess profits were taxed at eighty per cent. Here, as in the extent of the government's powers, the scale of its operations and the number of its civil servants and workers, Leviathan, big government, had taken over, never to retreat.

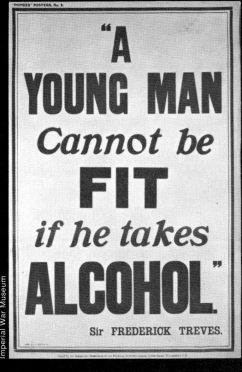

"**A YOUNG MAN** *Cannot be* **FIT** *if he takes* **ALCOHOL.**"

Sir FREDERICK TREVES.

Above: Temperance poster. Drunkenness and absenteeism led to government control of drinking habits. Right: Helpers on the agricultural front. Below: Munitions poster

THE WAR OF MUNITIONS

HOW GREAT BRITAIN HAS MOBILISED HER INDUSTRIES

WAR WORKERS

There are million persons engaged on Munition work, of whom nearly half a million are women.

MACHINE GUNS

The number of Machine Guns available for the British Army is now twenty times as great as it was at the end of the first year of the War.

HIGH EXPLOSIVES

In High Explosives the production is now more than 100 times what it was in January, 1915.

WOMEN in INDUSTRY

Of the 500 different processes in munition work, upon which women are engaged, two-thirds had never been performed by a woman previously to a year ago.

BOMBS

Between May, 1915, and December, 1916, the output of Bombs was increased 33-fold.

TRAINING SCHOOLS

Up to December, 1916, over 26,000 students had passed through Munition Training Schools, and at least 21,000 had been placed in employment.

SINCE the outbreak of war in August, 1914, Great Britain has grappled with the task of munitionment with astonishing success, and to-day she is one great Arsenal. Not only has she maintained her armies at the Front with ever-increasing supplies, but she has also materially assisted in the munitioning of her Allies. Despite the fact that more than five million men have been drafted to the Colours, she has raised a vast industrial army which is ceaselessly engaged upon the production of munitions. Her industries have been mobilised and placed upon a war footing, countless new factories have been erected, many old factories have been adapted for war purposes, and the output of munitions in the British Isles has been enormously increased. The workshops of Britain are at war, and they will know no truce till victory is secure.

THE ARMY

In 1914 275,000 than the Since million men have been enrolled British Army more the outbreak of war of the Crown.

NATIONAL ARSENALS

3 BEFORE THE WAR 100 WORKING TODAY

Before the War there were three National Arsenals working for the land service; to-day there are more than 100.

NATIONAL PROJECTILE FACTORIES

10,000 TONS

The New National Projectile Factories, which consist of bays of an average breadth of 45 feet, and a total length of 15 miles, are equipped with more than 10,000 machine tools, driven by 17 miles of shafting with an energy of 25,000 horse-power. The weekly output of this group of factories alone amounts to more than 10,000 tons weight of projectiles.

GUN AMMUNITION

The total amount of Shell produced during the first year of the War is now being produced in the following periods:—
Field Gun and Howitzer Shell ...... About 4 days
Medium Gun and Howitzer Shell ...... About 4 days
Heavy Gun and Howitzer Shell ...... About 4 days

HEAVY GUNS

The monthly output of Heavy Guns during 1916 was more than ten times what it was during 1915.

THE NAVY

To equip a sailor takes many workmen a sailor will the in the way of munitions. Since the outbreak of war the personnel of the British Navy has increased from 148,000 to 350,000.

The New Leaders

1916 brought a change of leadership in Great Britain and Germany. The men who were conducting their country's war efforts at the end of the year were: Lloyd George, a Welshman, and Ludendorff, a middle-class German general. In 1917, a former radical prime minister, Clemenceau, took office in France. They were very different from the traditional leaders of the past. But they were to lead their countries in the ruthless pursuit of total victory for the rest of the war

David Lloyd George / Kenneth Morgan

At Buckingham Palace on the evening of 6th December 1916, at an hour of supreme national crisis, David Lloyd George accepted the King's commission to form a government to win the war. So, at the age of fifty-three, Lloyd George reached the climax of an astonishing and dramatic career that had made him for over a decade the most colourful and controversial figure in British public life.

From the start, he had been an outsider in politics: a Welsh Baptist in a system run by and for the English ruling classes, a relatively poor man from a humble home thrusting his way through an aristocratic world. He had first emerged in the 1890's as a fiery young Nonconformist radical, dedicated to overthrowing the supremacy of the parson and the squire over the farming community. During the Boer War (1899-1902, Vol. 1, p. 8), he was a great opponent of British imperialism. When the Liberal Party came to power in 1905, he was the voice of radical dissent in the cabinet, first as president of the Board of Trade, later (from 1908) as chancellor of the exchequer. In this last office, he was the champion of social reform, of old age pensions, of the 'People's Budget', of national insurance, and other measures which helped to lay the foundations of the welfare state. Deep passions were stirred by his onslaughts on the landlords and on the House of Lords. And yet this extreme radical could also be the master of compromise: no one had a more notable record as conciliator in industrial disputes. It was said that he 'could charm a bird off a bough'. In 1910 he had even proposed a coalition government to promote social reform and rearmament.

When the First World War broke out in August 1914, Lloyd George was from the start a major figure in the great controversies that surrounded its course. Although he had been most reluctant to endorse a declaration of war, even as late as 2nd August 1914, he now threw himself unsparingly into a ruthless pursuit of total war, whatever the cost. He knew nothing of military affairs at first hand: in the past, he had been absorbed almost entirely in domestic rather than in foreign affairs. But his genius saw at once that this was a different kind of conflict, a total war, fought not just between armies but between peoples and civilizations. Here the intuition of a Welsh outsider might find a way through when the conventional wisdom of the generals would break down.

With Churchill, Lloyd George was throughout 1915 a vehement 'Easterner', urging a peripheral strategy in the Balkans and the eastern Mediterranean, instead of the useless stalemate on the Western Front. He developed an instinctive distrust of Robertson, the chief of the imperial general staff, and Haig, the commander-in-chief, which later events were to confirm. When Asquith's government was turned into a coalition in May 1915, Lloyd George took over the vitally important post of minister of munitions. Here he could employ all his dynamism and eloquence to provide mortars and machine-guns, and the 'mountains of shells' for which he had called. His 'men of push and go' helped transform the industrial sectors of the economy from a peacetime to a wartime basis. At the same time, he improved conditions for working men (and women) in the munitions factories, seeing that welfare and warfare went hand in hand. It was now total war at last.

As 1916 wore on, Lloyd George's impatience with Asquith's leadership became more acute. He was deeply disturbed by Asquith's delays in introducing general conscription in the early months of the year, and by his irrational faith in Kitchener, who in Mrs Asquith's view was only 'a magnificent poster'. When Kitchener was drowned at sea in June, Lloyd George succeeded him at the War Office. But his dissatisfaction continued. The war still went badly, notably, he thought, in the failure to launch a new expedition to Salonika or to aid Rumania, a 'little five-foot-five nation' like Wales itself. The climax came in the complicated political crisis of 1st-6th December 1916. On the 7th Lloyd George was able to find enough support to form an all-party government, and Asquith was pushed into opposition.

From the outset it was clear that Lloyd George's premiership marked a new era in British government. He set up a new war cabinet of only five members to run the war, a small and efficient body with its own secretariat, all under the direct control of the prime minister himself. But more important than the change in the machinery of government in December 1916 was the change in the style of leadership. The new premier seemed, in contrast to the fallen Asquith, alien and remote. His household at No 10 Downing Street was strange to English eyes—frugal,

Welsh in speech, with occasional evenings of hymn-singing around the hearth. He had little patience with high society and little faith in the 'experts'. His friends were drawn from outside the usual political circles—newspaper magnates and self-made industrialists prominent among them. Now there seemed in Great Britain a new will to victory, which the new leader's eloquence could harness. At the Aberystwyth National *eisteddfod* earlier in the year, he had urged his countrymen to sing during the gravest crisis of the war, as the nightingale sang in the darkest hour of the night. Buoyant, self-confident, the world crisis was now his opportunity.

Georges Clemenceau / J.M.Roberts

Snark International

On 20th November 1917, Georges Clemenceau presented himself to the Chamber of Deputies as the new prime minister of France. Called to office at last by an old enemy, Poincaré, President of the republic, he took up his new duties at a dark moment, but it was only because things looked so black that he was prime minister at all. Frenchmen with long memories remembered a man whose career had opened with great promise. Yet, somehow, time after time, it had run to seed in disappointment.

Clemenceau had been born in 1841, in a passionately republican family which still honoured the memory of the great heroes of the Revolution. He could remember his father being taken off in a Black Maria by the police of Napoleon III; as a young medical student in Paris he ran secret printing-presses and was soon prosecuted for it by the police. He was already committed to the republic as an ideal, and after 1871 he was faithful to the republic as an institution. Although deeply sceptical, Clemenceau, like a later great Frenchman, always cherished a certain idea of the grandeur of France. Unlike de Gaulle, however, Clemenceau saw France as the standard-bearer of reason and rationalism and the citadel of the republican democracy.

Besides passionate beliefs he had other

qualities which were likely to make a mark. He was fearless and willingly met his political and personal enemies on the duelling-ground. He soon earned his nickname 'The Tiger'; both a fine speaker and a fluent stylist, he was at his best in bitter invective. He had wide intellectual and artistic interests which appealed to the bourgeois elite of the Third Republic. His gifts should have brought him great success. Yet, indisputably, they did not.

During the siege of Paris in 1870 he was mayor of Montmartre. Nearly lynched himself, he failed to save the lives of officers seized by the enraged populace at the beginning of the Communard insurrection; it was years before gossip about this incident ceased to dog him. In the early years of the Republic he at first followed Gambetta, but soon moved over to become the leader of the radical left in the Chamber. He made many enemies as ministry after ministry fell apart under the hammering of his oratory. When he made a mistake, backing a war minister who turned out to be a would-be military dictator, his enemies were delighted. He was already acquiring the reputation of a man who was without judgement and unsound.

His enemies' chance came with the explosion of a great scandal. A company set up to build a canal in Panama collapsed in 1892. Friends of Clemenceau were deeply implicated in shady financial and political transactions connected with it. He could not explain away his relationship with them. At a time when anglophobia was rife in France, he was a known friend of Great Britain and was subjected to slanderous reports that he was a British agent. In his constituency he was greeted by peasants howling 'Aoh, yes', in heavily accented English and was soundly defeated. It seemed that his career was over.

He earned his living as a journalist. Then another scandal offered him the chance of getting back into politics, the Dreyfus Affair (Vol. 1, p. 120). His violent advocacy of Dreyfus's innocence took him back to the Chamber and the struggle with his old enemy, clericalism. Detested by the right, in 1906 he became minister of the interior, a post in which he then won the hatred of socialists by his skill and brutality in handling labour troubles. The left had now gone far beyond the once extreme Clemenceau; he harried the socialists. When he became prime minister in October 1906 another disappointment followed. Although in office for three years, he achieved almost nothing except the further embitterment of the social problem and the strengthening of his dubious repute as a strike breaker. Clemenceau retired to the Senate to grumble about his successors.

But once again a crisis saved Clemenceau. In 1914 he had refused office so that

he should not be muzzled in criticizing the conduct of the war. Fiercely patriotic, he used his newspaper and his position as president of the Senate Commission on the army to castigate and criticize incompetence and slackness. There was ambition in this. He longed to be prime minister and worked off personal vendettas in his investigations. But his contribution to morale was enormous. To all excuses and evasions he replied, implacably, 'the Germans are at Noyon'.

Finally, there was no one else to turn to. In the great ministry which began in November 1917, Clemenceau the politician was at last overshadowed by Clemenceau the statesman. He paid little attention to parliamentary politics and acted more or less as a dictator. At seventy-six, he was the oldest of the war leaders. He left the details to dim and shadowy ministers whose names have been forgotten, and to a great French patriot, Georges Mandel, his omniscient *chef du cabinet*. There were scandals and protests, as socialists, defeatists, German agents, and former ministers were scooped up pell-mell in his purges. Clemenceau was untroubled by the outcry: if the firing-squads of Vincennes helped to save the Republic in danger, they were justified. And they did. Meanwhile, the prime minister spent his happiest and some of his most valuable days in fortnightly visits to the trenches. One day a soldier gave him a bunch of flowers gathered on the battlefield. They remained, in a shell-case, in Clemenceau's room until the day of his death and his will directed that they should be buried with him. They are a reminder of the feeling that Clemenceau always strove to conceal under a biting cynicism. They may also stand for the key to the success of Clemenceau as a war leader: finally, at last, he found in the war a role which reconciled him to his countrymen.

Ludendorff / K.H.Janssen

Radio Times Hulton

'The war is lost,' cried Kaiser Wilhelm II when he heard of Rumania's astounding declaration of war on the Central powers.

So great was the shock that he lost confidence in the faithful chief of his general staff, Erich von Falkenhayn, and sacrificed him as scapegoat for the defeats of the summer of 1916. The court consoled the Kaiser with the promise that Germany could still be saved by her national heroes Hindenburg and Ludendorff.

The old Field Marshal von Hindenburg, who had defeated the Russians at Tannenberg, was an even more popular father-figure than the Kaiser. Only the initiated knew that he really owed his fame to his chief of staff, General Erich Ludendorff. Without the latter Hindenburg would have been insignificant and helpless; at the same time he himself, with his imperturbable serenity and his sagacious humour, was the ideal complement to the younger, highly emotional and impetuous Ludendorff. For this reason the post of chief of the general staff now had two occupants: Hindenburg carried the outward responsibility while the true leader of the German army in the field—indeed the secret dictator of Germany—was henceforth Ludendorff, in the guise of 'First Quartermaster General'.

However, there were a few people at general headquarters who expected no good to come of Ludendorff's appointment. Colonel von Marschall, in those August days, put in writing his view that 'Ludendorff in his limitless ambition and pride will wage war until the German people are totally exhausted; and then the monarchy will have to take the blame'. Ludendorff's colleague and later successor, General Groener, summed Ludendorff up perfectly: *'Er ist ganz Soldat—aber gar kein Diplomat'* ('He is everything of a soldier —but nothing of a diplomat'). The court was horrified by the general's coarse tone when dealing with the Kaiser. And older, tradition-conscious soldiers stood aghast when Hindenburg—at the instigation of Ludendorff and his following of young colonels—publicly issued orders and reproofs to the chancellor. In contrast to the Allies, whose peoples granted extraordinary powers to civilians like Lloyd George and Clemenceau, in Germany Kaiser and government bowed before the brute will of a soldier. After only three months the chancellor, Bethmann Hollweg, was complaining of Ludendorff's continual attacks: 'At the core of it lies a dictatorial thirst for power and a consequent intention to militarize the whole political scene.'

By an irony of fate it had been Bethmann Hollweg himself who had helped Ludendorff to power. Long before the misguided majority, the chancellor had realized that Germany could not dictate peace to her enemies, but could at best arrive at one on the basis of the *status quo ante*. But he did not believe he could answer to the people for these 'meagre, rotten peaces'

once the most popular soldier had been placed at the head. 'Even if we lost a battle, which God forbid, our people would accept it as long as Hindenburg was in command; similarly they would accept any peace graced by his name.' This was a fatal error, for in fact statesmanship stepped down when the power-obsessed but totally unpolitical Ludendorff took control.

Ludendorff overestimated wildly not only himself but also the strength of the German people. Even when he was responsible just for a section of the Eastern Front he had showed not the slightest appreciation of the problems of a high command that was only managing to live from hand to mouth through a three-front war for which Germany was far too weak. Falkenhayn was calculating on a long war of attrition; for this reason he was trying to be sparing with his reserves of men and materials. Ludendorff, on the other hand, who wanted 'just to win again', could only attribute to envy and jealousy Falkenhayn's refusal of the six divisions he needed to conquer Riga and Petrograd. The general seriously believed that Falkenhayn's conduct of the war was leading Germany to disaster. Not only because he aspired to the levers of power, not only because he considered himself a better commander, but also out of patriotic conviction, Ludendorff intrigued with the chancellor until they achieved Falkenhayn's downfall. 'I can only love or hate,' he said at the time, 'and General von Falkenhayn I hate. To work with him is impossible for me.'

Ludendorff's 'crusade'
But Ludendorff could not work with anyone who did not share his unlimited will to win. And, indeed, even he had to admit after a few weeks that the German army had so exhausted itself in the bloody battles at Verdun and the Somme that it would be incapable of any further offensive in the coming year—even the Central powers' successful campaign against Rumania could not hide that. For him too the only possible chance of victory now lay in the ruthless submarine war against Great Britain's overseas trade. Although the politicians feared rightly that such warfare, which was contrary to international law, would drive the United States of America into the enemy's camp, Ludendorff on 9th January 1917 launched the submarine war, promising himself results within a few months. Until then he hoped to hold out by mobilizing all the available resources of the German people—the sick, the war-wounded, children, women—for total war ('He who does not work shall not eat either').

Following the pattern of the Munitions of War Act Germany, too, was now going to double and treble her production of guns and munitions. But Ludendorff over-

looked the fact that Great Britain commanded quite different sources of raw materials from Germany, who was cut off from her overseas connexions. Production targets were not reached, and many construction projects had to be abandoned half way through. It was all very well for the general to make the Reichstag pass a 'Law concerning service to the Fatherland', rendering all male Germans between the ages of sixteen and sixty liable for service; but he was soon forced to realize that one cannot command an economy like an army. Also it proved impossible, in the face of resistance from the trade unions, to introduce a blanket compulsion to work. Moreover, Germany no longer had the resources at the same time to replace her war casualties (a million and a half in 1916 alone), to man new divisions, and to fill new jobs with trained workers.

In the end Ludendorff fell back on the idea of utilizing the Polish and Belgian 'human material'. In the autumn of 1916, to the plaudits of German heavy industry and heedless of world opinion, he had Belgian workers rounded up in thousands like cattle and deported to Germany in goods trains. Only worldwide protests gave the civil government the courage to put a stop to this slave traffic. Over the Polish question, however, it surrendered abjectly to the pressure of the military. On 5th November 1916, at Ludendorff's insistence, the Central powers declared Poland independent, even though the slight chance then existing of making a separate peace with Russia was thereby wrecked. But instead of the expected 750,000, only 5,000 Poles turned up at the German recruiting offices.

Ludendorff's 'crusade' for total victory over all Germany's enemies only led to available resources being overstrained and exhausted—a situation which had to rebound sooner or later. The political leadership had naturally opposed this course; but it was powerless against an alliance of military and public opinion, a majority in the Reichstag, heavy industry and Junkerdom, all of which were well pleased by Ludendorff's dictatorship. Already by the end of 1916 the military leadership was working towards the chancellor's downfall; however, they let him carry on in the hope that, if he remained even after the submarine war had been declared, his international prestige would impress the neutral countries favourably. But from the end of 1916 until his fall in the summer of 1917 Bethmann Hollweg was only chancellor by Ludendorff's leave. 'Never before was a harder task suddenly imposed on a man by Fate,' wrote Ludendorff, looking back at his life in 1916. Too true. For he aspired to the impossible—a German victory. *(Translation)*

Revolutionary Implications of the War

Chapter 22

Introduction by J.M.Roberts

Nationalism had never previously achieved successes such as were given to it within a few years by the Great War. In the end it swept away the old multi-national dynastic European empires and led to the reorganization of central and eastern Europe on the national lines which are still the basis of the states which exist today.

Many of these changes came because a few devoted and indefatigable leaders seized the chance the war offered them. While it was still going on, they exploited the leverage available to them because of the quarrels of the great powers. Four of these leaders are the subject of profiles in this chapter. **Venizelos**, the Greek, dreamed of reconstituting an Aegean empire at the expense of Turkey. **Masaryk**, the Czech, convinced President Wilson of the justice of his people's claim to independence of the Habsburgs. **Piłsudski**, the Pole, used first the Central powers and then the Entente to advance his countrymen's interests. **De Valera**, the Irishman, exploited the legendary contribution of the 1916 rebels to lead an intransigent Irish national movement.

That the only important armed national rising against any of the great powers in Europe should be in Ireland, where British rule was mild by the standards of Habsburg or Romanov, was ironical, though understandable. Constantine Fitz-Gibbon describes **The Easter Rising** in this chapter. Its significance was not that it achieved any immediate success. It failed in all its military objectives. But the long-term effects were considerable. Before the Rising the nation, though supporting Home Rule, did not support the extremists who went out to fight in 1916. After the Rising came a remarkable change of sentiment in Ireland: the old Irish Parliamentary Party, which up to then had had the support of the majority of Irishmen, was finished; the extreme Sinn Feiners now held the centre of the stage. The Easter Rising was the first and the greatest blow in the Irish Revolution. It was a revolution which inspired and foreshadowed revolutionary movements in Asia and in Africa. The leaders of Indian nationalism were greatly encouraged by the Rising, and as Christopher Falkus shows in **India at War**, the tide of nationalism was rising in India.

A very different sort of revolution is described in the article on **Lawrence and the Arabs**, by Major-General J.D.Lunt. The desert Arabs who revolted did so less under the influence of ideas drawn from the European doctrine of nationalism than as followers of their traditional tribal leaders. The man who moulded their enthusiasm into a movement of major strategic significance was T.E.Lawrence, about whom a personal legend was to grow.

The surrender of Jerusalem, 9th December 1917. British soldiers mingle with Turks

Countess Markievicz surrenders after the Rising. She was then put in Holloway Gaol

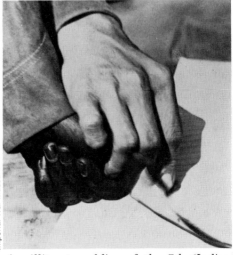
An illiterate soldier of the 7th (Indian) Division makes his mark on a pay sheet

Arabia

1916   5th June: princes of Hejaz rise against their Turkish overlords.
October: Storrs and Lawrence approach Abdulla and Feisal; Turks strengthen Medina.

1917   6th July: Lawrence, with Auda abu Tayi, takes Aqaba; Feisal places himself under Allenby's command.
9th December: Allenby enters Jerusalem.

1918   January: Lawrence advances through mountains of Moab and fights a fierce battle at Tafila.
In the spring Allenby crosses the Jordan, but the British fail to take Salt and the Arab attack on Ma'an fails.
17th September: Arabs attack Deraa railway junction.
19th September: British offensive against Turkish forces begins.
1st October: Feisal takes Damascus.
31st October: Allies sign Armistice with Turkey.

1919   Lawrence goes to the Versailles peace conference to plead for Arab independence.

Ireland

1905   Sinn Fein holds first annual convention.
1910   Irish Republican Brotherhood founds *Irish Freedom*.
1913   Irish Volunteers founded as a counter-poise to the Ulster Volunteers.
Connolly organizes his Citizen Army after an ITGWU strike is broken by strong-arm methods.
1914   On the outbreak of war Redmond accepts postponement of Home Rule; IRB decides that there must be an Irish insurrection before the end of the war.
1916   21st April: Casement lands from German submarine near Tralee in County Kerry and is arrested.
British navy intercepts German arms ship *Aud* carrying arms for the rebels.
23rd April: Wimborne orders the arrest of nationalist leaders; MacNeill calls for cancellation of the rising, but Pearse determines to continue.
24th April: Easter Rising begins; Pearse proclaims provisional government of Irish Republic from the captured General Post Office; the attempt to seize Dublin castle fails; the British call for reinforcements.
28th April: Pearse and Connolly surrender.
3rd May: Pearse executed in Kilmainham Gaol.
12th May: Connolly executed in Kilmainham.

Nationalism

Eamonn de Valera
1915   March: de Valera appointed commandant in Irish Volunteers.
1917   July: de Valera elected for East Clare.
October: de Valera replaces Griffith as president of Sinn Fein.
1918   December: de Valera effectively achieves leadership of the nation in the general election.
1919   3rd February: Michael Collins organises de Valera's escape from Lincoln Gaol.
1st April: at second session of Dail Eireann de Valera elected Priomh-Aire.
Eleutherios Venizelos
1910   October: Venizelos becomes Greek prime minister.
1912   March: Venizelist Liberals win 150 out of 181 seats.
1915   1st March: Venizelos proposes Greek troops aid Allies at Gallipoli.
25th September: Venizelos flees to Crete and proclaims a revolution.
1918   September; 250,000 troops engaged in Macedonia.
1920   November: Venizelos defeated at the polls.
Thomas Masaryk
1891   elected as member of the Young Czech Party to the Reichrat.
1906   accused but acquitted of anti-religious offences.
1917   May: Masaryk goes to Russia to plead Czech and Slovak cause.
1918   he goes to the United States on a similar mission.
Józef Piłsudski
1914   6th August: Pilsudski attempts to foment national uprising in Russian Poland.
1917   July: *Piłsudski* is interned in Magdeburg for refusal to swear oath of allegiance to the Reich.

India

1917   June: Indian government interns Mrs. Besant.
July: Edwin Montagu replaced Austen Chamberlain at the India Office.
20th August: Montagu announces that the British government aims to establish responsible government in India.
1918   influenza epidemic scourges India.
1919   13th April: Amritsar massacre.

The Arabs and Lawrence

Opposite page: Painting of T.E.Lawrence in Arab dress by Augustus John. He fixed the bird-like mind of the bedouin on a stable course and shared their hardships
Below: *Mecca to Aqaba, June 1916-July 1917. Mecca fell to Sherif Hussein's forces on June 10th 1916 and on 6th July 1917, Lawrence, with Auda abu Tayi, took Aqaba.* ***Bottom:*** *Aqaba to Damascus, July 1917-October 1918. Damascus fell to Lawrence and Feisal on 1st October 1918*

In the harsh world of the Arabian desert, T.E.Lawrence — Al Auruns as the bedouin called the small, fair-haired, blue-eyed man who led them — created two myths. To Englishmen he himself became an ambiguous hero, a figure of adventurous glamour who invited detractors and controversy. To Arabs he offered a vision of Arab unity that carried them to Damascus and helped Allenby defeat the Turks — a vision which has haunted the Middle East ever since

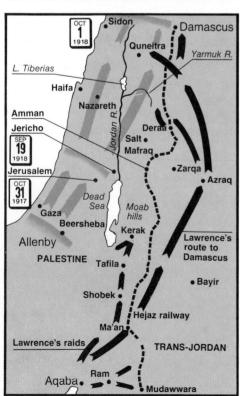

Arabia, the land with which T.E.Lawrence will always be associated, is reputed to be a harsh and barren mistress, rewarding those who serve her with sickness of the body and distress of the mind. Lawrence's connection with the Arabs brought him at least as much pain as profit, and was in large measure responsible for his decision to retire at an early age from public life, once he judged that his work for the Arabs had been completed.

He is one of the most interesting personalities of his times, as well as one of the most controversial. He possessed the ability to achieve distinction in many fields, and yet, after flashing across the skies like a comet, he chose to become a recluse. Here again he was original, choosing neither the monastery nor the hermit's cave, but the anonymity of life in the ranks as a private soldier, first in the Royal Air Force, then the army, and then once more in the RAF. He believed himself immune from most human weaknesses, renouncing women, drink, and tobacco, but he worshipped speed. A few months after his final retirement from the RAF in 1935, he was riding his motorbike along a Dorset lane when he came upon two cyclists and in a vain attempt to avoid them, crashed and met his death.

A man so varied in accomplishment, so complex in character, so untrammelled by convention, inevitably invited hostile criticism. Richard Aldington, the poet and novelist, sought to destroy the Lawrence legend finally and for ever in his *Lawrence of Arabia* (1955), but he wrecked his case by confusing his facts. Others, too, have belittled his contribution to Allenby's victory in Palestine, arguing that Lawrence was at most a gifted leader of guerrillas. Some believed that his desire for anonymity was inspired as much by a clever understanding of the media of publicity as by any genuine desire to withdraw from the hurly-burly of public life. But Lawrence was not an ordinary man. He did not fit, nor did he wish to fit, into the 'establishment'. If fame is a natural ambition, he achieved it, both in the world of action and in letters. If success is to be judged by the acquisition of wealth, he despised it; if it is to be determined by rank or status, he ignored it. The fact that throughout his life he enjoyed the friendship of such men as Churchill, Shaw, Liddell Hart, Wavell, E.M.Forster, and Trenchard is sufficient to demolish the charges brought against him by Aldington. These were not men

who admitted to their friendship the charlatan and the braggart.

The untidy subaltern

Thomas Edward Lawrence was born at Tremadoc in North Wales in 1888. He was the second son of Thomas Chapman, a rather eccentric Anglo-Irishman who later changed his name to Lawrence, and who subsequently inherited a baronetcy. T.E. Lawrence was born out of wedlock, a fact which undoubtedly affected him psychologically, but there is no evidence to suggest that he took the matter as seriously as Aldington has alleged. He discussed his illegitimacy quite openly with his more intimate friends. His father had sufficient private means to live comfortably, but not ostentatiously, and T.E.Lawrence gave early evidence of ability above the average. He learned to read at the age of four, and was learning Latin at six. He contributed towards the cost of his education by winning scholarships, first to Oxford High School, and then to the University. He was an omnivorous reader, with a particular interest in medieval and military history, and archaeology.

While reading history at Jesus College, Lawrence travelled in the Levant visiting Crusaders' castles, and subsequently took a first-class degree. Having been awarded a travelling scholarship, he joined D.G. Hogarth's expedition excavating Carchemish, and also worked with the archaeologist (Sir) Leonard Woolley. This brought him into contact with the Arabs, for whom he discovered he had a natural affinity, and he learned their language and as much as he could about their history and customs. On the outbreak of war in 1914, he tried to join the army, but was rejected at first, because he was below the minimum height of five feet five inches. It was several months before he was given a commission and employed in the intelligence branch of the general staff, where his knowledge of Arabic led to his posting to the 'Arab Bureau' at GHQ in Egypt. He was then a very junior and young-looking subaltern, whose untidiness in uniform and unconcern with the niceties of military protocol were not calculated to endear him to the more orthodox among his superiors.

The war against the Turks was going badly at the time. Their attack on the Suez Canal had been easily repulsed, but the ponderous British advance across Sinai had ground to a halt opposite Gaza. The failure at Gallipoli was fresh in men's

Above: *Painting of Australian troops at Rumani, Sinai, August 1916. The second Turkish attack on the Suez Canal was foiled here*

Below: *Feisal's tribesmen enter Damascus, October 1918. The Turks were now in flight*

Below: *One of Lawrence's desert warriors*

Below: *Typical follower of Lawrence. 'Al Auruns' won the love and respect of such men*

Imperial War Museum

memories, and was soon to be followed by Townshend's surrender at Kut in Mesopotamia (Vol. 4, p. 529). In south-west Arabia the Turks had reached the gates of Aden, where they were to remain for the rest of the war. They may have been corrupt and incompetent, but they were not faring too badly against the might of the British empire. It was at this moment, 5th June 1916, that the Hashimite princes of the Hejaz chose to rise against their Turkish overlords. The Arab Revolt, or, as some would prefer it, the Arab Awakening, had begun.

As a military operation, it was no more likely to succeed than some of the more recent military undertakings of the Arabs, in which performance has fallen far short of promise. Mecca, Jidda, and Taif were quickly captured, but the Arabs failed to take Medina, the principal Turkish garrison. The revolt lost impetus, and in the meantime the Turks sent reinforcements down the Hejaz railway, which the Arabs failed to interdict. In October 1916 the British sent Mr (later Sir Ronald) Storrs, accompanied by Lawrence, to investigate the situation at first-hand, and to consult with the Amir Abdullah, second son of Sherif Hussein, ruler of the Hejaz, whose tribal levies had captured Taif the previous month.

After preliminary discussions with Abdullah, Lawrence was dispatched to visit his younger brother, the Amir Feisal, whose tribesmen had been repulsed at Medina, but who was lying up in the hills nearby. The two men established an almost immediate *rapport,* but it was clear to Lawrence that Feisal's ill-disciplined and badly-armed tribesmen were no match for the Turks in conventional positional warfare. Meanwhile, the Turks continued to reinforce Medina, and the unruly bedouin, disappointed in their hopes for loot, began to drift back to their tents in the desert.

Lawrence was completely untrained in military staff work, but he at once appreciated that the key to the strategic situation was the Hejaz railway. So long as this continued operating, the Turks would be able to build up sufficient strength to reconquer the Hejaz. Moreover, the Arabs, although natural guerrillas, lacked the discipline, and even the will, to fight a pitched battle against the Turks, however incompetent the Turkish leadership. Some other use must be made of their natural military qualities and their ability to operate for long periods in the desert, and this could best be done by abandoning the siege of Medina and carrying the campaign into the north, raiding the railway, the Turks' lifeline, and reducing the flow of reinforcements to a trickle. Lawrence was not the first military leader in history to understand the potentialities of guerrilla warfare when operating against a conventionally-minded enemy, nor has he been the last, for Mao Tse-tung has been equally successful in China, and Giap in Vietnam. But he must at least be given the credit for appreciating how best the Arab Revolt could be harnessed to assist the Allied cause, and at the same time achieve the Arabs' aim, which was to win their independence from foreign rule.

In pursuit of his aim to tie down as many Turks as possible in the Hejaz, Lawrence launched a series of raids against the single-line, wood-burning railway linking Medina with Damascus. He sought not to destroy the railway, but to impede its working, and to compel the Turks to deploy an ever-increasing number of troops to guard it. Fakhri Pasha, the Turkish commander in Medina, lacked initiative, remaining static behind his defences, and clamouring for more and more reinforcements. As they trickled down to him, Lawrence moved steadily farther north, joining forces with the Trans-Jordan tribes, and carrying his raids against the railway nearer to the main British front in Palestine. On 6th July 1917, in company with the famous desert raider, Auda abu Tayi, and his Howeitat tribesmen, he captured Aqaba from the rear, having first overwhelmed a Turkish battalion moving down from Ma'an to reinforce Aqaba.

Feisal then moved his headquarters to Aqaba, which was nearer to the main front than Wejh on the Red Sea, and with Sherif Hussein's permission placed himself under the command of General Allenby, who had taken over command in Palestine. The mainly tribal contingents of Feisal were provided with a stiffening in the shape of armoured cars and light artillery; small detachments of British, French, and Indian troops were sent to Aqaba to support the Arabs; and above all, arms, ammunition, and gold were provided to keep the Arab tribesmen in the field. Allenby intended to employ the Arabs to protect his open flank east of the river Jordan, and to hinder Turkish attempts to reinforce their armies in Palestine. He also realized the political appeal of the Arab Revolt, and planned to harness it to his aim of destroying the Turkish armies, containing as they did large numbers of Arab officers and many thousands of Arab conscripts.

To Damascus

The British attack on the Gaza-Beersheba line was planned for early November 1917. The Arabs were asked to cut beforehand the Damascus-Haifa railway in the Yarmuk gorge, west of the junction of Deraa in Syria, in order to impede the flow of reinforcements to Palestine. The raid involved an approach march from Aqaba of over 350 miles through the desert, but the final stretch was through cultivated country where the peasants gave the Turks warning. The operation was unsuccessful, and nearly a disaster, but the raiders managed to get away and destroyed sections of the railway north of Amman before retreating to Aqaba. Meanwhile, Allenby had successfully broken through the Turkish defences and was advancing on Jerusalem.

Lawrence was present when Allenby entered Jerusalem on 9th December 1917. He greatly admired Allenby, just as Allenby, at their first meeting, had immediately appreciated Lawrence's qualities. He was also unmoved by Lawrence's preference for wearing Arab dress, a practice that reduced many British regular officers to apoplectic fury. Allenby now required the Arabs to move north from Aqaba, through the hills east of the Jordan valley, and establish contact with the British near Jericho. Lawrence thereupon advanced through the mountains of Moab, fighting a fierce battle at Tafila in January 1918, a masterpiece in minor tactics which resulted in the annihilation of a Turkish battalion. However, a farther advance to Kerak and beyond was prevented by the bitterly cold weather which affected the Arabs' morale.

Allenby crossed the Jordan in the spring of 1918 and attempted to capture Salt on the Trans-Jordan plateau. This failed, as did the Arab attack on Ma'an, intended to coincide with the British attack, but large sections of the railway were permanently destroyed and the Turkish army in the Hejaz was effectively isolated. Lawrence had set off for the north to link up with the British, but this too had failed, and he established himself far out in the desert at the oasis of Azraq. There he waited for the main British offensive to begin.

The British attack was due to start on 19th September 1918. Allenby had asked that it should be preceded by a diversionary attack by the Arabs on the important railway junction of Deraa. This was carried out under Lawrence on 17th September with complete success. When, two days later, Allenby fell with massive strength on the Turkish army, its way of retreat through Deraa to Damascus was blocked. Moreover, Lawrence and Feisal, moving north, had raised the tribes south of Damascus. The Turks gave no quarter, nor did they receive any from the Arabs, as they struggled in hopeless confusion across the Jordan into Syria. Feisal entered Damascus in triumph, and for some weeks Lawrence was responsible for civil and military order in the city. On 31st October 1918 an armistice was concluded with Turkey. ▷ 594

It has sometimes been said of Lawrence's campaign in the desert that it was 'a sideshow within a sideshow'. This may be true if war consists of a counting of heads, or 'cipherin' ', as Robert E.Lee described it, but Wavell, in his semi-official history of the Palestine Campaign, certainly does not underrate the valuable contribution made by the Arabs under Lawrence's leadership to Allenby's victory. He makes it clear that a force of barely 3,000 Arabs tied down 50,000 Turks at a crucial moment, and compelled the Turkish high command to deploy some 150,000 troops 'spread over the rest of the region in a futile effort to stem the tide of the Arab Revolt'. As General Glubb has since written: 'To the student of war, the whole Arab campaign provides a remarkable illustration of the extraordinary results which can be achieved by mobile guerrilla tactics. For the Arabs detained tens of thousands of regular Turkish troops with a force barely capable of engaging a brigade of infantry in a pitched battle.'

Al Aurens

When Lawrence arrived in the Hejaz he was junior in rank and untrained in formal military matters. It is the measure of his strategic insight that he was able to perceive how best the Arab Revolt could be utilized to assist the British strategy in the Middle East, and his understanding of the characteristics of Arab tribesmen enabled him to employ them to the best advantage in the war against the Turks. Whatever may be said to the contrary, and there has recently been published a book by an Arab author which seeks to belittle the part played by Lawrence in the Arab Revolt, anyone with experience of the Arabs as soldiers will know that they would never have chosen such tactics of their own volition. They would have met the Turks head-on, and they would have been defeated.

The way in which Lawrence established his leadership over the Arabs is a fascinating study in itself. He proved to them time and again that he could out-match them in their own hardiness. No people live in a harsher environment than the bedouin tribesmen of Arabia. Lawrence lived in the same fashion as they did, enduring the same hardships, and demanding no favours. He rode his camels harder, and farther, and for longer periods, than his Arab companions were accustomed to do. He trained himself to be patient during the interminable, and often fruitless, discussions around the coffee hearth. He ate their food, and drank their water, and suffered in consequence from a succession of debilitating stomach ailments. He was never a fluent Arabic speaker, like Glubb for example, nor could he hope to pass

himself off as an Arab, as Leachman did in Nejd; his piercing blue eyes, fair hair, and skin would soon have given him away. He could appreciate the Arabs' virtues without overlooking their weaknesses, as some Englishmen have done when subjected to the persuasive charm of the bedouin. No one who has lived with the bedouin can forget the attractive side of their characters, but very few men have possessed the ability to fix their bird-like minds on a stable course. Lawrence succeeded in doing this, and no amount of critical hindsight can detract from the part he played in maintaining the impetus of the Arab Revolt.

His work with the Arabs did not end with the conclusion of the armistice in 1918. He believed passionately that his own honour was committed to obtain for them the independence for which they had fought. He understood the force of Arab nationalism as did few others at that time. The Turks had hopelessly under-estimated the strength of the movement for Arab unity, just as the British and the French were to do in later years. The ramshackle Ottoman empire had no other solution for Arab nationalism than repression, but the Arabs' desire for unity is a burning faith, however distant its fulfilment may seem. Statesmen and politicians in London and Paris might scoff, but Lawrence was a visionary, and he understood the Arabs' longing. He gave himself body and soul to help them in their quest. This brought him into conflict with his own government after the war, since the aim of Great Britain and France was to substitute their influence for Turkey's in the Middle East.

Lawrence accompanied the Arab delegation to the Peace Conference at Versailles as an adviser, and found himself ensnarled in the tortuous negotiations conducted by Great Britain and France earlier in the war to carve up the former Turkish empire in Arabia into respective spheres of influence for themselves. It has been a dirty game, as power politics so often is, and Lawrence was soon to learn that pledges made in the stress of war are as likely to be overlooked as honoured after the peace. His practice of wearing Arab dress aroused hostile comment. It was far too unconventional for British tastes, but it was as good a way as any for Lawrence to demonstrate to the Arabs which side he was backing. Nonetheless, despite all his efforts, the outcome of the negotiations could have been predicted. The French received mandates in Syria and the Lebanon, and they at once ejected Feisal from his throne in Damascus. The British were given mandates in Iraq, and in Palestine and Trans-Jordan. Feisal was in due course to be given a throne in Iraq, and Abdullah in Trans-Jordan, but there had

been left a legacy of bitterness which has soured our relations with the Arabs ever since.

Lawrence was far from fit at the time, either physically or mentally. His physical resistance had been lowered by his years in the desert. He had been scarred mentally by the vicious sexual assault he had suffered at the hands of the Turkish commandant in Deraa, where he had been captured while reconnoitring the town. He had managed to escape, his identity still not suspected, but not until after he had been subjected to appalling indignities and a merciless beating. Exhausted though he was, he fought his hardest for the Arabs at Versailles. After the peace treaty had been concluded, and there was nothing more he could do in an official capacity, he resigned from the army, and in letters and articles in the press sought to persuade the British government to honour its obligations and give the Arabs real, instead of sham, independence.

Adviser to Churchill

His vision of the Commonwealth was years ahead of his time, though he expressed himself in contemporary terms. 'This new Imperialism,' he wrote in *The Round Table* in 1920, 'involves an active side of imposing responsibility on the local peoples. . . . We can only teach them by forcing them to try, while we stand by to give advice. . . . We have to be prepared to see them doing things by methods quite unlike our own, and less well; but on principle it is better that they half do it than that we do it perfectly for them.' Much blood, treasure, and heart-ache would have been saved had the colonial powers understood the truth of this. The Middle East was in a turmoil, while Curzon's policy at the Foreign Office was out of tune with the times, old-fashioned imperialism that had had its day. The situation only improved when the Colonial Office assumed responsibility for the Middle East. Churchill was the minister, and he took Lawrence with him as adviser on Arab affairs to a conference convened in Cairo in 1921.

The outcome of the conference was regarded at the time as being entirely satisfactory, almost universally so among the British, and only to a lesser extent among the Arabs. In Churchill's words in *The Aftermath,* 'The Arabs and Colonel Lawrence were appeased by the enthronement of King Feisal at Baghdad; the British Army, which had been costing thirty millions a year, had been brought home; and complete tranquillity was preserved under the thrifty Trenchard'. Lawrence, writing in 1932 a second inscription in the copy of *The Seven Pillars of Wisdom* he had presented to Churchill, had this to say: 'And eleven years after we set our

T.E.Lawrence in RAF uniform. He was killed in 1935 riding his motorbike along a Dorset lane when, coming upon two cyclists, he crashed in a vain attempt to avoid them

strong meat for some people's tastes.

The newspapers tracked him down, and unwelcome publicity forced him to leave the RAF. He promptly re-enlisted in the Royal Tank Corps under the name of T.E.Shaw, which he later adopted by deed poll, but found himself more suited to the RAF than the army. He wangled himself back into the RAF in 1925, pulling every string he could in order to overcome bureaucratic resistance, and he served in India from 1927 to 1929. After India Lawrence was at first posted to the flying-boat station at Cattewater near Plymouth, before being sent to Calshot on the south coast, where he indulged his love of speed by working with high-speed air-sea rescue launches. He invented his own engine and spent hours tinkering with his motor-cycle to get more power out of it. All this time he was corresponding, as a leading aircrafts-man, with the great in the land, and on every imaginable kind of topic from cabbages to kings. He was a brilliant letter-writer, as the publication of *The Letters of T.E.Lawrence to his Friends* has shown. These friends came from all walks of life, and he devoted as much care to a letter to an old comrade from the ranks as he did to one addressed to Field-Marshal Allenby, or George Bernard Shaw.

It was an extraordinary situation, and it is certainly arguable whether a man so gifted is justified in shutting himself away from the world, and avoiding his responsibilities. 'No man is an island,' wrote Donne, but that is what Lawrence was determined to be. Perhaps he had nearly come to terms with himself by the time his service in the RAF ended early in 1935. He had had time to work the bitter-ness and disillusionment out of his system, and he could hardly have expected to insulate himself from the rapidly-growing menace of Nazism. Had he lived, it is almost certain that Churchill would have sought—even commanded—his services. The two men had high regard for each other. But it was not to be, for he was killed the same year in May. He was only forty-seven.

Nearly twenty years after his death, while I was serving with the Arab Legion in Jordan, I retraced many of his journeys and operations, and sought out those who had ridden with him across the desert with Damascus as their lodestar. They were growing few and far between, and most of those I met had reached the stage where memory fails. But in a bedouin tent I found one elderly sheikh who had ridden with Lawrence to Deraa, and I asked what he had thought of him. For a while he was silent, staring out from the tent into the distance, and then he turned to me and said quietly—'Of all the men I have ever met, *Al Auruns* was the greatest Prince.'

hands to making an honest settlement, all our work still stands: the countries having gone forward, our interests having been saved, and nobody killed, either on our side or the other. To have planned for eleven years is statesmanship.' Unhappily, Anglo-Arab relations, which seemed 'set fair' in 1932, were soon to be wrecked on the rocks of Palestine, and Lawrence was fortunate in being spared witnessing the collapse of all he had striven for.

He had been elected a Fellow of All Souls in 1919, and most of his spare time immediately after the war was devoted to the writing of his book, *The Seven Pillars of Wisdom*. His style is modelled on Doughty's in *Arabia Deserta,* and it is curiously stilted in places, but he manages to catch, and convey, the spirit of Arabia as no other book, apart from the Bible, has succeeded in doing. Whether or not posterity remembers Lawrence as a gifted strategist and brilliant guerrilla leader, his name will live in his epic literary account of the Arab Revolt. But although he wrote un-ashamedly for literary fame, he did not seek fame in other fields. In 1922 he en-listed in the ranks of the RAF, taking the name J.H.Ross, and sought his personal seclusion in the barrack-room. He described his experience in the ranks in *The Mint,* written in 1928, which was rather too

The Easter Rising

Below: Raging fires silhouette the Dublin rooftops at the height of the Rising. Indiscriminate British artillery bombardments had started the conflagrations which laid waste large tracts of Dublin and wreaked millions of pounds' worth of damage. Centre: A row of British infantrymen fire on the Four Courts from behind an improvised barricade. It was no longer a police action but full-scale war in which no attempt was made to spare the civilians. Bottom: After the Rising, rebels in a British gaol. The Irish suffered some thousand casualties in the Rising and hundreds were imprisoned

Topix

George Morrison

George Morrison

The rebels knew they could not win. They were denounced by most of their countrymen. Yet this heroic, sacrificial gesture changed the history of Ireland – and perhaps the world?

The circumstances that led to the Irish rebellion of 1916 are of an intense complexity, historical, social, political, and perhaps above all psychological. Sean O'Faolain, that fine Irish writer, has written of his country: 'Most of our physical embodiments of the past are ruins, as most of our songs are songs of lament and defiance.' The Easter Rising was a complete failure, which left large parts of Dublin in ruins; yet without it Ireland might never have been free of English rule. The leaders, alive, had very few supporters even among the Irish patriots; dead, they became and have remained their country's heroes. It was a great historical paradox, and one that to this day the British have perhaps never really understood. Had they understood it, it is conceivable that the British might still have an empire, since the overthrow of British rule in Ireland became the model, the prototype, for the overthrow of imperial British might in Asia, in Africa, and elsewhere.

The historical complexity, from the British point of view, can be traced to a general misunderstanding of the Irish character and of Irish desires. The English were bewildered by the fact that most Irishmen, and all educated Irishmen, spoke English, and wrote it, as well as, and often better than, most Englishmen. They were further bewildered by the fact that a very large proportion of the Irish governing class was of English or Norman ancestry. In 1916, the English had not grasped the fact that for two centuries – since the brutal smashing of the old Irish governing class and the theft of their lands – it was precisely these people, Grattan, Tone, Parnell and so on, who had led the Irish in their longing to be free of alien rule. And the reason for this gross misunderstanding was that the English in England did not realize that the Irish way of life was in many ways – at least in terms of human relationships – culturally superior to the English way, less brutal, less materialistic, more spiritual, more dignified, with infinitely less snobbery and class distinction, directed more towards human happiness than to the acquisition of wealth or objects. Always technologically backward, the Irish were overwhelmed in the course of a thousand and more years by waves of conquerors. If those conquerors remained in Ireland, they became, as the English would and did say, seduced by the ease and pleasure of an Irish attitude that looks for charm, gaiety, and wit rather than for profit: they became 'more Irish than the Irish'.

And this the English, in England, dismissed as fecklessness. The fact that the Irish had different values from their own was regarded as funny – and the 'stage Irishman' was created in London. The fact that English might had always, eventually, crushed Irish rebellion was remembered; the fact that Irishmen had fought with immense distinction in all the major armies of Europe, and not least in that of Great Britain, was often forgotten. From the point of view of Whitehall at the turn of the century Paddy-and-his-pig was an essentially comical, child-like figure. He should know, in English terms, his proper station in life. Perhaps, at a pinch, the Anglo-Irish (an odious and meaningless term) might administer this province of Great Britain, but Paddy, never.

On the other hand, these people were politically troublesome and, furthermore, the English of the late Victorian age were a decent lot on the whole. During the Great Famine of 1846 the English liberals had let Ireland starve in the interests of their *laissez-faire* ideology – to have fed them would have interfered with the workings of the free market so far as corn chandlers were concerned – but later second thoughts prevailed. The Irish were to be given partial sovereignty over their own affairs, and a Home Rule Bill was passed. But then the First World War began. Home Rule was postponed until victory over the Germans should have been achieved. Paddy wouldn't mind, why should he? Paddy would join the British army, as he had always done and as scores of thousands of Irishmen did. Paddy wouldn't understand – and many, perhaps most, did not.

Mounting a revolution

But some Irishmen did understand. The most important of these were the members of the Irish Republican Brotherhood or IRB (which must not be confused with the Irish Republican Army, or IRA, a later creation). The IRB had been formed in 1858. It was a secret society which probably never numbered more than 2,000 including those Irishmen who belonged to it and who lived in England, America, or elsewhere. The majority of its members were what might be loosely called 'intellectuals' and in this, in their determination, and in their secrecy they bore a certain resemblance to their Russian contemporaries, Lenin's small Bolshevik Party. However, their aims were political rather than economic. They were patriots, dedicated to the ideal of national independence, and were prepared to use all means – including force – to achieve this ▷**599**

Above: One of the banners run up on the General Post Office, Dublin, after it had been seized by the rebels for their headquarters

Below: Irish Volunteers drilling in Dublin, 1915. One thousand men from this primitive army challenged the might of Great Britain

George Morrison

*Seeds of bitterness and resentment were sown in the 19th century when rapacious landlords, mostly Protestant Anglo-Irishmen who rarely visited their estates, authorized savage evictions of impoverished, land-hungry tenants. Unable to collect rents, they were more concerned with selling and rationalizing their estates than they were with the plight of the peasants who desperately wanted a few acres to grow potatoes. **Above:** An evicted family, Donegal. **Right:** Resisting eviction, 1881. The door is blocked with furze bushes through which the defenders hurl out boiling water. **Below:** British infantry at an eviction, 1890*

end. They provided, as it were, the general staff of the mass movement for Irish freedom from British rule, and their fortnightly publication, *Irish Freedom* (founded in 1910), advocated complete republican government for the whole of Ireland. It is significant that all the men who signed the proclamation of an Irish Republic on Easter Monday were members of the IRB.

When the First World War began, John Redmond, the leader of the Irish Nationalist Party and Parnell's heir, immediately proclaimed his acceptance of the postponement of Home Rule, both for himself and for his followers. These included the Irish Volunteers, perhaps then some 200,000 strong (of whom maybe a couple of thousand were trained and armed). This force had been created in November 1913 as a counter to the Ulster Volunteers (Vol. 3, p. 412), which were originally formed to fight Home Rule. The Ulster Volunteers were also prepared to postpone a struggle that had recently seemed both inevitable and imminent, and from the North of Ireland as from the South scores of thousands of young men went off to fight, and only too often to die, in Flanders. As volunteers. Indeed, Redmond suggested to the government in London that they could remove all British troops from Ireland: his Volunteer force and the Ulster Volunteers were quite capable of seeing that there were no disturbances in Ireland throughout the period of the war.

The IRB had other ideas. At a meeting of their supreme council, as early as August 1914, the decision was taken—in secret of course—that there must be an Irish insurrection before the end of Britain's war with Germany. Until Easter Week 1916 the active members of the IRB were fully occupied in mounting this revolution.

They had at their disposal brains, a fairly considerable amount of money—mostly from Irish Americans—and little else. They had to act through the Irish patriotic organizations, over many of which they had obtained partial control, and if the rising were to be a military success they had to acquire arms, either from British arsenals, or from abroad, which meant in effect from Germany. The balance sheet was roughly as follows: apart from Ulstermen and certain landlords and industrialists, the people of Ireland wanted their freedom from British rule. However, the people were temporarily agreeable to the Home Rule solution, even though the postponed bill gave Ireland less than Dominion status in fiscal and other matters. Furthermore, the farming community, even more important in Ireland then than it is now, was doing very well out of the war. Thus the IRB could rely on very considerable emotional sympathy but little, if any, practical help

from the mass of the people. And since the Irish are in some measure a volatile race, there was no telling how they would react to a rising. Certainly the Roman Catholic Church would be against such a deed: and the parish priests were and are very powerful spokesmen in Ireland.

So far as fighting men went, any insurrection would seem doomed to certain defeat. Redmond's huge numbers of Volunteers were mostly unarmed, or were fighting for the British in France. However, some of those who remained in Ireland and were armed and trained could be relied upon. Their chief-of-staff was the historian Eoin MacNeill, and their commandant a schoolmaster in his early thirties named Patrick Pearse. Both of these men were members of the IRB, but as events will show they did not see eye to eye on tactics. The Volunteers were scattered throughout Ireland.

Resources of David and Goliath
The other para-military force was James Connolly's Irish Citizen Army. Connolly was a socialist who in 1896 had founded the Socialist Republican Party. He was a trained soldier. In 1908 James Larkin had created the Irish Transport and General Workers' Union. When that union organized a strike in 1913, and the strike was broken by strong-arm methods, Connolly decided that a workers' defensive force was needed and created his Citizen Army. It was led by himself and by an ex-British Army officer named Jack White. It has been said that this was the most efficient military force at the disposal of the Republicans. It was, however, very small. When it came to the actual fighting, it was only some 250 men who went out, as opposed to about 1,000 from the Volunteers.

Supporting these was the women's organization. Countess Markievicz—an Irishwoman, born a Gore-Booth, and of aristocratic ancestry—was one of the most prominent. She fought as an officer of the Citizen Army throughout the Easter Rising for she was not only a patriot but a socialist. There were also the so-called 'Fianna Boys', lads who enjoyed the manoeuvring before the Rising, as most boys would, and who also showed guts and resourcefulness when the real thing happened. They were messengers, runners, and so on.

Against them they had what was, on paper at least, a most formidable force.

To maintain their control over Ireland, the British relied primarily on the Royal Irish Constabulary, an armed police force, living largely in barracks, and some 10,000 strong. They were almost all Irishmen, knew their districts thoroughly, and were in 1916, with a very few exceptions, entirely loyal to the Crown. They were well trained, well equipped, only moderately

unpopular (the Irish do not love police forces), and well informed. English HQ was Dublin Castle, and 'the Castle' relied on the RIC for its field intelligence.

In Dublin itself the police were not armed, though of course there were arms available. They numbered about 1,000 and were organized on the model of the London police. The Special Branch was concerned with politics. Through its investigations, and general infiltration of Irish republican politics, the Castle was supposed to know what the IRB was planning. The Special Branch did not seem, however, to have been particularly good at this job, nor to have infiltrated the IRB to any great extent. On the other hand the blame may rest with those in the Castle to whom they sent their reports. The evaluation of intelligence is infinitely more important than its accumulation.

And behind those 'occupation' forces there was a large British army in Ireland and what, in wartime and in Irish terms, were almost infinite reserves in Great Britain. If it were a mere question of manpower, the Irish had not a hope.

As for fire-arms, the David and Goliath ratio was even more vivid. Before the outbreak of the First World War the Ulster Volunteers had bought some 35,000 German rifles, the Irish Volunteers about 1,000. And of course the British army had everything, including artillery of all sorts. The Irish made an attempt to rectify this by getting rifles from Germany. Sir Roger Casement, an Irishman with a distinguished past, went to Germany from neutral America. He was to bring the weapons for the Easter Rising that the IRB had agreed on. His mission was a failure. British naval intelligence had broken some German cyphers. The British navy was thus able to intercept the German ship carrying the guns. Casement himself was immediately arrested when he came ashore from a U-boat near Tralee, in County Kerry, on Good Friday. Later the English tried him and hanged him as a traitor. The guns on which the Irish had been relying, even for this forlorn hope, had not arrived. Were they still to go on?

It is here that the different personalities and attitudes become important. We must pause to look at the men, English and Irish, involved; and also at the whole meaning of *Sinn Fein*.

Sinn Fein is usually translated as 'ourselves alone', and this is perhaps the best rendering in English of a complicated Irish concept. It means, first of all and above all, independence from British rule. But since Irish history was in those days so much bound up with contemporary Irish politics, it had a secondary meaning. For many centuries the Irish had hoped for the help of England's enemies to get rid of the ▷ 600

Patrick Pearse, in barrister's robe and wig

Above: *MacNeill – attempted to stop Rising*
Below: *Lord Wimborne – lord-lieutenant*

Below: *Countess Markievicz – a socialist*

English. The Spaniards and the French had let them down as the Germans were to do in 1916. This was not so much because Britain's enemies lacked the anxiety to defeat Britain in Ireland but because of geographical-military complications (tides, prevailing winds, and so on). Thus *Sinn Fein* also meant that the Irish must rely upon themselves alone in order to rid themselves of their British rulers. For the British, in the years to come, the 'Shinners' were to be the epitome of violent republicanism in Ireland. In fact the party, which only had its first annual convention as late as 1905, was essentially democratic. It had run a parliamentary candidate (who was defeated) in the Leitrim election of 1908. But as time went on it gained an increasing number of the extremists from Redmond's Nationalist Party. Arthur Griffith, its leader and also the editor of the *United Irishmen,* was never a fanatic. He believed in constitutional tactics – and was thus far less of an extremist than many of the IRB leaders – but, unlike Redmond's and Parnell's old party, he no longer trusted the alliance with the Liberal Party in Great Britain. Ourselves alone. To many young men it was a most attractive idea.

The British rulers were, on the whole, a shadowy lot. The Liberal government in London was inevitably devoting almost all its attention to the gigantic struggle on the Continent. Since Ireland appeared so placid in 1916, neither the best politicians nor by any means the best British soldiers were in the country. Augustine Birrell was Chief Secretary. Possessed, it was said, of extreme personal charm, he was a *belle lettrist* whose books, now forgotten, enjoyed in their time considerable esteem. He appears to have regarded his job in Dublin – which might be described as active head of the administration – as something of a sideline to his career as a *littérateur,* and spent a very large proportion of his time being charming in London. His principal Assistant Secretary, responsible for political affairs, was a civil servant experienced in colonial administration, Sir Matthew Nathan. He seems to have had little comprehension of the Irish temperament and to have been happiest behind his desk, dealing with routine paperwork. The general officer commanding the British army in Ireland was a Major-General Field. He, even more, seems to have had no idea of what was going on in Ireland at all. And finally there was Lord Wimborne, the lord-lieutenant and the King's representative, who presided over the British administration as a sort of constitutional monarch with all the powers, and most of the limitations, that that implies. However, he knew Ireland well. He had sponsored the land act of 1903,

which had pacified the Irish countrymen by further advantageous changes of the tenant-landlord relationship. He was popular with the Irish governing class, as was Birrell; but, unlike his Chief Secretary, he did not at all care for the situation that was developing.

The British intelligence services had, as we have seen, infiltrated the various Irish 'resistance' movements. The Volunteers, it must be assumed, had few secrets not known to Dublin Castle. And the Castle knew that a rising was planned to take place as soon as possible after the landing of Casement and his German guns. On 21st April 1916, Casement landed and was immediately arrested. Wimborne, who was to·have gone to Belfast, cancelled his visit and on Sunday the 23rd, that is to say only a matter of hours before the Rising took place, demanded of Nathan that he immediately arrest 'between sixty and a hundred' of the Irish leaders. Had this been done successfully, it seems unlikely that any Rising would have taken place *at that time.* However, it was probably too late for a mere police action by that date. The men of the Citizen Army and the more militant Volunteers were under arms and ready to fight. As it was, Nathan persuaded his 'constitutional monarch' that there was no need for action. And Birrell was in London.

It would seem probable that Nathan's intelligence service had briefed him as to what was happening within the high command of the Volunteers after the news of Casement's arrest, that he knew Eoin MacNeill had decided that without the guns the Rising must be cancelled or at least postponed. What Nathan presumably did not know was that this decision finally split the Volunteers, and that the IRB was almost solidly behind Patrick Pearse and those other Irish patriots who were prepared to go ahead with the Rising even in these disadvantageous, indeed well-nigh suicidal, circumstances. All this sounds very neat and staff-officerish when put down on paper, but of course the reality was far more chaotic, involving a clash of multiple personalities, orders and counter-orders, and very considerable bitterness. Indeed MacNeill's decision to call off the Rising, and Pearse's to go ahead, was really the death-knell of the Volunteers and of the Nationalist Party whose armed force they were supposed to be. After the Rising, the political leadership of those hostile to British rule in Ireland passed to *Sinn Fein,* while those who fought in Easter week became the nucleus of the Irish Republican Army.

Certainly MacNeill's last-minute proclamation that the Rising be cancelled – he had boys bicycling all over the country, and even announced this supposed non-

Some Irishmen chose to fight for 'country' rather than 'king'

George Morrison

Imperial War Museum

Above: A Dublin tram bedecked with British recruiting slogans, 1915. Home Rule now had to await German surrender. Paddy wouldn't mind, why should he? Paddy would join the British Army as he had always done—and as scores of thousands of Irishmen did. *Left:* Citizen Army parading outside Liberty Hall. When James Connolly assumed command of the Army he hung this provocative banner outside the building. The small Citizen Army contributed some 250 men to the rebel force. *Below:* Recruiting poster inviting young Irishmen to share the carnage of the trenches and die for Great Britain. By 1916 there was fierce opposition to conscription. Men felt they owed nothing to Great Britain. It was her war, not Ireland's

Above: Embattled rebels in the General Post Office, Sackville Street, Easter Monday, 1916

*Above: British troops searching the gutted GPO, 3rd May 1916. The rebels evacuated it when red-hot and just about to collapse. **Below:** Dublin slum-dwellers jeered at the rebels and carried off charred timbers from devastated buildings in Sackville Street as firewood*

happening in the Sunday papers—cannot possibly have been unknown to Nathan. He must have taken into account the fact that a few hot-heads were likely to ignore this order: he must also have known that the vast bulk of the Volunteers would breathe a sigh of relief and that the clergy—to whom the English have often attached an exaggerated political importance in Ireland owing to their ubiquity and their marked difference from the Anglican clergy in England—would support MacNeill and the mass of his supporters, content with the promise of eventual, diluted Home Rule. The handful of extremists could be dealt with—though not at all as easily as the English thought—by the overwhelming forces arraigned against them. No special precautions were taken, despite Lord Wimborne's fully justified fears. Indeed, on Easter Monday, the first day of the Rising, a great many British officers were at Fairyhouse Races.

The Easter Rising was suicidal. Patrick Pearse was well aware of this. Before ever it happened he said to his mother: 'The day is coming when I shall be shot, swept away, and my colleagues like me.' When his mother enquired about her other son, William, who was also an extreme nationalist, Pearse is reported to have replied: 'Willie? Shot like the others. We'll all be shot.' And James Connolly is said to have remarked: 'The chances against us are a thousand to one.' On the morning of the Rising, when asked by one of his men if there was any hope, he replied, cheerfully: 'None whatever!'

It was hard for the staff officers and colonial administrators of Dublin Castle, accustomed to weighing possibilities so far as their own actions were concerned, to realize that a group of men, perhaps 1,250 strong (the Citizen Army took no notice of MacNeill), was prepared to fight and die in such circumstances. But they should have been wiser in their age: Langemarck was recent, Verdun was going on, the Somme was about to happen. Seldom in history have men been so willing, indeed so eager, to throw away their lives for an ideal, almost any ideal, and the Irish ideal had long roots. The men went out and fought.

Easter week

The essence of the Irish plan was to seize certain key points in the city, and hold these for as long as possible, thus disrupting British control of the capital. It was then hoped that one of three things might happen: the country might rise in sympathy; the British might realize the ultimate impossibility of controlling Ireland and pull out; and last and faintest of hopes, the Germans might somehow come to the rescue of the rebels. Since the rebels had no artillery of any sort, their ▷**606**

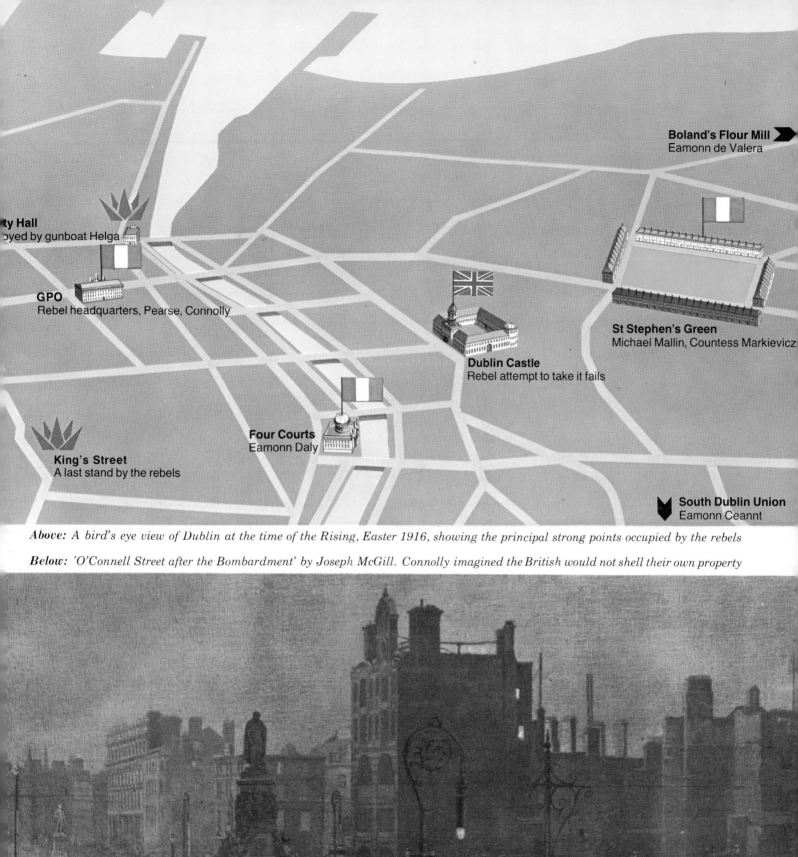

Boland's Flour Mill
Eamonn de Valera

ty Hall
oyed by gunboat Helga

GPO
Rebel headquarters, Pearse, Connolly

St Stephen's Green
Michael Mallin, Countess Markievicz

Dublin Castle
Rebel attempt to take it fails

Four Courts
Eamonn Daly

King's Street
A last stand by the rebels

South Dublin Union
Eamonn Ceannt

Above: A bird's eye view of Dublin at the time of the Rising, Easter 1916, showing the principal strong points occupied by the rebels

Below: 'O'Connell Street after the Bombardment' by Joseph McGill. Connolly imagined the British would not shell their own property

1 *Mementoes of resistance and revolt. Top row, left to right: Parnell on matchbox; badge and cap badge of Irish Volunteers; Pearse medallion; postcard depicting Pearse reading the proclamation of the provisional government. Bottom row, left to right: British military pass, 1916; Parnell memorial badge; Irish Volunteers button; 'Daughter of Erin' badge and Home Rule demonstration shamrock, 1912. **2** Pictured after the Rising: the women who fought so bravely during the siege of the GPO. **3** 'The Surrender of Countess Markievicz' painted by Kathleen Fox. **4** Plaque in Kilmainham Gaol commemorating the rebel leaders who were executed. **5** Portrait of Eamonn de Valera on an Irish Volunteers banner. Opposite: de Valera under arrest. His life was spared because he was of American birth*

George Morrison

strong-points could only hold out provided that the British did not use their artillery. Connolly and the socialists hoped that the British would, for capitalist reasons, not bombard Dublin and thus destroy their own – or largely their own – property. This, too, was an illusion.

H-hour was 12 noon and since this was a Bank Holiday there were crowds in the streets who witnessed the small bodies of Volunteers and of the Citizen Army marching, armed, through the city to seize their various strongpoints. It went, on the whole, remarkably smoothly. Five major buildings or groups of buildings were seized north of the River Liffey, nine south of it, and some of the railway stations were occupied. Headquarters were established in the massive General Post Office in Sackville Street (now O'Connell Street) from which Irish flags were flown and where Patrick Pearse announced the creation of a provisional government of the new Irish Republic. With him in the Post Office were Connolly as military commander, Joseph Plunkett (a very sick man), The O'Rahilly, Tom Clark, Sean MacDermott, and other leaders. There, too, was a young man named Michael Collins. The rebels immediately set about preparing the Post Office against the attack which they expected almost at once. The four other principal strong-points seized were the South Dublin Union, a congeries of poor-houses and the like (commanded by Eamonn Ceannt); the Four Courts, the headquarters of the legal profession, where heavy law books were used as sandbags (Eamonn Daly); St Stephen's Green, where trenches were dug and barricades of motor-cars erected (Michael Mallin and Countess Markievicz); and Boland's Flour Mill, which covered the approach roads from Kingstown, now Dun Laoghaire, where any reinforcements from England would almost certainly disembark (Eamonn de Valera).

An attempt to seize Dublin Castle failed. An attempt to capture a large quantity of arms and ammunition from the arsenal in Phoenix Park known as the Magazine Fort was only partially successful and merely a few rifles seized. On the other hand, the rebels successfully cut telephone lines, and the Castle was for a time almost isolated. A further success was that a troop of Lancers which attempted to charge down Sackville Street was repulsed with casualties.

The British had been taken by surprise and were now almost completely in the dark. The Castle immediately ordered troops up from the Curragh and other camps outside Dublin and appealed to London for reinforcements. There, Lord French was commander-in-chief. He was an Irishman and an ardent Unionist. He immediately ordered that no less than four divisions be alerted for transfer to Ireland.

British policy was in fact thrown into reverse. Appeasement of the Irish was out; the rebels were to be crushed, rapidly, and massively. But if the British in Dublin were in the dark, so were the rebels. They had no wireless links either between the strong-points they had seized or with the outside world. Communication by runner became difficult and eventually impossible when the fighting reached its peak.

From a military point of view, Tuesday was comparatively calm. The British were closing in cautiously. Their strategy was to throw a cordon around that area of Dublin where the rebels' strong-points were, then cut that area in two, and finally mop up. They moved artillery and troops into Trinity College, a natural fortress which the rebels had failed to seize, though they had planned to do so. The reason was the small number of fighting men available. Looting began by the crowds. Martial law was declared. British reinforcements arrived at Kingstown. A mad British officer, a Captain Bowen-Colthurst, had three harmless journalists shot 'while trying to escape' – a phrase to become hideously familiar, and not only in Ireland. The atrocities had begun.

Dublin burns, Dubliners starve

By Wednesday morning the rebels were outnumbered twenty to one. The British now began to attack in earnest. Their first major action was to destroy Liberty Hall, the headquarters of the Labour Party and of the trade unions, by shellfire from the gunboat *Helga*. As it happened, the rebels had anticipated this, and the building was entirely empty. The British gunfire was inaccurate and many other buildings were hit and many civilians killed. The army also was using artillery: a 9-pounder gun was fired against a single sniper. Dublin began to burn, and the Dubliners to starve, for there was no food coming into the city. This was no longer a police action but full-scale war in which no attempt was made to spare the civilians. Meanwhile, British reinforcements marching in from Kingstown were ambushed by de Valera's men and suffered heavy casualties, but by dint of numbers forced their way through. St Stephen's Green had been cleared of rebels, who retreated into the Royal College of Surgeons, and established a strong-point there.

On Thursday the new British commander-in-chief arrived. Since Ireland was under martial law, he held full powers there. This was General Sir John Maxwell, a soldier of some distinction who had returned the month before from Egypt, where he had been commander-in-chief of the Anglo-Egyptian armies. Although he numbered the Countess Markievicz among his relations, he had no knowledge of the

Patrick Pearse surrendering to the British

REBEL LEADERS SURRENDER.

THREE PRINCIPALS TRIED AND SHOT.

OTHERS ARRESTED & HELD FOR TRIAL UNCONDITIONALLY.

SERIOUS FIGHTING ALL ROUND THE CITY

HEAVY CASUALTIES IN DEAD AND WOUNDED.

CENTRE OF DUBLIN DEVASTATED BY FIRE; PALATIAL BUILDINGS IN ASHES.

The Sinn Fein insurrection, which broke out in Dublin City on Easter Monday at noon, has been effectively quelled.

The positions of vantage which the rebels took up in various parts of the city were reduced, and the leaders unconditionally surrendered.

Thomas J. Clarke, P. H. Pearse, and Thomas Macdonagh, three of the signatories to the poster proclaiming an Irish Republic, have been tried by court-martial and

Above: Headline in the *Irish Independent*
Below: Liberty Hall, Citizen Army HQ, in 1917. It was shelled by the gunboat, Helga

Photo: Alan Spain

current political mood in Ireland, and, indeed, as events were to prove, did more to undermine British rule in Ireland than all the rebels put together. He had been ordered by the British prime minister, Asquith, to put down the rebellion with all possible speed. And this he did regardless of political consequences.

The reinforcements from England were now in action. These were largely untrained men, and when they discovered that many of the men of the Irish Republican Army—as the rebels now and henceforth styled themselves—were not in uniform (how could they be?) they began shooting male civilians on sight.

On that day (Thursday) attacks were made on Boland's Mill, the men in the South Dublin Union were forced to give ground, and there was shelling of the General Post Office, which began to burn from the top down. Connolly was wounded twice. The first wound he hid from his men: the second was more serious, for one foot was shattered and he was in great pain. With the aid of morphia he carried on, directing the battle as best he could. The Dublin fires were now great conflagrations. With the streets full of small-arms fire and the water supplies often cut, these could not be dealt with. Still, no major rebel strong-point surrendered.

On Friday Connolly ordered the women who had fought so bravely to leave the General Post Office building, which was now cut off and burning. Later that day he and Pearse and the remaining rebels escaped from a building that was by now almost red-hot and about to collapse. They found temporary refuge nearby, while the British continued to shell the empty building. All knew that the end was near. A last battle was fought for King's Street near the Four Courts. It took some 5,000 British soldiers, equipped with armoured cars and artillery, twenty-eight hours to advance about 150 yards against some 200 rebels. It was then that the troops of the South Staffordshire Regiment bayoneted and shot civilians hiding in cellars. And now all was over. On Saturday morning Pearse and Connolly surrendered unconditionally.

Like so much else about the Easter Rising, casualties are hard to estimate. It would seem that those of the British were about 500; those of the Irish, including civilians, about twice that figure. Material damage was estimated at about £2½ million. Large parts of Dublin lay in ruins.

When, on Sunday, the arrested rebels were marched across Dublin from one prison compound to another, they were at times jeered at and booed by the crowds, and particularly in the slum areas the mass of public opinion had been against the rebels before the Rising and remained so until the reprisals began. ▷ **608**

Left: The rebellious capital was not allowed to forget that British military might had crushed the Easter Rising. Tanks clatter past the saluting base during General French's peace parade, Dublin 1919

On the direct orders of the cabinet in London, reprisals were swift, secret, and brutal. The leaders were tried by court martial and shot: only when they were dead were their deaths announced. Among those thus killed were Willie Pearse, who was no leader and who, it was generally believed in Ireland, was killed because he had followed his famous brother; the invalid Plunkett; and, most disgusting of all to Irish minds, Connolly, who was dying and who had to be propped up in bed for the court martial in his hospital room. He was shot in a chair, since he could not stand. A wave of disgust crossed all Ireland. That wave did not subside when Asquith defended these measures in the Commons; nor when he realized that a mistake had been made, and sacked Maxwell.

When London at last understood that its methods were uniting all Ireland against Britain, there was yet another change of British policy. Many of the three thousand-odd men arrested after the Rising were released from British gaols. They returned to Ireland and began immediately to reorganize a new and more powerful IRA, now with the backing of the people. This was a gesture of appeasement by Lloyd George, the new prime minister, who called an Irish Convention intended to solve 'the Irish problem'. Since *Sinn Fein* boycotted the Convention, it was a complete failure. Again British policy was thrown into reverse, and the leaders of the new independence movement were arrested in the spring of 1918. Michael Collins, however, escaped arrest, though there was a price on his head, dead or alive, which eventually reached the sum of £10,000. He was to be the great guerrilla leader in the next round of the struggle. The Irish leaders, with much backing from the United States, both emotional and financial, set about creating a viable alternative government which could and did take over when the British should have at last seen that they could not win. *Sinn Fein* triumphed, and won most of the Irish seats in the 1918 election. The elected members, however, formed their own 'parliament', *Dail Eireann,* rather than sit in Westminster. Collins drew up a strategy of resistance, first passive, then obstructive, and finally active, which has since been pursued elsewhere against British imperialism, and indeed against the imperialisms of other nations. And in January of 1919 the first shots of the new rebellion were fired in County Tipperary.

The Easter Rising was a total failure. And yet it was a total success. After Easter week 1916 permanent English rule in Ireland became an impossibility. One tragedy was a triumph. Other tragedies were to follow. But the Irish achieved it, and alone.

George Morrison

Four Nationalist Leaders

The First World War was a midwife of revolution. And this can be clearly seen in the careers of four European nationalist leaders – de Valera, Venizelos, Masaryk, and Piłsudski. The war was vital to them and their countrymen. The opportunities which were offered and taken were to shape the history of post-war Europe

EAMONN DE VALERA
– 'politician by accident'
David Thornley

If most revolutionaries are to some extent 'politicians by accident', the description is especially applicable to the men who carried on the 1916 struggle into its second phase of guerrilla war and international diplomacy. Mostly young men, often in their twenties, and without administrative experience, they came into their inheritance as the result of the prompt liquidation by General Maxwell's firing squads of almost the entire middle-age group of revolutionary leaders. And they were propelled into politics by a movement whose sole aim was independence and which had correspondingly avoided all but the most generalized ideas of social obligation.

Of no one was this more true than Eamonn de Valera. Born in New York on 14th October 1882 of a Spanish father and an Irish mother, he was sent back to Ireland at the age of two to be reared by a maternal uncle. A solemn, industrious child, he succeeded, through family self-sacrifice, part-time jobs, and scholarships, in educating himself to the attainment of the BA, BSc degrees of the old Royal University. He was drawn into nationalism through his devotion to the Irish language, joined the Irish Volunteers on its foundation in November 1913, and by the time of the rising had risen to the rank of commandant, with specific responsibility for the important Boland's Flour Mill outpost.

But there was still little hint of the power and adulation that were to come. At this period he was a teacher of mathematics, a tall, ascetic figure, withdrawn, and a poor speaker – which in a sense he always remained, his later magnetism being physical rather than rhetorical. In neither of the main organs into which revolutionary feeling was channelled was he in the top hierarchy. In the Volunteers, although appointed commandant in March 1915, he had remained outside the inner circle of the leadership; in October 1915 he refused Tomas MacDonagh's pressing invitation to join the executive council of the Volunteers. And of the Irish Republican Brotherhood, which master-minded the Rising, he was a passive member.

But a succession of factors, some of them deriving from the development of his personality and experience, some of them wholly coincidental, swept him to the leadership of the revolutionary movement in the period between May 1916 and April 1919. The first was the sheer fact of his survival. The first of the executed leaders was shot on 3rd May, the last on 12th May, the day after de Valera's own condemnation. By then a revulsion of public feeling, plus his American birth and arguable citizenship, saved his life. At once the aura descended upon him of 'the last surviving commandant' of the Easter Rising. The title was not quite technically accurate, but his seniority among the survivors was unquestionable and gave him, as Convict 95 in Dartmoor, and later in Lewes gaol, the *de jure* leadership of the Volunteer prisoners. Indeed, by comparison with many of them, he possessed, at thirty-four, the additional seniority of age. For over a year he occupied his time with mathematics and the maintenance of discipline and morale among his fellow-convicts.

Meanwhile, Irish opinion slowly changed. The heroism of the Volunteers and the savagery of the executions in the face of protests from sources as disparate as George Bernard Shaw and the *Manchester Guardian* pointed up the sacrificial role of Pearse and his little band. The continued failure of the Irish Parliamentary Party to make the smallest progress towards the peaceful attainment of independence except under the threat of partition discredited it. The Irish Republican Brotherhood was revived and reorganized by men like Michael Collins, back in Ireland in December 1916 with the first batch of 600 freed internees. Sheer war-weariness and the shadow of the introduction to Ireland of military conscription to sustain Great Britain's wasting armies fomented anti-British feeling. In February 1917 in Roscommon *Sinn Fein*, on an abstentionist platform and with Volunteer support, captured its first seat from the Irish Parliamentary Party; in May in Longford it took its second. In June the last of the prisoners were released. Cheering crowds greeted them as they stepped off the boat at Dun Laoghaire. For none was the reception so ecstatic as for de Valera. He was at once pressed into the *Sinn Fein* candidature in a third by-election in East Clare, and in July he was elected.

His informal public status as the surviving leader of the revolutionary tradition was now generally taken for granted. To give it formal expression he needed to assume the leadership of its institutional organizations, the Volunteers, *Sinn Fein*, the Irish Republican Brotherhood, and ultimately the revolutionary government. He never achieved leadership of the third, which remained effectively under Collins's control, and this dichotomy was to contri-

1 Eamonn de Valera – as a commandant during the Easter Rising, there was little hint of the power and adulation that were to come. 2 Eleutherios Venizelos – in self-imposed exile he watched his dream of a Greater Greece crumble. 3 Thomas Masaryk – a propagandist and conspirator in the cause of racial justice and human rights. 4 Józef Piłsudski – discovered that national unity created by the euphoria of independence had little substance

bute not a little to subsequent divisions. But within two years the leading positions in the other three were his. In October 1917 *Sinn Fein* held its tenth convention. This meeting abandoned Griffith's constitutional ideas in favour of an outright republican programme; Griffith stood down as president and de Valera was unanimously chosen to replace him. The Irish Volunteers nevertheless remained an independent and at times sceptical military movement, but the crucial personal status of de Valera, who had already been chosen as the spokesman of the released officers on the night of their return to Dublin, was further emphasized when the Volunteer Convention of November 1917 also elected him its president.

There remained only the leadership of the nation itself. This was effectively achieved in the general election of December 1918. De Valera himself was again in an English prison, but this, as with so many Irish leaders before him, served only to enhance his popularity. Mass excitement, the barrenness of the Parliamentary Party, Irish-American money, and enthusiastic organization, rising occasionally to intimidation, by the young men of the Volunteers, overcame the handicaps of censorship and the imprisonment of the principal leaders. *Sinn Fein* destroyed the old Party and won 73 seats out of 105. In January 1919 the nucleus of these members who were at liberty constituted themselves the first *Dail Eireann* (Assembly of Ireland) and declared the independence of Ireland. They appointed only an acting head of state; they were waiting for de Valera. They did not have long to wait; on 3rd February Collins successfully organized de Valera's rescue from Lincoln gaol and he was smuggled back to Ireland more than ever the symbol of Ireland's will to freedom. The second session of *Dail Eireann* was convened on 1st April and de Valera was formally elected *Priomh-Aire*. The precise meaning of that Irish term was to cause more than semantic confusion three years later. Some were to argue that it meant no more than the first minister of the Dail, others that it symbolized the Presidency not merely of the nation but of a formally-constituted sovereign republic. But that problem was in the future, as were civil war, imprisonment, the loss of power, and its recapture. In May 1919 de Valera set out on a publicity campaign to the United States; here he would sharpen his already developing tactical skill in the toughest school there was – Irish-American politics. Whatever *Priomh-Aire* meant, the bespectacled mathematician to whom Pearse entrusted the command of the 3rd Battalion of the Dublin Brigade in March 1915 was now the Chief, and the Chief he was to remain.

ELEUTHERIOS VENIZELOS
– and the dream of a Greater Greece
Michael Llewellyn Smith

A tall, thin man with a white beard, a black skull-cap, rimless glasses, infinite charm, and 'an inexhaustible eloquence', in Lord Curzon's words, 'which leaves no chink for a reply'. Such was Venizelos in the heyday of his power and influence, at the Paris Peace Conference in 1919. The mandate for a Greek occupation of Smyrna and its hinterland which he obtained at Paris was the reward for four years of unwavering support for the Allied cause in the First World War – support which Venizelos analysed with candour in a speech in September 1915: 'It must be understood that the great powers, every one of them, are out for their own interests. But over the Eastern Question, where our own interests lie, the two Western powers are, to my mind, those whose interests concur with our own.' This self-interested backing of the side which, providentially, won, to-

Venizelos arrives at Salonika. Within weeks Venizelist troops were fighting with the Allied forces along the Macedonian Front

gether with his three-year battle against a King of Greece who thought differently, won Venizelos a reputation as the greatest Greek statesman since Pericles, which even his shattering defeat at the polls in 1920 did not affect. The Greek people were dismissed as ungrateful, ready as always to turn to their greatest men and rend them.

Venizelos preached a Greek renaissance which British philhellenes – men like Harold Nicolson at the Foreign Office, steeped in the classical tradition – wanted to believe in. Certainly Venizelos's first four years in office gave grounds for confidence in his powers. He left his native Crete in September 1910, to become prime

minister of Greece within a month of his arrival on the mainland. In the next four years he succeeded in changing the face of the country, and almost doubling its surface area and population. First proving his 'respectability' by dropping the anti-dynastic tendencies which were expected of him by the Military League of revolutionary officers which brought him to power, and working in harmony with the King, he proceeded to build up support among the Greeks of all classes who were tired of the factional politics of his predecessors and the national humiliations of the last few years. The Venizelist Liberals won 150 out of 181 seats in March 1912.

Venizelos's appeal was a nationalist appeal, to all Greeks, for a national regeneration. Uninterested in theories of government, lacking any rigid political philosophy, he devoted his energies to the reorganization and strengthening of Greek institutions in preparation for the fulfilment of Greece's national dream – the expansion of the Greek kingdom so as to include all those parts of the Ottoman empire which the Greeks regarded as theirs by historical and ethnological right – Epirus, Macedonia, Thrace, the islands, Smyrna, and finally even Constantinople itself. This dream was the 'Great Idea' which, as the Greeks saw it, Venizelos had come from Crete to fulfil. The very successful Balkan Wars of 1912-13 (Vol. 3, p. 404) in which Greece extended her boundaries northwards to include Ioannina and southern Epirus, Salonika and western Macedonia, were a great leap forward towards its fulfilment. Venizelos, as architect of the alliance of Balkan states which launched the successful crusade against the Turks, shared the popularity for victory with Prince Constantine, commander of the victorious Greek army, who became King on the assassination of his father in newly liberated Salonika in 1913.

Thus at the outbreak of the First World War Venizelos presided over a country which needed a period of peace and quiet, as he himself admitted, in order to digest its territorial gains. The war, however, which Venizelos rightly saw would lead to the final disintegration of the Ottoman empire, gave Greece an unrepeatable opportunity to extend her frontiers still farther and embrace the still unredeemed Greeks of Thrace and Asia Minor. Venizelos's policy was, therefore, to support the Entente powers in the hope that the Allies would uphold Greek claims on Ottoman territory after the war. The view of the King, who believed that the Central powers would win, was that Greek neutrality should be preserved at all costs.

On 1st March 1915, in an attempt to engage Greece on the side of the Entente powers, Venizelos proposed to commit

Greek troops in support of the forthcoming Allied landing at Gallipoli. The King rejected the proposal, and Venizelos resigned. In the elections which followed Venizelos was returned with 184 out of 310 seats. In October, however, having attempted once more to commit Greece to war by inviting an Allied expeditionary force to land at Salonika, he was again dismissed by the King, who was by now opposed to Greek involvement even in the event of a Bulgarian attack on Serbia, with whom Greece had a defensive alliance.

The division of the country into Royalists and Venizelists was now acute and bitter. The King was obliged to impose his views through successive puppet Royalist governments. Allied pressure on the Greeks, and violations of Greek sovereignty by the Allied army at Salonika, became more and more flagrant—and for this Venizelos was later to be blamed. But it was not until summer 1916, when the Bulgarians invaded Macedonia and occupied Kavalla, and the Greek garrison of 8,000 men, laying down their arms, was sent to internment in Germany—all to maintain the dogma of neutrality—that Venizelos acted. On 25th September he fled to Crete, proclaimed a revolution, and ten days later, on arrival in Salonika, formed a pro-Allied 'Provisional Government'. Within weeks Venizelist troops were fighting with the Allies on the Macedonian Front. For eight months Greece was physically divided into a Venizelist and a Royalist camp; then the Allies, losing patience with the King, forced him to vacate the throne and retire to Switzerland, and reinstated Venizelos as prime minister over a united Greece. At last the country, freed from the blockade instituted by the Allies against Royalist Greece, was able to devote all its energies to war. By September 1918, 250,000 Greek troops were engaged in Macedonia, and played a brave part in the offensive which broke through the Bulgarian Front. Through this useful contribution to the Allied war effort Venizelos hoped to justify Greece's claims at the peace conference. In his success he overreached himself, claiming and gaining Smyrna and western Asia Minor, and thus committing Greece to a far more arduous war, against a rejuvenated Turkey, and to defeat.

In his unbounded faith in the vigour and 'civilizing mission' of the Greeks, Venizelos was a nationalist; but his nationalism was undisturbed by the extent of foreign influence and interference in Greek affairs. From his experience in Crete he knew how far Greek policy was affected by the pressures of the great powers. He knew that Greek finances, ever since the Graeco-Turkish war of 1897 had been controlled by an international financial commission. His reaction to this was not to complain of exploitation, or speak of 'Greece for the Greeks', as his opposite number Kemal fought for 'Turkey for the Turks'. On the contrary, Venizelos tried, by co-operating to the full with the Western powers, to *use* them to further his policy of Greek expansion. Thus during his first premiership he summoned a French military mission and an English naval mission to reorganize the Greek army and navy. Thus he supported the Allied powers. Thus after the armistice, in order to strengthen his claim on Allied gratitude, he sent two divisions of Greek troops to support the disastrous French expedition to south Russia, although no Greek interest was involved. Thus, because the island was British, he did not press the Greek claim to Cyprus at the conference. All this he did to win the support of France and Great Britain.

Spellbound by Venizelos's vision of a Greater Greece spanning two continents, his admirers often forgot that Greece remained in fact a war-weary, economically fragile, bitterly divided country, longing

Sarcastic German cartoon depicts Venizelos as a puppet of the Allies. It asserts he will be 'first played with and then broken'

Ulk/Tasiemka

for peace. Venizelos's colleagues, in his absence in Paris, did nothing to heal the divisions, and the opposition spoke convincingly of oppression and persecution of Royalists. Venizelos reassured his friends in Paris that as soon as the peace was settled he would devote himself, with startling results, to internal affairs. For the Greeks that was too long to wait. At the general elections of November 1920 Venizelos fell, his Royalist enemies triumphed, and King Constantine returned to Greece. In self-imposed exile in western Europe, Venizelos watched his dream of a Greater Greece crumble in September 1922 when the Greek army was broken by Turkish troops, and Smyrna went up in flames. This for Greece was the end of the great war, and the end of five centuries of dreams. Venizelos died in France in 1936.

THOMAS MASARYK
— father of Czechoslovakia
Elizabeth Wiskemann

Thomas Masaryk's parents were German-speaking working people of Slav descent; they lived in Austrian Moravia near Hungarian Slovakia from which they came. After some elementary schooling they managed to send their son to the German grammar school in Brno, and later he embarked upon a classical course at the University of Vienna. He was prodigiously intelligent and industrious, and uncompromisingly upright. He picked up Czech and Slovak at an early age, and soon read French, Russian, and English. His marriage in 1878 to Charlotte Garrigue, an American girl studying music in Leipzig, brought him closer to the English-speaking world. In 1879 he began to teach philosophy in the University of Vienna. Finally, after publishing a book on the sociology of suicide, in 1882 Masaryk was appointed to lecture in Prague, a city which he then scarcely knew, at the new Czech University. His first lecture there was on the philosopher Hume and his scepticism, a new subject for a Central European university. He introduced another novelty by inviting his students to his home and taking a helpful interest in their lives. At the same time he was soon directing two periodicals in addition to writing on philosophy, history, and politics.

His name first became known to a wide public in 1886 when he helped to expose as forgeries some Czech manuscripts claimed to derive from the early Middle Ages. As a Czech patriot he repudiated faked origins, but many Czechs denounced him as a traitor to his people. This controversy drew him into the racial quarrels of Austria-Hungary in those days. Masaryk advocated what he called a realist's approach and was followed as a realist by two leading young men, Kramář and Kaizl. The three of them were elected as members of the Young Czech Party to the Austrian Parliament or Reichsrat, in 1891. As a deputy Masaryk mostly spoke on educational matters, but he also expressed advanced views on universal suffrage for men and women, and on social reform. He was in fact too liberal for the Young Czechs, who were chauvinist, and in 1893 he resigned from the Reichsrat and also from the Bohemian Diet to which he had belonged.

In the following years, back at the University in Prague, Masaryk became a centre of attraction not only for the more liberally-minded Czech students, but also for Croats and Serbs who looked to him for advice over their own national problem, that of the Southern (or Yugo) Slavs. Serb and Croat students from Bosnia (occupied by Austria-Hungary since 1878) and Herzegovina were forbidden by the authorities there to visit the University of Prague, but some of them came to Masaryk's lectures. Masaryk, who felt himself to be a Slovak rather than a Czech, also in the 'nineties helped the Slovak nationalists to survive the oppressive rule of the Hungarians. Thus he became the leading intellectual of the Slavonic nationalities in Austria-Hungary. This was an important part of his preparation for the future. In the world of those days it was almost unprecedented that a man should rise from the lowest ranks of society to Masaryk's eminence.

Masaryk waged two typical battles for enlightenment in 1899 and 1906 respectively. In 1899 he, who had grown up in the anti-semitic atmosphere of provincial Austria in the 1860's, protested against the sentence to death of a Jew called Hilsner who was accused of a ritual murder: the sentence was commuted to penal servitude for life and was ended only by the amnesty of 1916. In 1906 Masaryk himself was charged with anti-religious offences, for he had 'accused Catholicism of being a degenerate religion which needs politics for its defence'. The case against

him broke down and he was acquitted. Throughout both episodes he was ferociously attacked and showed unshaken courage.

In 1907 Masaryk was again elected to the Reichsrat, this time as a 'progressive realist'. A year later Austria-Hungary annexed Bosnia and Herzegovina (Vol. 2, p. 214). This was a blow to South Slav hopes, for it brought the direct subjection of many more Serbs and Croats to the Habsburg monarchy and seemed a step backwards in the evolution of the nationalities. Masaryk condemned this move out of hand; it had been greeted with enthusiasm by the Austrian Pan-Germans as a triumph for them. The annexation was followed by the arrest of fifty-three Croats as Pan-Serb agents; they were brought to trial at Zagreb in May 1909. Some of them were former students of Masaryk and he spoke in their favour in the Reichsrat. In the end no death sentences were pronounced and a case was brought later in the year in Vienna against Dr Friedjung. The latter was the author of an article in the *Neue Freie Presse* on 24th March 1909: this had accused the Zagreb defendants of conspiracy, quoting 'official' documents which Masaryk was able to prove had been forged.

Thus on the eve of the First World War Masaryk had challenged the chief vested interests in Austrian life, the chauvinist

Germans and the Catholic Church. It is not surprising that even he, since the retrograde measure of the annexation of Bosnia, had developed bitter feelings against the Habsburg monarchy. Although he would have regarded any attempt to establish an independent Czechoslovakia as unrealistic before the war, he decided that the possibility of destroying Austria-Hungary must be used once war had broken out. The dynasty had failed to reconcile its nationalities, and it was clear to Masaryk that if the Central powers won the war the dominion of the Germans and Magyars over the Slavs and Rumanians was likely to be accentuated.

At the age of sixty-four Masaryk set out to plead the cause first and foremost of the Czechs and Slovaks, but also of the others, before the outside world. He went first to Switzerland, then to Paris and London, then, in May 1917, to Russia, and finally, in 1918, to the United States. In the cause of racial justice and human rights Thomas Masaryk became a propagandist and even a conspirator. His idea of propaganda was, however, unusual: 'not to abuse the Germans, not to underestimate the enemy, to distort nothing, and not to exaggerate; not to make empty promises and not to beg for favours; to let facts speak for themselves. . . .' His former pupil Edvard Beneš, was his representative

Thomas Masaryk with volunteers for the Czech force in the French army at the recruiting camp, Stamford, Connecticut, 1918

in Paris. Unlike some of their countrymen, Masaryk and Beneš had always looked to the Western powers for leadership, rather than to Slavonic Russia; thus the Russian revolution did not disturb their plans, although it meant disentangling a Czech volunteer army from Russia. Both the Czech leaders were social reformers but not Marxists.

In December 1918 he returned to Prague where his supporters had taken over from the Austrian authorities. A democratic republic was founded with German, Magyar, and Ruthene citizens to whom the new Minorities Treaty and the Czechoslovak constitution guaranteed education and justice in their own languages. It should be noted that many of the new Czechoslovak officials were former Austrian ones and often administered the regulations in much the same way but in reverse.

JÓZEF PIŁSUDSKI
—the indomitable Pole
Antony Polonsky

The First World War radically changed the nature of the 'Polish Question'. For the first time since 1815 all three powers which had effected the partition of Poland were at war, and it soon became clear that the struggle would be a long one. As the conflict dragged on, both sides looked to the Poles for support. The promises each made, in an attempt to outbid the other, raised again the issue of Polish national status.

The political orientations of the different Polish groupings had become crystallized in the decade preceding the outbreak of the war (Vol. 1, p. 60). Piłsudski and his followers had seen in the revolutionary crisis in Russia between 1904 and 1907 the opportunity they had longed for to launch a new insurrection to regain Poland's lost independence. Piłsudski even went to Japan in 1904, during the Russo-Japanese War, to seek support from the Japanese high command. During the revolution he assumed control of the almost completely autonomous 'Military Organization' of the Polish Socialist Party (PPS), and led a series of attacks on Russian government outposts which culminated in the seizure of the railway station at Bezdany, north of Wilno, in September 1908.

Piłsudski's devotion to terrorism and his belief in the precedence of national liberation over social revolution provoked considerable dissatisfaction within the PPS. By 1906 it had become obvious that his activities would not spark off a national revolt; in addition, the strength of the Russian revolutionary and socialist movements was contradicting his view that Russia was one uniformly reactionary mass. The discontent within the PPS came to a head at the party's 9th Congress in November 1906, when a large group

seceded, creating the Polish Socialist Party —Left Wing. This group advocated close co-operation between the Polish and Russian revolutionary movements and held that the establishment of a constituent assembly in Warsaw would satisfy Polish national demands. Yet, even so modest a proposal was to prove a bar to co-operation with Rosa Luxemburg's Social Democracy, absolutely opposed to any notion of Polish national separateness.

Piłsudski himself was dissatisfied with the results of terrorism and became more and more convinced that only war between the partitioning powers, which by now seemed increasingly likely, could change Poland's position. But he saw that if Polish desires were to be given any consideration, a Polish military force, capable of playing an independent part in such a conflict, would have to be created. Already in June 1908 he had formed the League of Active Struggle to organize and train military units. Soon afterwards he moved to Galicia (Austrian Poland) where political conditions were least restrictive and where the Austrian government was not unsympathetic to his anti-Russian aims. His pre-war military activity reached its peak in November 1912, with the formation of the Provisional Committee of Confederated Parties Demanding Independence which united in support of a Polish independent military force almost all the Galician parties except the Conservatives (a grouping of large landowners) and the National Democrats. By the outbreak of the war, in spite of Piłsudski's disputes with the Committee and the internal divisions which plagued it, it could put nearly 7,000 Polish Legionaries in the field.

The National Democrats, under Dmowski, had bitterly opposed Piłsudski's attempts to initiate a national revolt in 1905, regarding them as a futile and dangerous echo of the activities of the 19th-century gentry revolutionaries. Dmowski even followed Piłsudski to Japan to dissuade the Japanese from giving him any assistance. In the elections for the First Duma in March and April 1906 the National Democrats won every seat in Russian Poland (the Congress Kingdom). But although they had some success in convincing both Russian public opinion and some officials that Polish aspirations were not necessarily hostile to the interests of the Russian state, their activity had little practical result. Nevertheless, by 1914 they had become the strongest political force both in the Congress Kingdom and in Prussian Poland, where a policy of germanization was being energetically pursued during this period. In Galicia they were less successful. Their pro-Russian orientation was unpopular, and politics here were still to a great extent dominated

by the Galician Conservatives. This group, mainly upper class and landowning in its support, which had been instrumental in obtaining self-government for Galicia in the 1860's, advocated strong links with the Habsburgs. The most it demanded in national terms was the incorporation of the Congress Kingdom into Austria-Hungary. National Democratic strength grew in Galicia, particularly after the introduction of universal suffrage in 1907.

On the outbreak of war, Piłsudski attempted to foment a national uprising in Russian Poland. On 6th August 1914 he crossed the Austro-Russian border near Cracow with his troops, hoping in this way to gain a certain freedom in relation to the Central powers, whom he had not consulted before acting. His plans failed utterly. The Poles in the Congress Kingdom, for the most part sympathetic to the National Democrats and even to the Russian war effort, greeted his troops with a mixture of hostility and indifference. He was thus faced with the alternative of either disbanding his legions or co-operating with the General National Committee, a rival organization set up in Galicia by the pro-Austrian Conservatives at the beginning of the war. He decided on co-operation, and became still firmer in his resolve when the Central powers' successful offensive in the summer of 1915 led to the Russian evacuation of the Congress Kingdom. It is true that Piłsudski still had serious reservations about the Austrians (indeed, by August the Germans were tentatively suggesting to Austria that she eventually annex the Congress Kingdom) and that he tried to prevent the Central powers from recruiting Polish soldiers in Russian Poland, but he was probably sincere when he wrote to Władysław Jaworski, a leading Galician Conservative, in August 1915: '. . . the political aim of the War . . . was and is the incorporation of Galicia and the Congress Kingdom into the framework of the Austro-Hungarian Monarchy.'

Piłsudski remained true to the policy of turning to Austria until mid-1916, when the increasing weakness of Austria and the hostility of the Hungarians, the Germans, and the Austrian army to the Austro-Polish solution had become evident. Already in August 1916 Bethmann Hollweg, the German chancellor, had forced the Austrians to agree to the setting up of an 'independent' Polish state. Piłsudski now became convinced that a satisfactory resolution of the 'Polish Question' depended on an agreement with Germany. When the Germans established a rump Polish state on 5th November 1916, Piłsudski supported their action; however, he demanded the setting up of a civilian government before he would help in the creation of an army. When this condition was met in January 1917 by the formation of a Provisional Council of State, he went ahead. He realized very quickly, however, that the Germans were interested only in a puppet state, and he refused to take the oath of allegiance to the Reich which was demanded of the army, and counselled his supporters to follow his example. In July 1917 he was arrested and interned in Magdeburg for the duration of the war. After his arrest the Council of State, soon renamed the Regency Council, was controlled by groups in the Congress Kingdom similar in character to the Galician Conservatives.

Since the beginning of the war the point of view of the National Democrats had also undergone important changes. Already in 1912 a secret party conference with delegates from all three parts of Poland meeting in Cracow had decided that in the event of war the party would support the Entente powers. Thus in August 1914 the party accepted enthusiastically the Manifesto to the Poles issued by Grand Duke Nicholas, which promised the Poles national unification under the sceptre of the Romanovs. In November it formed a pro-Entente Polish National Committee to counteract the influence of the pro-Austrian General National Committee. The Polish National Committee strongly attacked the Piłsudski legions and formed Polish

units, the so-called Gorczynski legions, to fight beside the Russian forces. Yet once again little was achieved, and the self-government promised to the Congress Kingdom had still not been granted when the Russians were forced to withdraw.

The situation changed somewhat after the February Revolution of 1917. The Provisional Government of Prince Lvov issued a manifesto on 30th March 1917 promising to set up a Polish state composed of the Congress Kingdom, Galicia, and Prussian Poland linked to Russia in a military union. However, it was clear that Russia was by now a less significant part of the Allied coalition, and in August 1917 the Polish National Committee moved to western Europe. It was first reconstituted in Lausanne, then adopted Paris as its headquarters, where it was headed by Dmowski himself. During 1918 the Allies committed themselves to the re-establishment of a Polish state and in November recognized the Polish National Committee as the future government.

Yet although the National Democrats had gained recognition abroad as the predominant Polish group, in Poland itself Piłsudski was in a strong position. His internment in Magdeburg allowed him to return to Poland in November 1918, following the collapse of the Central powers, with the aura of a martyr and the reputation of

an indomitable fighter for independence, unsullied by compromises. When the Austrian occupying authority in the southern part of the Congress Kingdom collapsed, the PPS, the Galician Polish Socialist Party, and a number of radical peasant groups set up a People's Government in Lublin led by the veteran Galician Socialist, Ignacy Daszyński, which was intended to supplant the still existing Regency Council established by the Germans in Warsaw. However, when Pilsudski returned from Magdeburg, he was rather surprisingly recognized by the Regency Council as its legal successor. He also enjoyed the overwhelming support of the armed forces maintaining the Lublin government. As a result, Daszyński resigned, acquiescing in the formation of a new People's Government controlled by Piłsudski.

Piłsudski decided to try to come to terms with the National Democrats. He accepted the formation of a compromise government headed by Ignacy Paderewski and agreed that the delegation of the Polish National Committee, with some Piłsudski-ite additions, should represent Poland at Versailles. Nevertheless, the next few years were to show that the bitter antagonisms of the pre-war and wartime period could not be overcome so easily, and that the illusion of national unity created by the euphoria of independence had little substance.

Below: Piłsudski leading the Polish Legion across the frontier between Austrian Poland and Russian Poland on 6th August 1914

India, 1914-18/Christopher Falkus

India at War

Indians, spontaneously, and almost unanimously, embraced Great Britain's cause in the war. Nearly one million men fought on the Western Front, in East Africa, and in the Middle East and it was scarcely any wonder that they considered such efforts entitled them to higher status in the empire

The outbreak of the First World War found India in a state of political unrest. Growing dissatisfaction with her status as a dependency was expressed by increasing demands for self-government, an aspiration shared by both 'moderate' and 'extremist' members of the National Congress. This body, formerly little more than a glorified debating society for educated Indians, was rapidly becoming a focus of agitation as the British government persisted on an exasperating course. For no clear policy regarding India's future had been laid down, though some statesmen made matters worse with remarks like that of Lord Milner in 1908: 'The idea of extending what is described as colonial self-government to India which seems to have a fascination for some untutored minds, is a hopeless absurdity.' The Germans hoped for great things from Indian discontent, and in the years before the war tried to spread ideas of rebellion among the Indian people. There were many in Great Britain who shared the opinion of author William Archer that 'the moment Britain gets into trouble elsewhere, India, in her present temper, would burst into a blaze of rebellion'.

But in the event these fears proved groundless. Many Indians still prized the imperial connexion and some members of Great Britain's Liberal government showed themselves more tolerant of Indian hopes than imperialists like Milner, or the autocratic Curzon, who described them as 'fantastic and futile dreams'. Edwin Montagu, for example, later to become secretary of state for India, did not condemn the winds of change out of hand: 'A new generation, a new school of thought, fostered by our education and new European learning has grown up, and it asks "what are you going to do with us?"'

Encouraged by what they hoped was a growing sympathy for their aims, the Indians, spontaneously, and almost unanimously, embraced Great Britain's cause in the war. Offers of military and financial help poured in from all over the subcontinent both within and outside the territory of British India. The great Indian princes pledged their services and made massive financial donations. Nepal offered its resources; even the Dalai Lama in Tibet offered a thousand troops; while the Congress expressed enthusiastic support. Instead of having to reinforce India to combat sedition, Great Britain was able to denude India of almost all of her troops and equipment, while Indian forces were able to take their places on the battlefield before contingents from the dominions were trained and ready. In unfamiliar, bitterly cold conditions Indians reached the Western Front during the critical winter of 1914, symbolizing not only the wider imperial contributions which were to follow but also, in their own eyes, their right to be considered as free and equal members of a community fighting in a common cause. Altogether over 800,000 Indian soldiers fought on the Western Front, in East Africa, and in the Middle East. Their fatal casualties numbered 65,000, and their economy was brought to the verge of bankruptcy. It was scarcely any wonder that they considered such efforts entitled them to a higher status within the empire they were sacrificing so much to maintain.

Initial response in Great Britain was slightly incredulous. The public was both surprised and dazzled by the nature of India's effort and *The Times* wrote in 1914 that 'the Indian Empire has overwhelmed the British nation by the completeness and unanimity of its enthusiastic aid'. Nationalists in India were quick to emphasize what they expected in return. The famous theosophist Mrs Annie Besant, social worker, radical, and sometime Christian, atheist, and Hindu, said at the Congress in 1914 that India was 'not content to be any longer a child in the nursery of the Empire . . . She is showing the responsibility of the man in the Empire. Give her the freedom of the man in India'.

Perhaps British statesmen were at fault in allowing Indian expectations to rise too rapidly. Whatever the reason, a mood of uneasiness replaced the excitement of the early months. Educated Indians noted with concern that the imperial government could not be persuaded to define their long-term plans for India. Agitation increased when Mrs Besant and Mr Bal Gangadhar Tilak, the extremist leader, launched 'home rule' movements. Muslims in India were disconcerted by Turkey's entry on the side of the Central powers. Projected schemes for some kind of imperial parliament or council alarmed Indians who feared that their affairs would be controlled not only by Great Britain but by the white dominions. In view of the humiliating racialist policies pursued by South Africa and Australia this was not a pleasant prospect.

By 1917, though most Indians continued loyal to the empire, tension was rising as Great Britain remained silent on plans for Indian self-government. Moderates were struggling to restrain the militant policies of extremists. Sir Satyendra Sinha, the

Below: *Blunt Indian recruiting technique. The accompanying exhortation read: 'This soldier is guarding India. He is guarding his home and his household. Thus we are guarding your home. You have to join the army.' Nearly a million men joined up, suffering 65,000 casualties, while India was brought to the verge of bankruptcy*

A woman offers flowers to British Indian troops marching through Paris, 14th July 1915

great moderate leader, had already appealed for 'a frank and full statement of the policy of the government as regards the future of India so that hope may come where despair holds sway and faith where doubt spreads its darkening shadow'. All the diverse elements in Indian society were slowly uniting at least in their insistence on a definition of British aims. The Hindu-dominated Congress signed a concordat with the Muslim League; the Maharajah of Bikaner approved of 'the legitimate aspirations of our brother Indians'; Mrs Besant continued her agitation to such an extent that the Indian government foolishly had her interned in June 1917. Demonstrations against this action threatened an ugly situation when, in July 1917, Edwin Montagu replaced Austen Chamberlain at the India Office. On 20th August he made a pronouncement which was of epoch-making importance for the whole empire. In the Commons, he defined his government's aim as 'the progressive realization of responsible government in India as an integral part of the British empire'.

Exactly what the British government was committed to, and by when, was unclear. But obviously some form of parliamentary government was foreshadowed.

It cannot be denied that by the time of this announcement a great deal of India's earlier enthusiasm for war had been allowed to evaporate. Nevertheless, despite her enormous sacrifices and frustrations, the war ended with Indian opinion on a rising tide of expectancy. War fever had been rekindled after the Russian collapse threatened to open a land route for German armies to march on India; Montagu's declaration, and his subsequent arrival to make an on-the-spot report, aroused new hopes; the principles of self-determination preached in Europe seemed applicable to India; even the future nationalist leader, Mahatma Gandhi, was opposed to the activities of Tilak and Mrs Besant. In July 1918 he wrote, in support of the war effort, 'seek ye first the recruiting office, and everything will be added unto you'.

But of course there were difficulties. The British government was, perhaps inevitably, expected to make her intangible promises a reality too quickly. Failure to grant self-government was rapidly to alienate Gandhi and begin a new era in non-violent agitation. The very impetus given to nationalist aspirations alarmed the Muslims who feared a Hindu-dominated administration. A more sombre mood rapidly took the place of earlier hopes, darkened by the Amritsar massacre and by the terrible epidemic of influenza which killed more Indians than had perished in more than four years of war. This mood was rarely to be absent from Indian politics in the inter-war period.

Chapter 23

'Business as usual', a slogan said to have been launched by Winston Churchill, was one the British used with pride in the early months of the war. They drew from it reassurance; things were going to go on much as before, with, perhaps, a little added excitement. But as the war unrolled, one settled institution after another was shaken to its foundations. Every side of the national life was gradually permeated by the business of war-making. In every country the story was the same. This slow but tremendous revolution is the subject of this Chapter.

Christopher Falkus's article on **The Dominions at War** shows how widespread in a purely geographical sense were these repercussions. It was at first sight extraordinary that the domestic politics of Australia and Canada should be disturbed by a quarrel over the way Habsburgs treated their Slav subjects. Yet this happened, because of the nature of the British empire at that time and the relations of the dominions to the mother country. It was full of significance for the future; the dominions were not to forget the cost to them of involvement in Great Britain's war.

The home fronts of the European combatants showed, even more quickly, startling changes in both economic and social life. Colin Cross's article on **The Meaning of Total War** outlines the most important changes in Great Britain, France, and Germany down to the end of 1916. After that time, with the intensifying of the war (of which the adoption of conscription by Great Britain may be taken as the supreme symbol) these changes were accelerated. In 1918 men would find themselves living in a world undreamed of in 1914. And this was even more true for women. In **Women at Work and War** Louise Black describes the war's lasting impact on one half of the human race.

When so many rapid and violent changes occurred in the external world of material culture and institutions, it was inevitable that culture and artistic life should also respond to them. The cultural history of the war is a vast theme. Here we can discuss only two of its many aspects. T.G.Rosenthal's article on **War and the Artist** describes the response of the visual and plastic arts to the war. **The War Poets** are the subject of an article by Michael Llewellyn-Smith.Perhaps because of the concentration of emotion which it can impose, poetry has claim to be, of all the arts, the one in which the Great War left behind most of enduring value. To English readers that legacy is easily available in the poems of Owen, Sassoon, Blunden, and Graves. To remind our readers of what is available in other languages, we have printed also a poem by Apollinaire.

Ulk/Tasiemka

German cartoon ridiculing British reliance upon Australia, as 'England's last hope'

Roger Viollet

A French family amuses itself in a cellar during a night air raid alert in Paris

Imperial War Museum

British girls humping coke. Behind every fighting soldier—three civilian workers

British War Poets

'The subject of it is War, and the pity of War,' wrote Wilfred Owen in his preface to the book of poems he was writing in the trenches. The British poets appointed themselves spokesmen for the generation who died in northern France, gassed, demoralized by shell shock, their lives thrown heedlessly away by ignorant patriotism. The following poems show the preoccupations of these poets of the trenches.

Anthem for Doomed Youth

What passing-bells for those who die as cattle?
 Only the monstrous anger of the guns.
 Only the stuttering rifles' rapid rattle
Can patter out their hasty orisons.
No mockeries for them; no prayers nor bells,
Nor any voice of mourning save the choirs—
The shrill, demented choirs of wailing shells;
And bugles calling for them from sad shires.

What candles may be held to speed them all?
 Not in the hands of boys, but in their eyes
Shall shine the holy glimmers of goodbyes.
 The pallor of girls' brows shall be their pall;
Their flowers the tenderness of patient minds
And each slow dusk a drawing-down of blinds.

Wilfred Owen
(By permission of Mr Harold Owen
and Chatto & Windus Ltd)

The General

'Good morning, good morning' the general said,
When we met him last week on our way to the line.
Now the soldiers he smiled at are most of them dead,
And we're cursing his staff for incompetent swine.
'He's a cheery old card,' grunted Harry to Jack
As they slogged up to Arras with rifle and pack.

But he did for them both by his plan of attack.

Siegfried Sassoon
(By permission of the author)

Break of Day in the Trenches

The darkness crumbles away—
It is the same old druid Time as ever.
Only a live thing leaps my hand—
A queer sardonic rat—
As I pull the parapet's poppy
To stick behind my ear.
Droll rat, they would shoot you if they knew
Your cosmopolitan sympathies
(And God knows what antipathies).
Now you have touched this English hand
You will do the same to a German—
Soon, no doubt, if it be your pleasure
To cross the sleeping green between.
It seems you inwardly grin as you pass
Strong eyes, fine limbs, haughty athletes
Less chanced than you for life,
Bonds to the whims of murder,
Sprawled in the bowels of the earth,
The torn fields of France.
What do you see in our eyes
At the shrieking iron and flame
Hurled through still heavens?
What quaver—what heart aghast?
Poppies whose roots are in man's veins
 Drop, and are ever dropping;
 But mine in my ear is safe,
 Just a little white with the dust.

Isaac Rosenberg
(By permission of the author's literary
estate and Chatto & Windus Ltd)

The Meaning of Total War

'Keep the home fires burning' sang the British Tommies at the front in the first years of the war. But even at home the war had its effects. Ersatz coffee, coupons and war loans, paper money and censored newspapers were superficial signs of strain. Other changes were more profound. And over everything hung the shadow of the casualty lists, appearing with terrible monotony week after week

On 5th September 1917 Miss Barbara Adam, a twenty-year-old student at Cambridge University, married Captain Jack Wootton, aged twenty-six. According to the conventions of their era and class, neither was yet ready for marriage. It was simply because of the war that their families gave consent.

They had a twenty-four-hour honeymoon in the country and then a night at the Rubens Hotel, London, before Captain Wootton set off from Victoria Station to join his regiment at the front. Five weeks later, without his wife ever having seen him again, he died of wounds. The army sent his blood-stained kit to Mrs Wootton and she resumed her studies at Cambridge. She went on to make a considerable public career, ending as one of the first women to become a member of the House of Lords. She married again. Yet, describing her brief first marriage in her autobiography half a century later, she wrote that she still avoided any occasion for entering the Rubens Hotel.

In ordinary times, such a story would stand out as being especially tragic. But during the First World War it was routine; something of the kind happened to tens of thousands of couples. The most direct and most devastating result of the war was the wholesale killing of young men. Great Britain lost 680,000, France lost 1,300,000 and Germany lost 1,700,000. The point is not that the total numbers were particularly large—the warfare of the 1939-45 period accounted for many more deaths—but that the casualties were almost all of the same kind. It was as if some Pied Piper had travelled across Europe carrying off the young men.

There were so many widows and bereaved parents that, in Great Britain, a movement was started to make white the colour for mourning, lest the streets appear too gloomy. This did not catch on and the old mourning rituals were curtailed to a simple armband or dropped altogether. They never really returned. The Germans were rather

more traditional. 'For weeks past the town [Berlin] seems to have been enveloped in an impenetrable veil of sadness, grey in grey, which no golden ray of sunlight seems to pierce, and which forms a fit setting for the white-faced, black-robed women who glide so sadly through the streets,' wrote Countess Evelyn Blücher, in her diary for 27th December 1915.

It would be false, however, to suppose that the mood in the combatant countries was one entirely of gloom. By 1916 the expectation cherished at the beginning by both sides, that the war would be a short one, had faded. But each side, convinced that it was fighting in self-defence against an evil enemy, was confident of ultimate victory. The roistering energies which over the previous period had revolutionized the European way of life were now turned inwards, to destruction. The war was not so much the end of 19th-century Europe as its consequence.

Land of Hope and Glory

The deepest impact was upon Great Britain where the war acted as an accelerator and distorter of social changes which had already begun in the unstable Edwardian period.

The key decision, from which every other change derived, was the novel one of creating a mass British army on a scale comparable to the gigantic conscript forces on the mainland of Europe. That army was intended to end the war by overwhelming Germany on the Western Front. (Unfortunately neither its training nor its higher leadership matched the enthusiasm of its recruits.)

During the first two years of the war the whole resources of public propaganda were used to recruit the army. The country was saturated with patriotic appeals. 'Land of Hope and Glory' became a second national anthem. 'God Save the King' was introduced as a customary item in theatre and cinema performances, a custom which still survives. Kitchener's poster 'Your King and Country Need YOU', with its pointed finger, can still be counted as the most memorable piece of outdoor advertising ever designed. Every locality had its own recruiting committee. There were private-enterprise recruiters, notably the outrageous Horatio Bottomley. Some clergymen preached sermons urging young men to join the army. Music-hall stars ended performances with patriotic tableaux and appeals for recruits. Military bands paraded the streets and young men fell

1 Parisians queuing for coal in the Place de L'Opéra, March 1917. While their menfolk died women queued for the necessities of life. 2 A Hyde Park investiture. Widows and next of kin seen waiting to receive posthumous awards. There were very few families who did not know personal grief. 3 Horatio Bottomley, 1915. Popular jingoistic orator. He made patriotism pay, earning some £27,000 as a private enterprise recruiter

in behind them to march to the recruiting sergeant. 'We don't want to lose you, but we think you ought to go' became an important popular song. The basic pay was a shilling a day, and many recruits did their first drills in public parks, with civilian spectators proudly looking on.

It became embarrassing to be a male civilian of military age. An admiral in Folkestone started a movement organizing girls to present white feathers to young men they saw in the streets in civilian dress. In one case, it was said, a winner of the VC got one while on leave. Some women went a stage farther. The romantic novelist, Baroness Orczy, founded the 'Women of England's Active Service League', every member of which pledged herself to have nothing to do with any man eligible to join up who had not done so. She aimed at 100,000 members; she actually achieved 10,000, and sent the names of all of them to the King.

The flaw, which by 1916 had become glaringly apparent, was that an army on such a scale required enormous industrial support to equip and clothe it. At least three civilian workers were required for every fighting soldier. By 1915 the shortage of artillery shells had become a national scandal and even so elementary a thing as soldiers' boots was presenting problems. Thousands of skilled workers had followed the band into the army and they were hard to replace.

The government takes over

So, on a makeshift and temporary basis, began the characteristically 20th-century phenomenon of wholesale government direction of industry, Lloyd George as minister of munitions directing the initial stages. Until the war the condition of the economy had been considered hardly more the responsibility of the government than the weather. Even socialists had thought more about distributing wealth and resources than about managing them. Although after the war most of the controls were to be removed, the idea remained that the government was ultimately responsible for the economy.

To an increasing extent party politics and elections were to centre around economic questions. Unemployment between the wars was to become a political issue on a scale which would previously have been impossible. Recruitment propaganda also had some influence in this direction. It was hinted, without any precise explanation of how it was to come about, that the military defeat of Germany would raise British living standards. The soldiers who came back tended to look to the politicians to raise them.

The aim in 1915 and 1916 was to create a tri-partnership of government, trade

Soup kitchen for the people of Berlin, 1917

Above: *Fashions rising to the occasion—a French reflection on German privations.*
Below: *Boiling bones for fats, Berlin 1917*

unions, and employers in which output, wages, and profits would be settled by negotiation instead of by the free play of the market. This had the incidental effect of increasing the size, status, and power of the unions. Instead of being pressure groups in the class war, they tended to become a recognized organ of the community, with rights and responsibilities to the whole nation as well as to their own members. Their membership rose dramatically, from 4,100,000 in 1914 to 6,500,000 in 1918; and when the soldiers returned it shot up to over 8,000,000. The effect was permanent (although numbers were to fall later) and it was one factor in the post-war displacement of the Liberal Party by the Labour Party.

By 1916 the war had become a way of life. The streets were curiously silent; the German bands and itinerant salesmen who in 1914 had enlivened them were now gone. There were short skirts and widows and multitudes of young men in uniform. For an army officer in uniform to have appeared in a tram or bus would in 1914 have been unknown; by 1916 it was commonplace for subalterns with their toothbrush moustaches to be handing their fares to girl conductors. Every issue of every newspaper carried lists of names of men who had been killed. Soldiers on leave sought to enjoy themselves before they died and nightclubs, previously furtive, almost unmentionable places, had become prominent features of the London scene. There were said to be 150 in Soho alone; in them the customers danced to the new jazz music which had just crossed the Atlantic. The older institution, the public house, had begun to decline; under emergency legislation the government had regulated the hours at which they could serve liquor and the phrase 'Time, gentlemen, please' had entered the language. The daytime thoughts of the nation were of the permanent battle which was being waged from trenches in France; sometimes in southern England the actual sound of the guns could be heard as a distant thunder.

Deadlock and disappointment

France and Germany, unlike Great Britain, had long prepared for the war in the sense that they had for generations run a system of universal military service and could, without improvisation, immediately mobilize a mass army. Neither, however, had reckoned on a long war. The German aim was a quick knock-out of France and then a switch of forces to the east to defeat the armies of archaic Tsarist Russia. The French, equally, had looked forward to dashing victories and the reconquest of the provinces of Alsace and Lorraine which they had lost to Germany forty-four years earlier. The outcome, a deadlock in France,

Musée de l'Armée, Brussels

Above: German poster exhorting women to save hair for making machine belting. Left: Berliners exchange firewood for potato peelings, Berlin 1917

Above: Substitute for rubber. Sprung metal 'tyres' on a German car. Left: Parisians in a bread queue, 1917. Despite hardships there was bread for all. Below: German poster appeals for aluminium, copper, brass, nickel, tin

Bibliothek für Zeitgeschichte, Stuttgart

was a disappointment to both sides.

The fighting on the Western Front was on French (and Belgian) soil, so that the French, unlike the Germans and the British, were on their home ground. Much of the industrial north-east of France was under German occupation. The result was that the French became less idealistic about the war than the British and Germans; they saw it as a plague rather than as an adventure. It was not until late 1917 that they found in Clemenceau an apt warlike leader. The French were drearily conscious of having been defeated in the initial battles of 1914, and by 1916 they feared that they were bleeding to death. The following year large segments of the French army were to mutiny in favour of a negotiated peace. German propaganda to the effect that Great Britain was willing to fight to the last Frenchman had its effect; the Germans actually subsidized the leading French left-wing paper, the *Bonnet Rouge*.

There was in France a special wartime drabness, save among the minority of industrial workers and their employers who made more money than ever before. In Paris the politicians quarrelled and at the front the soldiers died in thousands. Unlike the British and Germans, the French felt a widespread distrust of both politicians and generals, a distrust justified by some of the facts. There was no proper attempt at financial or industrial management. Since the richest industrial area was under German occupation, France had to rely upon imports from Great Britain, the United States, and Japan for the sinews of war and these were paid for by contracting debts. The internal debt also grew—in 1915 French revenue from taxes was actually lower than the ordinary peacetime level—and more and more paper money was printed. A crudely inefficient method was adopted by the government to finance munitions production. It lent capital, interest-free, to entrepreneurs; this, naturally, gave them enormous profits at the public expense. Few proper accounts were kept and by 1916 there was virtually no reliable information on the state of the public finances.

The mass French army consisted largely of peasants conscripted from their smallholdings and sent to the front. The women left behind continued to work the holdings, but the total food output, in peacetime sufficient to meet French needs, fell sharply. By 1916 sugar had become a luxury, there were two meatless days a week, and restaurants were restricted to serving three courses. According to historic practice, the government concentrated on controlling the supply and price of bread, and success in this was the civil population's great palliative; no matter what other hardships existed, there was bread for all. Other matters of price control and rationing were left to the departmental prefects, with the result that what supplies were available oscillated around France to the *départements* which momentarily allowed the highest prices. The Paris municipality incurred huge losses through trading in food; they were written off as 'insurance against public disorder'.

Paris in the early 20th century was at its peak as the international capital for the arts, culture, and the amenities of luxurious living. Every cultivated European and American regarded Paris as in some way his spiritual home. The war, if anything, increased this prestige. Although the street lights were extinguished and the city was on the edge of the war zone, Paris acquired extra glamour as an international city. By an odd compromise, the *Opéra* was allowed to stage performances on condition that the audiences did not wear evening dress.

The war struck deeply into French family and social life. The depreciation in money —by 1916 the cost of living had risen by forty per cent—was beginning to wreck the *rentier* class which, by tradition, had its savings in fixed interest bonds. Secure employment as a public official had, until 1914, been the most respectable thing to which a Frenchman could aspire. By 1916 the officials were losing their social prestige and being overtaken by businessmen, a process which was to continue.

French war-weariness, which was already apparent in 1916, seemed to sap the spirit of the nation. In the occupied sector the people were cowed by strict German administration; there was no attempt at a resistance movement. Although eventually France emerged as a nominal victor, and got back her lost provinces, there remained a loss of national confidence and a deep-rooted distrust of war. The seeds of the disaster of 1940 were being sown.

Ersatz *coffee and 'means-test' clothes*
In Germany in 1916 something still remained of the elation caused by the great victories of 1914. With the United States not yet in the war and the Russian empire obviously crumbling, it was reasonable for Germans to expect victory. The strategy was to be defensive in the west until forces could be brought from the Russian front to overwhelm the French and the British.

The main effect of the war on the national life was, apart from the enormous casualties, the shortages caused by the British blockade. Bread rationing had started as early as January 1915, and there was an agonizing dilemma, whether to use scarce nitrates to fertilize agricultural land or to make explosives. Generally the claims of

German appeal for acorns, chestnuts, 1917

the explosives got priority and so agricultural production, which in any case was insufficient for the nation's needs, declined. Further difficulty came because of bad weather—the winter of 1916-17 was known as the 'turnip winter' because early frosts had spoiled the potato harvest.

German ingenuity concentrated on producing substitute—'ersatz'—foods and some, although they sound dreadful, were quite palatable. It was possible to make an eatable cake from clover meal and chestnut flour. 'Ersatz' coffee, made from roasted barley, rye, chicory, and figs, became a national drink. Schoolchildren were lectured on the need for thorough mastication to prevent the substitutes from harming their digestions.

The virtual dictator of the German economy was the Jewish industrialist, Walther Rathenau, a brilliant administrator brought in by the war office to organize supplies for the army. Step by step Rathenau brought the principal industries under government control and set up an elaborate bureaucracy to run them. As in Great Britain, this was public control without public ownership, but Rathenau's methods were more thorough than those of the British; government 'kommissars' participated in the actual management of companies, and the plan allotted everyone his place. In 1916 the Rathenau machine had reached the peak of its efficiency and the whole of Germany was organized for fighting the war.

To accompany Rathenau's economic planning there were elaborate rationing schemes, with everyone ticketed and docketed for what he was entitled to receive. Clothes were distributed in part on a 'means-test' system—a customer had to prove to an official that he needed a new suit.

The political effect of the war was still, in 1916, to reinforce confidence in the German imperial system. Germany consisted of twenty-five states, each with its ruling dynasty, the whole under the dominance of the largest state, Prussia, of which

the Kaiser was King. It was an authoritarian and hierarchical system with a strong infusion of democracy—the imperial parliament was elected on universal manhood suffrage. (In Great Britain only fifty-eight per cent of adult males had the right to vote.) Although a strong Social Democrat opposition existed in parliament, the imperial and hierarchical system worked because the average German worker trusted his social superiors and was willing to vote for them.

Even the Social Democrat deputies had voted in favour of war credits. The military victories had engendered further confidence in the system and war weariness had hardly begun. Shortages, hardships, and even casualty lists were tolerable as the price of a certain German victory.

Of course the vast self-confidence of 1916 turned out to be a mistake. Within two years the Kaiser and the authorities under him were simply to vanish from German politics. German success and German power proved to have been a delusion. The psychological shock was to be enormous and lasting and it helped to cause the strange and national mood in which so eccentric a figure as Hitler was able to rise to power.

Debts and death
All the combatant countries financed the war by loans rather than by taxation. In Great Britain, for example, the highest wartime rate of income tax reached only 6s. in the pound. The theory was to lay the cost of the war upon the future generations it was being fought to protect. What it really meant was that, instead of being taxed outright, people subscribed to war loans and so received the right to an annual payment of interest.

After the war, France was to lessen the burden of debt by allowing the franc to depreciate in value. Germany got rid of it altogether in the great inflation of 1923. In Great Britain, however, where the value of money remained stable or even increased, the war debt was a continuing burden which contributed towards a sense of national ill-being and inability to afford costly projects, either for military defence or for the promotion of living standards.

But the greatest single effect of the war, clearly apparent in 1916, was the killing of young men. Public imaginations exaggerated the effect of the casualties far beyond statistical realities. In Great Britain and Germany, particularly, appeared a cult of youth which has continued ever since. There was impatience and even contempt for the past. Jeremy Bentham's plea that we should look to our ancestors, not for their wisdom, but for their follies became the fashionable mode of thought, and even half a century later it is still continuing.

Women at Work and War

'The ordinary male disbelief in our capacity cannot be argued away,' wrote a tired Englishwoman trying to persuade Russian officers to let her start up field hospitals in Rumania. 'It can only be worked away.' During the First World War munition girls and policewomen, Métro workers and bank clerks worked it away

The new Amazon—French war-time postcard. As their husbands, brothers, and sweethearts went off to die, the women came forward to 'do their bit' for their countries

'"That men must fight and women must weep" is an old story now being told again,' mourned *The Lady* in August 1914. Alongside patterns for that autumn's becoming tea-gown appeared instructions for making bandages. 'Old underwear can be cut up into good-sized handkerchiefs which are often so useful to the man in action. For instance he can wrap his handkerchief round a superficial wound and go on.'

It was a gentle note. The militant feminists reacted more positively. Mrs Pankhurst and her formidable daughter, Christabel, diverted their crusading energy to the war effort, and 'the Cause' was

1 German lady shoemaker. Shortage of labour introduced many women to unaccustomed trades. **2** Workroom of a British war hospital supply depot, painted by J.B.Davis. **3** War working party, painted by J.B.Gibbs. Well-bred leisured ladies volunteered for hard work sewing comforts and uniforms, or serving in canteens. **4** Munition girls painted by E.F.Skinner

5 French tram driver. **6** 'A Land Girl Ploughing' by Cecil Allen. On the Continent the peasants' wives took over in the fields. The British were startled by the land girls, who worked as hired farm hands. By the end of 1917 there were 260,000 women, part-time and full-time, in the Land Army. **7** Woman in the uniform of the City of London Red Cross ambulance column

In factories, hospitals, public services, women's work was winning the praise of society

almost overlooked in their impassioned appeals to British patriotism. Mrs Fawcett, the head of the National Union of Women's Suffrage Societies, approached the situation more sedately: 'Let us,' she said, 'prove ourselves worthy of citizenship whether our claim is recognized or not.' Many of the able and under-valued women who formed the backbone of the movement for women's rights saw the war as an opportunity to use their abilities to the full. Within a week the London branch of the NUWSS had converted itself into a women's employment agency in response to the thousands of women wanting to know where they could 'do their bit' for King and country. But as yet there was little for them to do, except gather 'comforts' for the wounded, and welcome Belgian refugees.

'The doctors is ladies'

The most obvious opening for women was in the hospitals. In August 1914 Mrs St Clair Stobart offered the services of the Women's Convoy Corps to the British Red Cross. They rejected her offer. In the same month Dr Elsie Inglis, founder of the Scottish Women's Suffrage Federation, suggested to the War Office that Scottish Women's Hospital Units should be formed for overseas service. Her offer was also refused. Nothing daunted, Mrs Stobart and Dr Inglis set to work and got together teams to go to Serbia. Dr Flora Murray and Dr Louisa Garret Anderson did not bother to go to the British authorities, but offered the services of an all-woman hospital to the French, who accepted with alacrity. By September a team of women doctors and nurses, most of them veteran suffragettes, was installed in the Hotel Claridge, Paris; the ladies' cloakroom had been converted into an operating theatre, and men suffering from sepsis, tetanus, and shock, were gazing up at the gilded halls and writing home that 'the doctors is ladies'.

In 1915 they were offered a hospital in London at Endell Street by the British authorities. A total of about 26,000 patients passed through the hospital before it was closed in 1919, and the high standards it maintained, and the excellence of its surgeons, in particular of Dr Anderson herself, excited the admiration not only of their grateful patients but also of the authorities themselves.

Dr Inglis and her all-woman team took part in the fight against the typhus epidemic in Serbia in 1915, and in the flight of the Serbian nation to the sea. As soon as she could she returned to help the Serbian units fighting with the Russians in Rumania. 'We do not see much of the glamour of war here,' she wrote. But her exploits showed a curious mixture of practicality and love of adventure, hard

work and heroism. Few of the women who went to war had to cope with the problems Dr Inglis coped with (these varied from difficulties over transport, which not all her skilled lies could quite extort from the Russians, to the behaviour of Mrs X, a transport driver, who had taken to dressing like a man and flirting with the local Rumanian peasant girls). Few got as far from home as Russia. Few died of overwork. None received such a tribute—the Serbs dedicated a public fountain to the woman who had wanted every village to have clean drinking water, and whom some had come to venerate as a saint.

But for many of the women from the upper and middle classes who volunteered in their thousands for the Voluntary Aid Detachments and the other nursing services the war provided the same opportunity for useful action and patriotic adventure as it had for Dr Inglis.

For lower-class women the immediate effect of the war was unemployment. Large numbers of women had been employed in the cotton mills and cotton suffered a rapid slump. Many more were in luxury trades related to dress-making. In the hectic months of the autumn of 1914 the demand was for cartridge belts and khaki, not gloves and embroidery. In London women's employment dropped by ten and a half per cent in October.

In Germany the government had foreseen the problem, and enlisted the help of Dr Gertrude Baumer, the head of the *Bund Deutscher Frauenvereine*, one of the largest women's rights organizations in Germany. An order was issued organizing women district by district for 'the duration of the war', and making them responsible for providing cheap eating places, setting up nurseries, and helping the government to 'keep up an even supply of foodstuffs, and controlling the buying and selling of food'. Within the first month of the war the *Frauendienst* (as this wartime organization of women was called) had set up workrooms in all the larger cities to cope with the problem of unemployment. In the Berlin workrooms alone 23,000 women were employed within a week, sewing cartridge belts, bread sacks, and sheets for hospitals.

In Great Britain the only initiative to relieve the plight of unemployed women was taken by Queen Mary who hastily re-christened her Needlework Guild Queen Mary's Workshops. In the workshops women were employed at 3d an hour for a maximum of forty hours a week. Though this was condemned as 'sweated labour' (a weekly wage of 10s was intended to be less than that of regularly employed women, who supposedly earned 11s 6d a week) it was better than nothing.

By the summer of 1915 the situation had

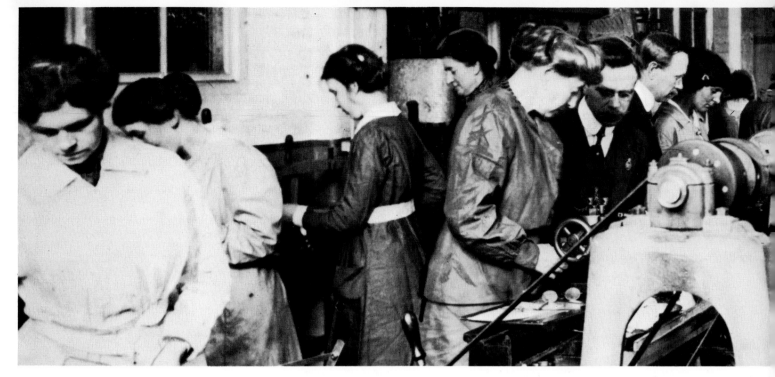

changed completely. As the men went to the trenches to die in their thousands, the women had to take over. In France, Great Britain, and Germany the munitions factories demanded more and more workers. Women who had been unemployed moved in. Only in Great Britain does this appear to have caused hostility. The trade unions were sharply opposed to the threatened competition of unskilled and, in particular, female labour, which had always been cheaper than their own. At some factories the men refused to work with women, and in March 1915 the government had to promise that wage rates would be protected, and that women doing the same job as men would be paid the same piece rates. Furthermore, it was specifically stated that after the war the pre-war practices of industry would be restored. In July 1915 Lloyd George appealed for women to work in the munitions factories. The response seemed enormous. The increase of women in industry in Great Britain was in fact about 800,000, most of them employed in the munitions industry. Sixty per cent of those in the shell industry were women.

The skill and the patriotism of the women workers were praised rapturously in the British press. Women, it turned out, could work in the supposedly unfeminine world of the engineering industry as efficiently as men. Where manual dexterity was required they could work more efficiently. Where the work was too heavy or too complicated, it had been reorganized. In France the numbers of women employed in industry forced the introduction of mass-production techniques, in Great Britain they accelerated it.

The general attitude of the country was reflected in the instruction issued to the munitionettes in Woolwich Arsenal. 'A munition worker is as important as the soldier in the trenches and on her his life depends.' 'Output. Anyone who limits this is a traitor to sweethearts, husbands, and brothers fighting.' Under the pressure of patriotism and the war the munition girls were working twelve-hour shifts seven

days a week. But since the making of shells was essential for the country, the government was at least careful of its workers. Women welfare supervisors were compulsory in the danger zones of the munitions factories, and recommended whenever large numbers of women were employed. They insisted on better cloakroom facilities, better rest rooms, ambulance rooms where accidents and illness could be treated immediately and better health regulations. There was constant supervision of those working with dangerous materials, and the food in the canteens was checked for its nutritional value. Many of the girls, despite their hard work, were healthier than they had been before.

The vast numbers of women workers, many of them working several miles from their homes, had to have somewhere to live. Sometimes whole new residential areas were built. Sometimes they lived in hostels. Nurseries also had to be found, and some of them were partly financed by the ministry of munitions. The nurseries became a recognized institution.

But it was not only in the munitions factories that women replaced men. They ran the Métro in Paris, the buses in London; they hammered plates on to ships in the Clyde, and worked in the shipbuilding plants of the German navy. They acted as electricians, plumbers, undertakers. Two of Lloyd George's secretaries were women and over 200,000 extra women were employed in government establishments. Over 1,300,000 more women were employed in Great Britain in July 1918 than in 1914, and it was estimated that 700,000 of these were directly replacing men.

In Great Britain women also became police and served in the forces. Volunteer policewomen discouraged 'provocative loitering', and indecent behaviour in cinemas, parks, pubs, and the darkened streets. By 1916 the Women's Police Service had been sought out by town authorities and the ministry of munitions, and was proving invaluable in controlling crowds during air raids and

helping checking that munition girls obeyed the safety regulations.

The first of the women's forces, the Women's Army Auxiliary Corps, was organized in 1917 to replace fit men doing jobs in what was called the line of communications. Although some drove ambulances, most were employed in the kitchens, the offices, and as gardeners in the cemeteries. They wore smart khaki uniforms, with peaked caps and skirts a daring twelve inches off the ground, slept in dormitories, and were submitted to drill and discipline by their officers. By the end of the war about 57,000 had enrolled. About 3,000 women served in the Women's Royal Naval Service and about 32,000 in the Women's Royal Air Force.

Women's battalions were also formed in Russia in early 1917. They were on guard in the Winter Palace the night the Provisional Government surrendered to the Bolsheviks.

The 'restless feeling'

When the war was over most of the women went quietly or reluctantly back to their original jobs, or to their homes. The figures for women employed in 1921 were no larger than those in 1914. Women had not won the right to equal pay or equal opportunity.

Despite the agreement that men and women should be paid equally for piece work, women had still usually been paid less than men. In the National Shell Factories women earned up to £2 4s. 6d. a week, men up to £4 6s. 6d. Women had usually worked under the supervision of men. Although women had occasionally been promoted, where they were available, men were automatically preferred. Few women had managed to get any lengthy training. The NUWSS had established a training school for oxy-acetylene welders, and by December 1917 there were twice as many women as men in forty government-run training schools for engineering work. But these were exceptions. Women had remained a source of comparatively unskilled and temporary labour.

Similarly 400,000 women had left domestic service during the war, but in the mass unemployment for women that followed the return of the troops, most probably returned to their old jobs. There were no fewer servants after the war than before it. But, as one of the bus conductresses, who were mainly recruited from the better class of domestic servants, put it: 'The Company has promised all the men who are fighting that their places shall be kept open and we would not have it otherwise . . . but it's going to be a big problem. You see . . . we have all got a contagious restless feeling.'

The contagious restless feeling, the desire for the new way of life they had experienced was not easily buried. Though prices in Great Britain had doubled, many working-class women had been earning up to four times as much as they had earned before the war. Their children were better clothed, better fed, and in better health.

Even more important than the money was their increase in self-respect. The *New Statesman* commented 'they appear more alert, more critical of the conditions under which they work, more ready to make a stand against injustice than their pre-war selves or their prototypes'.

This was reflected in the increasing figures of trade union membership. The National Federation of Women Workers increased its membership to 50,000, but the total number of women in trade unions increased from 350,000 before the war to nearly 600,000 by the end of 1917. On the whole women tended to join the mixed general unions rather than the NFWW, and their admission into most unions (though not all) gradually made separate trade unions for women seem redundant. In France there was the same general tendency. Trade union activity among women increased, more women became prominent trade unionists, and the need for separate trade unions for women lessened.

In some ways the upper classes had gained even more. The nurses, the VAD's, and the WAAC officers, had been liberated from their restricted and over-protected lives. Any idea that it was unladylike to work was dissipated in the wave of patriotic fervour, and 'those peaceful days in the Midlands when one had lived for one's amusement and to kill time seemed to date back to one's infancy. The war turned one topsy-turvy, altered one's whole outlook on life. I felt I could never be "pre-war" again. None of us ought ever to have been like that'. Some went nursing only for a good time or to get their names into society papers. 'Miss Flapperton' was a recognized figure. But many led a tougher life than they had ever known. They left the shelter of the parental wings, and self reliance had to take the place of protection. There was much greater freedom between the sexes. During the war men and women were 'so thrown into daily contact with each other that conventional notions of a certain reserve as between the sexes have been very largely modified'. Chaperones disappeared, and so did the delicate ignorance in which upper-class girls were kept.

The outward signs of their freedom were flaunted gaily. Many used language that would have shocked their mothers; many started to wear cosmetics, smoking became widespread, and women bought drinks in public houses. Before the war short skirts and brassières had come in. During the war they completely ousted long dresses and camisoles. Well-meaning committees tried to discourage Land Girls, who, like most women doing heavy work or working outside, wore trousers, from wearing them off duty, but without success.

In defiance of the ever-present casualty figures, England was gripped by a feverish gaiety. 'Give the boys on leave a good time' was the universal sentiment. As one woman remembered it: 'If these young women who, as they read the casualty lists, felt fear in their hearts, did not seize experience at once, they knew that for many of them it would elude them for ever. Sex became both precious and unimportant: precious as a desired personal experience; unimportant as something without impli-

A new feminine occupation—women training for work in the engineering industry

cations.' Young girls were gripped by 'khaki fever' and hovered round army camps. By the end of the war the illegitimacy rate had increased by thirty per cent. The marriage rate also increased sharply. Many marriages swiftly contracted, swiftly broke up. There were three times as many divorces in 1920 as in 1910.

The vote

Women's participation in the war effort had definitely shaken society. 'It would have been utterly impossible for us to have waged a successful war,' said Lloyd George, 'had it not been for the skill and ardour, enthusiasm and industry which the women of this country have thrown into the war.' In both Germany and France women talked more hopefully of getting the vote. In Great Britain they got it. The voting laws had to be changed to enfranchise the soldiers who were either not entitled to vote at all under the old system, or who had disfranchised themselves by moving from their homes to distant factories or the front. Women were enfranchised at the same time, though an age limit of thirty was imposed so that they would not become a majority of the electorate as they were of the population.

'Topping about your bill,' said the younger nurses to the veteran suffragettes at the Endell Street Hospital. The old valour for 'the Cause' had gone. To the short-skirted, self-reliant, uninhibited war girls of 1918 the romantic hysteria of the Pankhursts' championship of pure victimized women was as irrelevant as *The Lady's* advice on handkerchiefs. 'The ordinary male disbelief in our capacity,' Elsie Inglis had written from Rumania, 'cannot be argued away. It can only be worked away.' It had been. Women had been acknowledged as equal citizens. But most of all, women's understanding of what they were, and what they would like to be, had radically changed.

War and the Artist

The horrors and futility of the war provided artists with new and terrible subject matter. Different lessons, increasingly bitter and disillusioned, could be drawn from it

The First World War, as everyone knows, was the 'war to end wars', and because of this somewhat feeble built-in excuse allowed itself to become, in human terms, one of the biggest wars in history. Out of such a self-styled definitive war, one would expect, some kind of definitive artistic statement. But, alas, just as the war itself was not the last word, nor was the art it produced. The moral is, of course, all too obvious; to make great art you need not great wars but great artists. The Peninsular War in Spain was a mild skirmish compared to Flanders Field, but it had Goya to chronicle it and etch into our memories images of war, such as the firing squad scene in *The Third of May,* which make the 20th-century equivalent seem feeble by comparison.

Only once in this century have we had an artistic statement of comparable force and then again it came from a Catalan, Pablo Picasso. But, perhaps significantly, *Guernica,* the delineation of the destruction by German bombers of the ancient capital of the Basques, was a part of the Spanish Civil War. It was a direct and specific protest against one direct and specific event that could burn itself into the mind of a great creative artist in a way that no part of that huge sprawling shambles which was the First World War ever could. In many ways the First World War was so ungraspable and so amorphous that it took the writers to do it full justice because they could more readily distil its essence into words than the painters could into visual images.

Yet, if there is no portrait of a soldier from the First World War to match Leonardo's drawing of a *Condottiere* and if there is no evocation of the undoubted physical excitement of war to compare with Uccello's *The Battle of San Romano,* the First World War did, nevertheless, yield a very large number of works of art which deserve to be remembered as much for themselves as for their subject matter.

There are basically two kinds of war art; the purely 'artistic' done with no motives other than to create good art and, perhaps, simultaneously preach an appropriate message and the 'official' art which sets out to record for governments, for regiments, or for posterity, particular

Left: 'The First German Gas Attack at Ypres' by William Roberts. **Opposite page:** *Perhaps the most important single English war painting – 'Merry-go-round' by Mark Gertler, painted after the Somme, 1916. D.H.Lawrence described it as 'a terrifying coloured flame of decomposition'*

military engagements or groups of people and which also sets out, often too frequently, to propagandize at the same time.

A typical piece of official art is Sir William Orpen's massive group portrait *A Peace Conference at the Quai d'Orsay.* This is routine, somewhat dull academic work containing conventional portraits of the victorious world leaders, Clemenceau, Lloyd George, and Woodrow Wilson. Neither this picture, nor its companion piece by the same artist, *The Signing of Peace in the Hall of Mirrors, Versailles, June 28th 1919,* can be called, in any acceptable sense of the word, art. Yet both pictures record factually what those momentously bungled scenes must have looked like to the detached observer; what they fail to do is re-create the heady, pompous, and self-satisfied atmosphere, and the exquisitely subtle hypocrisy which dominated the aftermath of the war.

Similarly there is no artistic joy to be had in looking at the serried and immaculately dressed ranks of official portraits of admirals and generals that one finds in war museums and portrait galleries the world over. Almost invariably the portraitist takes the easy way out and paints, often with much bravura, the uniform and the decorations and surmounts them with the best looking head he can produce in the circumstances. This, and the Great War produced an inordinate quantity of this kind of portraiture, is patriotism, glorification of the military leader, and anything else one cares to call it; but it is not art. Only rarely did the official or semi-official portrait produce anything of genuine intrinsic artistic quality. Oddly enough it was some of the lesser known theatres of war whose artistic by-products were the most interesting.

The desert war, for instance, produced a number of fascinating portraits, either during its progress or in retrospect. One of the most painted characters was T.E. Lawrence, Lawrence of Arabia (Vol. 5, p. 590), and there are many studies of him, notably Eric Kennington's romanticized head and shoulders bust and Augustus John's much more ambiguous and enigmatic oil painting of the quasi-mystical, quasi-charlatan, desert leader in full Arab dress. The same campaign gave rise to Sydney Carline's painting of Turkish troops being bombed at Wadi Fara and to the bust of Feisal by Meštrović. Ivan Meštrović, who was Serbia's leading sculptor and probably that country's only 20th-century artist of European stature, also did a moving bust of Elsie Inglis. This bust is a memorial to a heroic woman who organized ambulance and other medical services on the ▷ 632

1 'The Armoured Train' by Severini, a Futurist who was fascinated by speed, the machine, and by violence. Here he is excited by the force of the train, the shapes of weapons. 2 'La Mitrailleuse'—French machine-gunners painted by an Englishman, C.R.W.Nevinson

3 'Sappers at work: a Canadian Tunnelling Company' by David Bomberg. 4 'Some Day the People Will Return' by F.H.Varley, a battlefield not of glory but a waste of uprooted tombstones. 5 'A Battery Shelled' by Wyndham Lewis. This most important war painting shows a strong influence of Cubism

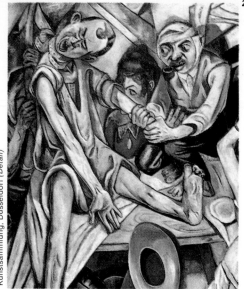

1 'We are making a New World' by Paul Nash — an ironic title for a picture of the devastation war had brought to the old world. 2 'The Night' by the German Expressionist, Max Beckmann. The war had imprinted on his mind images of killing and the wounded

Serbian, Rumanian, and Russian fronts, and died in 1917 after leading a unit across Russia. It is, in a sense, official art but it is executed by a powerful and mature sculptor, and is thus infinitely more effective than the academic sculpture spawned by the war and its millions of casualties.

Sculpture has always presented particular problems for the 'official' artist since, at least until the 1920's, sculpture was traditionally a more rigid and disciplined art form than painting and, consequently, fewer liberties could be taken. Good war sculpture is therefore extremely rare and, all too often, one is restricted to life-size, or larger-than-life-size, models of artillery or machine-guns as memorials to the fallen. One of the few sculptors who managed to do work which was not wholly traditional was the American-born Jacob Epstein. His portrait of Admiral of the Fleet Lord Fisher is a distinguished piece of portrait sculpture by any standards and succeeds in bringing out the formidable intelligence and personality of the architect of the modern British navy in the first quarter of this century. Another Epstein bronze, *The American Soldier,* displays the classic difficulty of the military form, since even Epstein can do nothing with the unyielding shape of the steel helmet, but when one gets below the helmet one sees the vigour of the sculptured face.

The official art of the Great War obviously had its limitations, and the most interesting art engendered by the war is that born of genuine conviction rather than a government commission. Thus, in France, for example, most of the best artists seemed to spend their war fighting rather than painting, and much of France's war art is therefore official and bad. A perfect example is *The Restoration of Alsace-Lorraine to France* a lithograph by Maurice Greiffenhagen. This is simply crude, bombastic propaganda showing two shawled girls, fetters sundered, clasping the noble, sword-carrying and buxom figure of the eternal Marianne. Other artists, however, contributed rather more although Picasso did surprisingly little. It is hard to think of any Picasso work directly connected with the First World War apart from

his delightful 1916 drawing of the artist and poet Guillaume Apollinaire in uniform and with his head-wound bandaged.

But Braque, with Picasso the co-founder of Cubism, and one of the artists who fought in the war is quoted as saying, 'I was very happy when, in 1914, I realized that the army had used the principles of my Cubist paintings for camouflage.' One can see why Braque thought as he did, since the pre-war Cubist pictures painted by him and Picasso were, in their colouring and their fragmentation, not at all unlike camouflage netting and sheeting, being predominantly brown, green, and grey. That, apparently, was a case of art affecting war. For Fernand Léger it was the other way round. Léger fought in the French Engineers Corps and both his service in the army and his contact with the machinery of war had a profound influence on his post-war artistic development. Douglas Cooper, in his book on Léger, has quoted him as saying that: 'I was dazzled by the breach of a 75-millimetre gun which was standing uncovered in the sunlight: the magic of white light on metal. This was enough to make me forget the abstract art of 1912-1913.' It is difficult to say how much Léger's work after 1918 owes to the war and how much simply to the paraphernalia of the mechanistic age in which he lived. Clearly, however, he became obsessed with the harsh shapes of industrial products and the most often repeated images in his work are those of cylinders, pistons, and rods which belong to the battlefield almost as much as they belong to the factory. A typical example is his work of 1916 entitled *Soldier with Pipe.*

A French painter who recollected the war in retrospect was Georges Rouault. In his remarkable series of etchings entitled *Miserere* and *Guerre,* Rouault included one or two subjects which recalled the war with dreadful poignancy, most notably in *Mon Doux Pays, où êtes-vous?* (My sweet homeland, what has become of you?). This grim, brooding picture epitomizes the destruction of France, with its shattered buildings still burning and its gaunt soldiers lying listlessly in the foreground, wounded, bewildered, and

apathetic. Another French artist who recalled the horrors of the Great War was Georges Leroux who, in *L'Enfer* (Hell), re-creates the inferno of battle with broken and uprooted trees, fire and explosions, mud-filled shell-holes and twisted corpses. In many ways this painting is typical of the art of the Great War in that it records the horrors without too much questioning. It was the English war artists, as we shall see later, who raised the largest doubts about this whole disastrous period.

One of the paradoxes of the time was the artistic role of the Germans. Strangely enough this ultra militaristic nation produced hardly any war art of any distinction, despite the fact that the period from about 1914 to 1933 was one of the most exciting in the whole history of German painting. Significant German artists like Lovis Corinth and Max Liebermann did some etchings for the German Red Cross and there is a good etching by Otto Dix called *Lens Bombed* which is a classic piece of Expressionist drawing, filled with terror and foreboding. But there are relatively few paintings of any distinction which deal with the war. One of the few exceptions is, in fact, only loosely connected: Max Beckmann's *The Night.* Beckmann fought in the war and was invalided out, after a spell in hospital, and the memory of the maimed and wounded was, for him, an indelible one. *The Night* is a nightmarish composition. The images of torture, wounding, and killing are clearly inspired partly by his dread of the Second World War, whose seeds he already saw in the late 1920's, and partly by his haunting remembrance of the First.

In Italy there were a number of artists who wanted Italy to come to the aid of France. These included in particular, men like Marinetti and Carrà, who were the pioneers and theorists of Futurism, a short-lived art movement which came to an end early in the war. A leading member of the Futurist group was Gino Severini, who has contributed two notable paintings to the art associated with the First World War. In *Guns in Action* he has managed to combine a visually exciting picture with a witty composition, using actual artillery

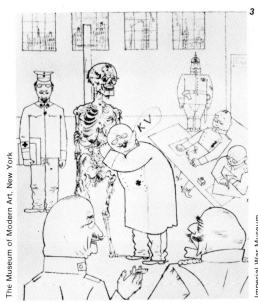

3 'Fit for Active Service' says the doctor of the skeleton. German cartoon by George Grosz. 4 Admiral Fisher – sculpture by Jacob Epstein.
5 Official art, factually correct, but not evocative: William Orpen's 'The Signing of Peace in the Hall of Mirrors, Versailles, June 28th 1919'

phrases and humorous corruptions of those terms. His other major war picture, *The Armoured Train*, is much more straightforward, and juxtaposes the force of the train, the shapes of the weapons and the typical, explosive fragmentation of Futurism to make an image of great excitement and power. The metaphysical painter Giorgio de Chirico also made his contribution, in the form of a splendid version of *Hector*. This work, done in 1916, could well be interpreted as an ironic call to arms. The martial figure of Hector is shown sightless, faceless and, presumably, brainless, consisting only of his metal armour and, instead of having a proud military bearing, standing slumped forward, needing the support of struts. Apart from being an archetypal de Chirico, *Hector* is also a telling image of war.

Understandably, because of her relatively late entry into the war, the United States' contribution to the visual arts of the First World War is not a very substantial one. The most important American artist of the period was the society painter John Singer Sargent who painted a huge canvas during his visit to the front in 1918 called *Gassed*. It shows the Dressing Station at Le Bac-de-Sud on the Doullens-Arras Road and measures 7 ft 6 ins by 20 ins. Painted in predominantly subdued, gas-like colours of mustard, brown, and green it is an ambitious picture in which files of wounded, blinded, and bandaged men, clinging to each other, walk through groups of similarly afflicted soldiers lying on the ground on either side of the road. It is a brave effort at a major work of art but it fails because the grandness of scale is not matched by any equivalent grandeur of either design or emotion. Yet it is, for all that, an honest attempt to record the disasters of war and, in a sense, a tribute to the pull of the war itself that this sophisticate, who became rich from painting the beautiful and the famous on both sides of the Atlantic, should endure the discomfort of the war to paint what he did.

The Canadians, who came into the war much earlier, made a quite remarkable contribution to the art of the period, chiefly because they had two outstandingly talented artists in F.H.Varley, a direct descendant of the English painter John Varley, and Wyndham Lewis. Lewis, the founder of Vorticism, the founder-editor of *Blast,* iconoclastic novelist and brilliant draftsman, painted some quite remarkable war scenes. His *A Battery Shelled* of 1918 is probably one of the most important pictures to come out of the First World War. It shows the influence of Cubism and does not yet show the distinctive characteristics of the Vorticism that was to come later. It is remarkable for the division between the calm of the observers on the left and the chaos of the running men on the right, and for the stylization of the figures, the guns and the buildings, apparently fragmented, but actually integrated. Varley's major painting is *Some Day the People will Return*. This monumental battlefield picture is a kind of visual counterpart to the second act of Sean O'Casey's anti-war play *The Silver Tassie*. It actually bears a strange relationship to O'Casey's stage directions: 'a scene of jagged and lacerated ruins . . . spiky stumps of trees which were once a small wood. Every feature of the scene seems a little distorted from its original appearance'. The irony of Varley's title is hammered home by the fact that a large part of his shattered landscape is a graveyard erupting with fragmented and grotesquely leaning tombstones.

Perhaps the most remarkable contribution to the art of the First World War is that of the British artists, not least because British art is, with a few obvious exceptions, less highly developed than in the European countries. Yet, for some reason, that old cliché about war bringing out the best in people applies more to British painters than to anyone else. C.R.W.Nevinson, for example, is a relatively unimportant English painter, but the war enabled him to paint a handful of pictures which entitle him to a respectful backward glance from his successors. His *La Mitrailleuse* (The Machine Gun) is a marvellous evocation of men in battle and *La Patrie* (The Fatherland) is probably his major work.

Paul Nash is another painter who did his best work during the First World War, as one can see from his deeply ironical *We are Making a New World* in which he almost brutally displays the destroyed old world which is the legacy of the war to end wars. Nash and Nevinson excelled in the depiction of the desolate, non-active aspects of war. David Bomberg, on the other hand, brilliantly caught the frenetic quality of hurried military activity in *Sappers at Work: a Canadian Tunnelling Company* and William Roberts has exactly caught the moment of horrified confusion in *The First German Gas Attack at Ypres*.

In some ways the most important single English war painting of this period is Mark Gertler's symbolic *Merry-go-round* in which a group of military and civilian figures are hopelessly caught on the vicious circle of the roundabout which goes on crazily turning for ever. Gertler painted this picture in 1916 after the tragedy of the Somme. When D.H.Lawrence saw it he wrote to Gertler that it was 'a terrible and dreadful picture . . . a terrifying coloured flame of decomposition'. *Merry-go-round*, with its robot-like figures, mindlessly revolving and going nowhere, is a coherent and protesting voice crying out against the wickedness of war. It is the voice of the non-participant shouting at those too stupid to see the needless waste.

The war pictures of Stanley Spencer are altogether different. His moving series of paintings in Burghclere Chapel is a series of semi-visionary and visionary recollections of his own military service as a hospital orderly, first in England and then in Macedonia, and then, for a brief period, as an infantryman, also in Macedonia. For him the military life is a strange mixture of floor scrubbing and of soldiers being resurrected after dying in battle.

All these painters, in their widely differing ways, have set down the few glories and the many horrors of the Great War which, whatever else it may have failed to achieve, did produce some very interesting art. But perhaps the last word should be left to that Swiftian caricaturist George Grosz who served in the German army during the First World War. In his cartoon *Fit for Active Service* a half-witted doctor is pronouncing a skeleton fit for military duty.

The Dominions at War

Although the fate of the war would have to be decided in Europe, this was bound to be a world war. This survey shows how the war affected the dominions of the British empire: Australia, New Zealand, Canada, and South Africa

The Great War was a world war from the moment of Great Britain's entry on 4th August 1914. For she declared war not only on behalf of the 45,000,000 inhabitants of the British Isles, but also of the 400,000,000 members of a far-flung empire which was near the zenith of its extent and self-confidence. Within that empire the self-governing dominions could, if they chose, decline active support. But none did choose, and soon troops were on their way from remote corners of the world to battlefields many thousands of miles from home. Cana-

dians, Australians, New Zealanders, and South Africans, representing the dominions, took their places in the trenches beside their European allies, as did the Sikhs, Gurkhas, Mussalmans and others from the Indian sub-continent (Vol. 5, p. 615).

The participation of the British empire involved all the non-European continents in the war, and in time the entry of Japan and the United States would transform it into a global conflict on a grand scale. Inevitably such a war brought a whole series of problems. In countries far from the

Australians wave an enthusiastic farewell to troops leaving Melbourne to help preserve the 'security of the Empire'. They were to win for Australia a sense of national identity and national pride

Western Front it was sometimes difficult to promote that sense of urgency needed for supreme effort. The vagaries of colonization had left some countries, like South Africa and Canada, with ethnic divisions which threatened grave crises under the stresses of war. In India growing nationalism foreshadowed a transformation in the character of the empire, while for all 'emerging' nations the question was raised of the part they were to play in the post-war world.

This article will deal with the effect of war on the political developments and ambitions of the dominions of the British empire which, geographically, were among the numerous countries on the perimeter of the conflict. A full list of participants – active and passive – would include not only the dominions and colonies of Great Britain but also the colonies of other European powers as well as numerous South and Central American countries who declared war in the wake of the United States. These were Cuba, Panama, Brazil, Guatemala, Nicaragua, Costa Rica, Haiti, and Honduras, while Siam, Liberia, and China also declared war on the Central powers. The contributions of the dominions considered here, while statistically smaller than those of the leading nations, were nevertheless of great significance, and emphasize the merging of European history into that of a widening world.

Australia

More than most other countries of the empire, Australia was able to boast that she entered the war a united people. The majority of her 5,000,000 inhabitants were bound by strong ties of race and sentiment to the mother country, and the major political parties vied with each other in expressions of support for Great Britain's policy. Joseph Cook, the Liberal leader, said: 'Whatever happens, Australia is part of the Empire right to the full. When the Empire is at war, so is Australia at war. All our resources are in the Empire and for the preservation and security of the Empire.' His Labour opponent, Andrew Fisher, declared that 'should the worst happen, after everything has been done that honour will permit, Australia will stand behind the mother country to help and defend her to our last man and our last shilling'. Such statements echoed the country's eager, even exuberant, mood. The governor-general cabled that there was 'indescribable enthusiasm and entire unanimity throughout Australia in support of all that tends to provide for the security of the Empire in war'.

The outbreak of war coincided with an election which resulted in a decisive Labour victory. Fisher was thus called upon to preside over the early stages of a war

effort which involved measures quite out of keeping with Australian experiences and traditions. Sweeping powers over aliens, settlers of enemy origin or recent ancestry, censorship of the press, and control of publications were acquired by such measures as the War Precautions Act which gave the government authority to impose virtually a military regime. Inevitably the exercise of such authority in a country proud of its democratic way of life caused problems. Overzealous censorship, for example, caused friction between the government and press, while at times the rights of states seemed threatened by the powers of the federal government. When the Queensland premier, T.J.Ryan, spoke against conscription the federal government forbade publication of the speech and seized numerous copies. Ryan thereupon initiated action against the government for alleged violation of the rights of his sovereign state and found himself summoned before a Brisbane police court on charges of having prejudiced the public interest. The charges and counter-charges were allowed to drop, but Ryan's speech was nevertheless printed in the Parliamentary Debates with the 'censored' extracts appearing in heavy type.

Dealing with aliens was no great problem for Australia and only in the later stages of the war was there much prejudice shown against Germans in matters of employment and other forms of discrimination. South Australia, and other states to a lesser extent, assisted the war effort by appointing committees to replace traditional Germanic place-names with neutral or patriotic substitutes like Mount Kitchener in place of Kaiserstuhl.

These were trivial matters, however, compared with the great crisis of Australia's war effort, the struggle over conscription.

As the first enthusiasm faded, and as the Western Front added to the toll of Gallipoli, Australia was faced with a man-power shortage which had become acute by the end of 1916. Recruiting figures dropped so rapidly that, whereas in June 1915, for example, recruits had numbered over 12,000, a year later the figure was little more than half that. To one man, at least, it was clear that something would have to be done: that man was William Morris Hughes, the former attorney-general, who became prime minister in October 1915.

Hughes was one of the most colourful, as well as capable, statesmen in Australian history. Born into a poor Welsh family, at an early age he emigrated to Australia, where he studied law, entered politics, and with the aid of administrative gifts and fervent oratory rose to the highest position at a critical time. In more ways than one his career resembled that of his great contemporary, Lloyd George, though even the

latter would probably have been incapable of Hughes's characteristic effrontery when, at the post-war peace conference, he was rebuked by no less a figure than President Wilson for his insistence on retaining New Guinea. Wilson said: 'Mr Prime Minister of Australia, do I understand your attitude aright? If I do, it is this, that the opinion of the whole civilized world is to be set at naught. This conference, fraught with such infinite consequences to mankind for good or evil, is to break up with results which may well be disastrous to the future happiness of 18 hundred millions of the human race, in order to satisfy the whim of 5 million people in this remote southern continent whom you claim to represent.' Hughes smartly replied: 'Very well put, Mr President, you have guessed it. That's just so.'

In March 1916 Hughes visited Great Britain for four months, a visit which, with the passage of time, has taken on the qualities of legend. His aggressive, uncompromising speeches made him a figure of international fame and the Australian press rejoiced in the triumphs of their leader. He spoke of 'the happy privilege of Australians now in France to fight alongside the men of my native country'. He declared that 'we must win! We are fighting for a deathless principle. And though we walk for a time through the valley of the shadow of death, yet our cause is right and it shall prevail'. Such words hit the right note when Great Britain herself was searching for resolute leadership, and the *Evening Standard* asked 'who are the two men amongst us today wielding the biggest sway over the minds and the hearts of the British people? Surely Mr Lloyd George and Mr W.M.Hughes, the Australian prime minister. Both are Welshmen of fervid imagination who appeal by their eloquence, their fire, their patriotism'.

But on his return Hughes was to embark on a policy which split, not only his party, but the nation, and threatened seriously to jeopardize the Australian war effort. This policy, to extend compulsory service to overseas duty, met with a humiliating rebuff in a national referendum held in October 1916. The Australian people rejected his proposals by a majority of over 72,000, though for reasons which are not easy to discover. Hughes enjoyed the support of the press and of most prominent figures which, together with his own Herculean labours, indicated a 'Yes' majority. But the combination of war-weariness, remoteness from the main areas of conflict, a developing and perhaps healthy national tradition of defeating the government on referenda, all combined to defeat the forecasts. In addition there was the remorseless figure of Dr Mannix, Roman Catholic coadjutor archbishop of Melbourne, campaigning tirelessly against conscription. He did not scruple to play on Irish feelings in the aftermath of the Easter Rising (Vol. 5, p. 596), or to suggest that Australia had already done more than her fair share in the war.

The referendum divided party and nation. Anti-conscriptionists resigned from the government; Hughes left the Labour party. He was able to carry on only with the support of the Liberals, and when his government shortly became a Nationalist coalition, headed by himself but maintained by his political opponents, his position was indeed strangely similar to that of the prime minister of Great Britain.

Hughes's Nationalists won an overwhelming victory in the 1917 election, which encouraged him to appeal once more for powers to enforce conscription. By this time recruiting figures had dropped to below half the figure of 7,000 a month considered necessary. The prime minister said bluntly: 'I tell you plainly that the government must have this power. It cannot govern the country without it, and will not attempt to do so.' Yet again he was disappointed, this time by an even larger adverse vote. He resigned as he had promised, but, with no alternative government possible, came back on the following day with the identical cabinet which had resigned with him. Compulsion was now impossible, and the government tried to make the best of things with a vigorous recruiting campaign. But they were hampered by growing opposition, particularly from trades unionists and a militant body called International Workers of the World, which demanded immediate peace through negotiation. It is probable that a serious division within Australian society on the war issue was averted only by the unexpected collapse of the German armies in the autumn of 1918.

Australia's political crisis was to remain significant long after the conclusion of the war. But despite these troubles her contribution to the final victory was remarkable. Her proportion of troops in the field and of casualties sustained compared favourably with those of other dominions and of Great Britain herself. Moreover in the 'Anzac spirit' she discovered, in conjunction with the New Zealanders, a sense of national identity as well as of national pride.

New Zealand

The First World War presented fewer problems in New Zealand than in the other dominions. Her political life was not disrupted by minority problems, social cleavages, or conscription debates. The country as a whole vigorously supported the war, and compulsory overseas service was adopted in 1916 not because of any lack of re-

cruits but out of a sense of 'fair play'. The coalition government which had been created the previous year reflected no crisis, as in Great Britain and Australia, but rather the desire for national unity at a time of national effort.

By 1914, New Zealand politics were undergoing a process of transition. Until recently the Liberal party had reigned supreme under the impetus given by the extraordinary Richard Seddon — gross, uncultivated, far from high-principled, yet firmly entrenched prime minister from 1893 to 1906. His successor, Joseph Ward, continued to enjoy a success which had been built on strong support from the farmers, and it was a right-wing defection among the farmers which allowed the recently created Reform Party to form its first government in 1912.

The prime minister, William Ferguson Massey, was in many ways an uninspiring figure. He continued the 'Seddon tradition' of lack of refinement and intellectualism, but was without Seddon's overpowering personality. Narrow, bigoted, but resolute and energetic, Massey managed to remain prime minister continuously for thirteen years, though it is probable that Ward, his coalition partner and treasurer, exercised a greater control in wartime.

New Zealand entered the war with alacrity. Her traditions, recent though they were, were decidedly imperialistic. She had urged Great Britain to pursue a more active policy in the Pacific and her adoption of compulsory military service for home defence in 1909 involved calling up all males over the age of 12. She took pride in being the first dominion to offer troops, and throughout the war maintained a 'pro-British' sentiment which has become part of her national characteristic. She is regarded as considerably more 'British' than her Australian neighbour.

There was little social unrest to hamper her war effort. In the years preceding 1914 there had been, it is true, some violent incidents when Massey ruthlessly crushed a series of strikes. But the Labour movement, which would one day destroy the Liberals, was in its infancy; only half a dozen Labour members formed a party in opposition to the war. On the whole the war was a period of prosperity for New Zealand's agriculture. Her promise to feed Great Britain was profitable to both sides of the agreement, and her exportable wool, meat, and dairy produce was commandeered by the government to be sold at guaranteed high prices. The military effort was, for a country with such a small population, astonishing.

Altogether about 120,000 New Zealanders saw active service, of whom 17,000 were killed — a vast number of young men whose loss was severely felt in the difficult

inter-war years. The Maoris, at first understandably reluctant to enlist, served with distinction, whether as volunteers or conscripts. Despite the smallness of her population and her distance from Europe, New Zealand's contribution to the Allied victory was far from negligible.

New Zealanders were proud of their war effort. The performance of their troops at Gallipoli (Vol. 4, p. 506), their occupation of German Samoa, their voice in the counsels of the empire and in the League of Nations all assisted that growth of identity so important in the evolution of a colony into a nation.

Canada

As in Australia and New Zealand, in Canada both major political parties were outspoken in their support for the war. The Conservative prime minister, Sir Robert Borden, said that 'as to our duty, we are all agreed: we stand shoulder to shoulder with Britain and the other British Dominions in this quarrel, and that duty we shall not fail to fulfil as the honour of Canada demands'. Sir Wilfrid Laurier, leader of the Liberals and spokesman for the majority of French Canadians, claimed that 'this war is for as noble a cause as ever impelled a nation to risk her all upon the arbitrament of the sword'.

Such assertions hid a fundamental division in Canadian society which was to loom larger as the war progressed. The so-called Anglo-Canadians, together with British-born immigrants, had a vastly different outlook from that of the insular, tightly-knit community of French-speaking *Canadiens*. Naturally enough the French-speaking settlers felt less attachment to the British empire than their countrymen. Less obviously, but equally important, the French community retained fewer ties with their own 'mother country' and their support for the war was, on the whole, passive rather than overtly enthusiastic. This situation was not helped by the attitude of the administration. The minister of militia, Sam Hughes, made no pretence of his disgust at the low recruiting figures from the French-speaking provinces. Efforts to create specifically *Canadien* forces were usually obstructed; English was uniformly adopted as the language of command; and *Canadien* recruits seemed to suffer almost insuperable difficulties when it came to promotion.

These problems lay in the future, however, when Canada, in common with the rest of the empire, embarked on her struggle of unprecedented magnitude. Borden's greatest tasks, as he saw them, were two-fold. First he had to mobilize the nation for war, second, to ensure that his country participated in the direction of the effort to which he committed so many of ▷ **639**

THE EMPIRE NEEDS MEN!

AUSTRALIA
CANADA
INDIA
NEW ZEALAND

All answer the call.

Helped by the YOUNG LIONS
The OLD LION defies his Foes.

ENLIST NOW.

'GOD BLESS DADDY'
45,000 AUSTRALIAN FATHERS ARE FIGHTING!
WILL YOU HELP?

1 *Maori butcher at his work in France.*
2 *Australian recruiting poster. In the earlier part of the war as many as 12,000 Australians volunteered each month.*
3 *Canadians at the time of the battle of the Somme tend German wounded*

Boys Come over here
you're wanted

4 *Australian poster asking for recruits for Gallipoli.* 5 *West Indians clean their rifles on the road to Amiens.* 6 *Appeal for money for a European war from the hungry people of British India. Poster says 'Give money to help our warriors'*

युद्ध ऋणमें कर्ज दो

जिससे लड़ाई जितने में सहायना हो ।

300,000 CANADIANS

HAVE JOINED THE COLORS

AND ARE HELPING TO CRUSH THIS VENOMOUS REPTILE.

Two hundred thousand will yet answer the call that says:

Your King and Country Need You

Will YOU Be One of These?

The Forces of the ALLIES are Exerting Every Ounce of Their Strength to CHAIN this DRAGON.

Will YOU HELP Along With the Other LOYAL SONS of Britain?

JOIN the 99th ESSEX BATTALION and HELP CRUSH the GERMAN MONSTER The World-wide Menace to Humanity and Civilization.

For particulars Apply to Lieut. Morton Wellington Barracks or W. T. Gregory at 141 Talbot St.

7 Canadian recruiting poster. 8 General Botha (sitting on the stool) personally directs operations in South West Africa. 9 An Australian and a New Zealander make friends with children on Lemnos, a base for soldiers fighting at Gallipoli

10 Canadian prime minister Massey enters a captured German dug-out, 1916. 11 Scene during riots in Johannesburg, where opposition to fighting a war for the English never died down. 12 W.M.Hughes, Australian prime minister

Great Britain's declaration of war brought 450,000,000 people from all continents into the conflict

his country's resources. Raising sufficient troops was far from easy. Canadian traditions were non-military; the pre-war permanent army numbered mere 3,000. No doubt a feeling of security due to the nearness of her powerful neighbour with its protective Monroe Doctrine played its part in this lack of preparedness, but it meant that Canada felt the war-time dislocation even more severely than other countries.

In view of her traditions, Canada's achievements were formidable. Though the target of 500,000 troops had become evidently unattainable by 1917, Canada played her full share in the war effort. Lloyd George's verdict on the quality of the Canadian troops after their exploits on the Somme (Vol. 5, p. 562) was that they 'played a part of such distinction that thenceforward they were marked out as storm troops; for the remainder of the war they were brought along to head the assault in one great battle after another. Whenever the Germans found the Canadian Corps coming into the line, they prepared for the worst'.

With his country performing such feats, Borden considered that he should play some part in formulating the policies for which his troops were committed. When told by Bonar Law, the colonial secretary, that his schemes were impractical, he retorted that 'it can hardly be expected that we shall put 400,000 or 500,000 men in the field and willingly accept the position of having no more voice and receiving no more consideration than if we were toy automata. Any person cherishing such an expectation harbours an unfortunate and even dangerous delusion. Is this war being waged by the United Kingdom alone or is it a war waged by the whole Empire?' His language had its effect, and after Lloyd George became prime minister in December 1916 the dominions found themselves consulted to a much greater extent. An Imperial War Cabinet was set up in March 1917, the same month for which the Imperial War Conference was summoned. It was Borden, appropriately enough, who moved the famous resolution at the conference, claiming for the dominions 'a right to an adequate voice in foreign policy and in foreign relations'. After the war Borden led the dominions' demand for representation at the peace conference and for their individual membership of the League of Nations.

But while Sir Robert was demanding more influence for Canada, his country was being torn by a grave crisis over conscription in 1917. The enormous losses sustained in Europe during the previous year made man-power shortages general throughout all belligerent countries. Recruiting figures high in the early months of the war, fell alarmingly until they were less, month by month, than the casualties. By 1917 not only was conscription an urgent problem, but party politics had been renewed in a way which lent considerable bitterness to the struggle.

The growing opposition of the *Canadiens,* which was fostered by the treatment of their recruits, long-standing grievances over the exclusive use of English in schools in Ontario, and a series of frauds at governmental level all helped to create a dangerous political climate. Moreover, Laurier was determined to maintain the separate identity and different ideals of the French-Canadians, and these seemed threatened, not only by conscription, but by the coalition government advocated by the prime minister. So the Liberal leader fought the Military Service Act every inch of the way until it became law in August 1917; but the issue split his party and Borden was able to form his coalition in October with the help of Liberal defections. Moreover in the December elections, fought, like the parliamentary battle, over conscription, along racial lines, Laurier was heavily defeated by the government. Quebec, however, solidly supported him with 62 out of 65 seats. There is much truth in the accusation that the election was at least partly influenced by 'shameless manipulation'. For example, special legislation enfranchised those who were most committed to the war and therefore likely to be conscriptionist, but disenfranchised others who would be expected to vote the other way. In addition the soldiers' vote, which was solidly conscriptionist, was distributed in those provinces where it was most likely to show the best results for the government.

Perhaps the worst feature of the conscription crisis was that the political victory committed the country to a goal it was unable to achieve. Mass pleas for exemption, together with evasion and desertion cut the projected figure of 100,000 by nearly forty per cent, and most of those were too late to reach Europe anyway. Quebec was, of course, the most recalcitrant province, but farmers and trades unionists were to be found objecting in all parts of Canada.

So Canada's war effort was achieved at the cost of a deepening antagonism within her mixed population. But she had at least managed to sustain that effort without major disunity on the issue of the war itself. This no doubt had its effect on bringing the insular *Canadiens* to a fuller realization of the part they were compelled to play in world events. And that part had significantly grown when, in these years, Canada took the lead in asserting that the daughters of the mother country had come of age.

South Africa

South Africa's role in the war was dominated by two factors peculiar to her among the dominions. She alone had a military front line bordering her territory; and she alone had a large minority of settlers not only opposed to war but actively seeking a German victory as a means of throwing off the British connexion.

Causes of unrest in South Africa are not hard to find. Memories of the Jameson raid and the Boer War (Vol. 1, p. 13) remained strong, particularly among the Dutch farmers of Transvaal and the Orange Free State. All their lives these men had learned to regard the British as their chief enemies, and it was too much to expect that the grant of dominion status in the Union of 1910 would at once dispel the antagonism of generations. That despite these cleavages the Union remained intact under the stresses of war was due in large measure to the loyalty of two men. Louis Botha and Jan Smuts, South Africa's greatest soldier-statesmen, both pursued a policy of uniting their country within the framework of empire. The extent of their success must rank both men in the forefront of the world's leaders of the 20th century.

The existence of a strategically important German colony in South West Africa made any prospect of South African neutrality impossible. On the contrary, Great Britain immediately asked South Africa to undertake the conquest of the neighbouring territory, and Botha, the prime minister, was quick to agree. But his initial plans were scarcely completed when operations had to be suspended. For a serious rebellion among anti-British and pro-German elements threatened to undermine the war effort and perhaps to topple the government itself. The rebels included soldiers of the calibre of Colonel Maritz, commander of the frontier forces, General Beyers, and General de Wet. Suppressing this revolt was thus South Africa's first major achievement of the war, though the personal anguish of Botha, as he relentlessly pursued those who had formerly been comrades-in-arms against the British, can only be imagined. Smuts, the minister of defence, who directed from headquarters this destruction of former colleagues, said that 'few know what Botha went through in the rebellion. He lost friendships of a lifetime, friendships he valued perhaps more than anything in life. But Botha's line remained absolutely consistent. No one else in South Africa could have stuck it out. You wanted a man for that . . .'

Botha's statesmanship was never more clearly revealed than by his measures after the surrender of the rebels in February 1915. He was so lenient that only one man was executed – surely a record for a large-scale revolt in wartime. Meanwhile, he was able personally to conduct a campaign against German South West Africa, which has been called 'one of the neatest and most successful campaigns of the Great War'. Troops were also sent under Smuts to co-operate with British and Indian troops in German East Africa against the redoubtable Lettow Vorbeck, a campaign which was virtually over when Smuts left for London to represent his country at the Imperial War Conference.

Arriving in March 1917, Smuts originally intended to stay only a few weeks. He remained in Europe for two-and-a-half years, proving himself both militarily and politically among the ablest and most visionary of the British government's advisers. He was consulted by Lloyd George on tactics and strategy in Europe, spoke on imperial affairs so effectively that he was dubbed 'Orator for the Empire', recommended the creation of an independent command for the RAF, and was even used to end a strike of Welsh miners at Tonypandy. On that famous occasion he quietened the tumult by asking the miners to sing. They returned the compliment by returning to work. Lloyd George paid tribute to him as a man of 'rare and fine gifts of mind and heart', and that 'of his practical contributions to our councils during these trying years it is difficult to speak too highly'.

Besides serving on their own continent, South Africans also saw duty in the Middle East and on the Western Front where they enjoyed some notable triumphs. In all, some 136,000 white South Africans saw active service in a greater variety of conditions than the troops of any of the other dominions. But while the troops were winning distinction, and Smuts was earning unique prestige as an imperial statesman, Botha was severely troubled at home. Republicans, hostile to the empire, kept up constant pressure. Their party, the Nationalists, led by J.B.M.Hertzog, continually tried to obstruct the prosecution of the war, even to the extent of opposing, in 1918, Botha's motion hoping that God would grant victory to Great Britain.

South Africa's war effort had very mixed results. On the one hand the Union remained intact, South African prestige grew with the magnitude of her efforts, and her statesmen demonstrated the calibre which could be brought to British councils from distant parts of the empire. But numbers of her population remained unreconciled to the imperial connexion, and many who sought to protect the Afrikaner against the British extended this policy to seek greater protection for the white South African against the black. The war deepened rifts in South African loyalties and foreshadowed later internal developments which were to have important consequences for the nation's future.

The War Poets

When you see millions of the mouthless dead
Across your dreams in pale battalions go,
Say not soft things as other men have said...
Charles Sorley, killed in the battle of Loos, 1915

Bottom: Charles Péguy (sitting on right), a French poet who had warned his country of the impending German menace. 'Happy are they who died in a just war,' he wrote. He died in 1914, in the battle of the Marne
Below: Rupert Brooke, spokesman and symbol of the generation of young men who volunteered gladly at the outbreak of war. To him the war seemed to offer an opportunity to cleanse Europe from the stagnation and corruption of peace

Bibliothèque Nationale, Paris

Radio Times Hulton

'The very phrase *War Poet*,' wrote Osbert Sitwell, a war poet himself, in *Noble Essences*, 'indicates a strange twentieth-century phenomenon, the attempt to combine two incompatibles. There had been no War Poets in the Peninsular, Crimean or Boer wars. But war had suddenly become transformed by the effort of scientist and mechanician into something so infernal, so inhuman, that it was recognised that only their natural enemy, the poet, could pierce through the armour of horror . . . to the pity at the human core.' There was a further, more prosaic reason for the phenomenon: this was the first war which sucked a whole generation into battle. The likelihood of a young poet fighting in the Crimea was slight. Almost the only young men of letters who escaped the First World War were those who were medically unfit, like Aldous Huxley.

The war generated two kinds of verse, belonging to a written and an oral tradition. The editor of an anthology of war poetry which appeared in 1916 referred to the 'scores of slim volumes and hundreds of separate poems' which had come from men in the army — most of them officers. Most of this verse is now totally forgotten. To the oral tradition belong the songs produced for and by the ordinary soldiers of each country involved in the war, and especially perhaps the British. Ironic, funny, obscene, and self-mocking, these songs are a wonderful reflection of the private soldier's views of the generals, the trenches, the food, the shells, his mates, and himself. They helped to make the almost intolerable tolerable. 'Send out the army and the navy, but for God's sake don't send me.' Exactly. Though some songs became universal, there were regimental preferences depending on temperament and origin. 'The men were singing,' wrote Robert Graves in *Goodbye to All That*, his account of his experiences in the war. 'Being mostly from the midlands, they sang comic songs rather than Welsh hymns: *Slippery Sam, When we've Wound up the Watch on the Rhine*, and *I do like a S'nice S'mince Pie* . . . The Second Welsh would never have sung a song like *When we've Wound up the Watch on the Rhine*. Their only songs about the war were defeatist:

I want to go home,
I want to go home.
The coal-box and shrapnel they whistle and
  roar,
I don't want to go to the trenches no more,
I want to go over the sea

Where the Kayser can't shoot bombs at me.
Oh, I
Don't want to die,
I want to go home.

This was the voice of the 'men'. It is the first category, the written verse, which most people mean when they speak of war poetry. Osbert Sitwell's quotation refers to a conception of war poetry which developed only towards the end of the war, when the full horror of it could not be camouflaged in rhetoric. In August 1914 the poetical voices which the public wished to hear were romantic, patriotic, and innocent. Convinced as each nation was of the rightness of its cause, it wished to have this confirmed by the poets. After a peace which had lasted in western Europe since 1871, no one, and poets no more than anyone else, knew what war would be like. Hence the idealization of war and death in much of the verse produced in the first months of the war. In England Rupert Brooke thanked God. In France the socialist, Charles Péguy, who had been warning the French of the German menace since the Morocco crisis of 1905 (Vol. 2, p. 163), had just time to respond to the war — 'Heureux ceux qui sont morts dans une juste guerre!' ('Happy are they who died in a just war') — before falling in the battle of the Marne.

Many European poets half-welcomed the war, not merely as an opportunity for self-sacrifice in a just cause, but in a deeper sense. In Russia Valery Bryusov in the decade 1900 to 1910 had called, in *The Coming Huns*, for some great catastrophe to purge a world grown rotten. In Germany Stefan George, anxious for the regeneration of German youth, whom he saw as corrupted by the false material values of the age, had foreseen, approvingly, a 'Holy War'. The war when it came fulfilled the prophecies of George and of many others.

Though some of these men would have claimed personally to abhor violence, they helped to create an atmosphere in which violence — and violence on a cosmic scale — was expected. The Futurists, led by the Italian poet, Filippo Marinetti, went farther. Marinetti's Futurist Manifesto of 1909 proclaimed the necessity of a new art drawing inspiration from the new and unforeseen, the rhythms of machines, the beauty of aggression. War for Marinetti was the bloody and necessary test of a people's force, 'the world's only hygiene'. It was as if men were tiring of peace.

The 'hygienic' view of war, echoed by Brooke in his reference to 'swimmers into cleanness leaping', was common. War was

Jonathan Cape

Robert Graves. He, like other British poets in the trenches, wanted to tell of the real horrors of war, realistically

to be a kind of surgical operation on the rotten body of a society corrupted by materialism and complacency. A new, young, better society would emerge from under the knife. On these grounds, and as a release from uncertainty, the war could be welcomed. Even those who saw the magnitude of the catastrophe laboured to extract some good from it. The English poet, Wilfred Owen, wrote of 'the need /Of sowings for new Spring, and blood for seed'.

Disillusion, of course, followed. On the Western Front the slaughter on the Somme in the summer of 1916 destroyed for ever the romantic innocence with which the young had gone to war. The process of disenchantment is seen most clearly in the British poets, who set out in 1914 with perhaps more illusions than their continental cousins, and reacted more sharply in consequence. Every country had its soldier poets. Only among the British did war poetry develop an autonomous life of its own, so that one can fairly speak of a 'school' or 'movement'. Of the continental poets caught up in the war, some took it as their subject, others, preoccupied by aesthetic demands of their own conception of poetry, preserved the 'purity' of their art by retreating into silence or writing on other themes.

Thus the history of war poetry on the continent is the history of individuals. In Russia the moving descriptions of the Eastern Front by Viktor Khlebnikov, who served as a private, and the condemnation of the 'capitalist' war by Mayakovsky, were overtaken by the revolution, which undammed a torrent of verse from these two and their elders. Here, is seemed for a time, was the rebirth for which poets had been calling. In Italy, which came into the war late, the veteran romantic poet, Gabriele d'Annunzio, devoted his immense energy and rhetorical talents to involving

his country on the side of the Allied powers, pointing to the example of France, who had 'donned her purple robe of war, / Ready to sing like a lark / On all the peaks of death'. He devoted the war years to playing the part of the poet-hero, the superman of action, losing an eye when crash-landing his aircraft, seeing his hour of glory when he captured Fiume in defiance of his own government in 1919. The war poems of Giuseppe Ungaretti expose with quiet honesty the morbid vanity of d'Annunzio's cult of blood and death.

France had her celebrator of war as Italy had d'Annunzio – Drieu la Rochelle, who found in the war a gratifying escape from bourgeois mediocrity to a life in which he hoped to find vitality, danger, and chivalry. War became his religion: 'Guerre . . . il faut que je m'abandonne à toi, corps et biens . . . Je ne saurais plus vivre hors de toi'. (War . . . let me abandon myself to you, body and all . . . I couldn't live without you now.) Such mystical enthusiasm was mercifully rare. It is lacking in France's greatest war poet, Guillaume Apollinaire, who wrote about the war, as he wrote about everything else, simply because it happened to him; too humane to glorify it; too honest to suppress its strange moments of beauty –

Ah Dieu! que la guerre est jolie
Avec ses chants ses longs loisirs.

(Ah God! how pretty war is
With its songs and its long hours of leisure)

He was too engrossed in the exploration of his own sensations and reactions to the war to preach about it. Apollinaire, a corpulent, generous figure, the champion of Picasso and the Cubists, was already an established poet at the outbreak of war.

Bibliothèque Nationale, Paris

A drawing by Apollinaire of himself as an artillery-man. He was a vivid reporter in poetry of the experience of war

After some unavoidable delay – being the son of a Polish mother and Italian father, he had to take out naturalization papers before he could join the French army – he enlisted in the ranks, was promoted sublieutenant in November 1915, and served at the front from then on. To the surprise of his literary friends, he adapted himself easily to army life. Neither the danger nor the tedium of war dulled his vitality. He bombarded his friends with letters and postcards in verse from the front:

The war-enthusiast D'Annunzio. Italian cartoon captioned: 'If we had guns as big as his mouth we'd have no trouble'

Je t'écris de dessous la tente
Tandis que meurt ce jour d'été
Où floraison éblouissante
Dans le ciel à peine bleuté
Une canonnade éclatante
Se fane avant d'avoir été

(I write to you from under the tent
While this summer day is dying
In which like a dazzling blossoming
In the hardly bluish sky
A cannonade bursts out
And fades before it has ever been)

Yet, though he was one of the most vivid reporters of the experience of war, he remained apart from it, not engaged in the way that Sassoon and Owen were morally engaged. After a head wound from a shell fragment ended his war service on 17th March 1916, Apollinaire lived out the war in Paris, and was adopted as the hero of the *avant-garde*, the 'little magazines', *Sic* and *Nord-Sud*, the young poets such as André Breton, Paul Eluard, and Louis Aragon, now serving in the army, who a few years later were to assist at the birth of Surrealism. It was for his techniques, his joyful experimentation, and his modern sensibility (he once wrote that artillery gave birth to the modern literary spirit) that these men took him as leader, not for his attitude to the war. Their poetic concerns, and his, were aesthetic. Thus Aragon, who won the *Croix de Guerre* in 1917, was later to reproach himself for passing through the war without writing a single word about it. Apollinaire died of Spanish 'flu on 9th November 1918.

The graceful, exuberant spirit of Apollinaire is very far from the spirit of the British war poets. When the war broke out in August 1914, men were agreed that it would not last long; it would be over in months. This made it easy for young men

Siegfried Sassoon: a recklessly brave soldier, an angry satirist of the 'callous complacency' of the patriots at home

like Rupert Brooke to see the war as a short, clean, painless break with the complacent materialism of the past. There is in the early war poems a paradoxical insistence on the irrelevance of death. We find it in *Into Battle* of Julian Grenfell, who died of wounds on 27th May 1915:

And life is colour and warmth and light,
* And a striving evermore for these;*
And he is dead who will not fight;
* And who dies fighting has increase. . . .*
The thundering line of battle stands,
* And in the air death moans and sings,*
But Day shall clasp him with strong hands,
* And Night shall fold him in soft wings.*

We find it also in the work of Brooke himself, who after his early death from septicaemia on a hospital ship in the Aegean was taken to be the ideal representative of the brave youth of Great Britain who sacrificed their lives:

War knows no power. Safe shall be my going,
Secretly armed against all death's
* endeavour;*
Safe though all safety's lost; safe where men
* fall;*
And if these poor limbs die, safest of all.

Brooke never experienced the trenches; he died in April 1915, just missing the

Gallipoli campaign. It is therefore unfair to reproach him with failing to appreciate the awful reality of modern war. No one appreciated this before it was experienced. The point is that Brooke was typical. He expressed the thoughts of 'the plain recruit who had not the gift of a style', in the words of C.E.Montague, himself a far from plain recruit (he dyed his grey hair in order to be accepted into the army); of the 'officer-class' volunteers, at any rate. And when these views ceased to appeal to the fighting men as they discovered what war was really like, they continued dear to those at home who had lost their sons. Twenty thousand copies of Brooke's *1914, Five Sonnets* were printed in 1915.

After the Somme, a new, tougher group of poets began to make their voices heard. These men—Edmund Blunden, Robert Graves, Wilfred Owen, Herbert Read, Isaac Rosenberg, Siegfried Sassoon, and others—had a number of points in common. They were all, except Rosenberg, junior officers—among whom casualties were heaviest. They all hated the war, hated the profiteering and the jingoist propaganda of wartime Great Britain, and wished to confound the lies and the complacency with a true vision of the trenches. Blunden described the difficulty thus: 'Among the multitudes of us shipped to the Pas de Calais a few months before the Great Push (or Drive) of the British army in 1916, I was a verse-writer; my interests were not yet changed from what life had formed before all this chaos . . . In May and June 1916, in my notebooks, the grimness of war began to compete as a subject with the pastorals of peace. By the end of the year, when madness seemed totally to rule the hour, I was almost a part of the shell-holes, of ruin and of mortification. But the stanzas then written were left in the pocket-book: what good were they, who cared, who would

Wilfred Owen, the greatest of the British war poets. 'I shall be better able to cry my outcry, playing my part'

Charles Sorley, killed in the battle of Loos. He was the first poet who tried to express the futility and horror of the war

agree?' To spread the bad news was hard. 'National interests were, understandably, in the way.'

The precursor of these poets, Charles Sorley, who was killed in the battle of Loos in 1915, and who was the first to present an image of the war which came near to comprehending its full horror and futility, left behind him a sonnet:

When you see millions of the mouthless dead
Across your dreams in pale battalions go,
Say not soft things as other men have said...

His successors had to find a language and a style for the hard things they had to say. When Graves first met Sassoon near Béthune, and showed him some of his poems, Sassoon 'frowned and said that war should not be written about in such a realistic way. In return, he showed me some of his own poems. One of them began:

Return to greet me, Colours that were my
* joy,*
Not in the woeful crimson of men slain . . .

Siegfried had not yet been in the trenches. . . . I told him . . . he would soon change his style'.

Sassoon did. By 1917 he was totally opposed to the war. His verses were circulating rapidly among his fellow poets, but had not filtered through to the consciousness of the public. Sassoon, a recklessly brave soldier, decided to make a direct protest against the war. Having discussed his stand with the editor of *The Nation*, which was banned from foreign circulation on the grounds that its attitude to the war prejudiced recruiting, and with Bertrand Russell, whose opposition to the war lost him his Cambridge fellowship, Sassoon made public a statement repudiating the war.

Sassoon's statement was not pacifist, but a protest at the continuation of this particular war. The other trench poets, though they too had turned 'against the war', continued to fight; and even Sassoon, in the end, went back to war. Wilfred Owen moved close to pacifism, writing in a letter in 1917, that he now understood 'that one of Christ's essential commands was: passivity at any price! Suffer dishonour and disgrace, but never resort to arms. Be bullied, be outraged, be killed; but do not kill. . . . Am I not myself a conscientious objector with a very seared conscience?' But the desire to stand by his men in the trenches, the feeling that the true protest against the war could come only from those engaged in it, overcame the pacifism. 'I shall be better able to cry my outcry, playing my part.'

And though the trenches were desolate, in some ways home seemed even worse. England moved the poets to angry frustration. Sassoon wrote of the cheap music-hall show:

I'd like to see a Tank come down the
*   stalls,*
Lurching to rag-time tunes, or 'Home,
*   Sweet Home' —*
And there'd be no more jokes in Music-
*   Halls*
To mock the riddled corpses round
*   Bapaume.*

Owen wrote from Scarborough in July 1918: 'I wish the Boche would have the pluck to come right in and make a clean sweep of the pleasure boats, and the promenaders on the Spa, and all the stinking Leeds and Bradford war-profiteers, now reading *John Bull* on Scarborough Sands.' England and the trenches were different worlds. The poets' hate was reserved not for the Germans but for the profiteers and the general staff. At home everyone was patriotic. 'Patriotism, in the trenches,' wrote Graves, 'was too remote a sentiment, and at once rejected as fit only for civilians. . . . Great Britain was a quiet, easy place for getting back to out of the present foreign misery; but as a nation it included not only the trench-soldiers themselves and those who had gone home wounded, but the staff, Army Service Corps, lines of communication troops, base units, home-service units, and all civilians down to the detested grades of journalists, profiteers, "starred" men exempted from enlistment, conscientious objectors, and members of the Government.' If the trench-soldiers were fighting for anyone, it was for each other. The trench poets were on their side.

After his protest, Sassoon was sent to Craiglockhart War Hospital to recover from neurasthenia. There Wilfred Owen, also convalescent, showed him his early war poems. Sassoon's encouragement and

friendship gave Owen the self-confidence and inspiration he needed. With Sassoon's approval, Owen returned to the front in August 1918. He was killed on 4th November, a week before the armistice, while taking his company across the Sambre canal in the face of determined German machine-gun fire. In the few months before his death Owen produced most of those poems which mark him out as the greatest war poet of the First World War. He embraced the futility, the waste of life and spirit, the boredom, the blood, and the pity of the trenches in a vision which raised his verses high above the outraged satire of his master Sassoon. He saw his function as to warn his generation, by depicting the truth and the pity of war. From one side of the front, Owen pictured a 'sad land. . . . Gray, cratered like the moon with hollow woe,/ And pitted with great pocks and scabs of plagues'; from the other, the German poet Anton Schnack described the dead, 'heavy, fossilized, their hands full of spiders, their mouths red with scabs'. It was the same no man's land, the same corpses, for both. They felt the same horror, yet they fought. Political protest, like Sassoon's, had proved useless. In the end, all the poet could do was to describe.

Exercise

Vers un village de l'arrière
S'en allaient quatre bombardiers
Ils étaient couverts de poussière
Depuis la tête jusqu'aux pieds

Ils regardaient la vaste plaine
En parlant entre eux du passé
Et ne se retournaient qu'à peine
Quand un obus avait toussé

Tous quatre de la classe seize
Parlaient d'antan non d'avenir
Ainsi se prolongeait l'ascèse
Qui les exerçait à mourir

(Four gunners were going towards a village behind the front. They were covered with dust from head to foot. They looked at the vast plain, talking among themselves of the past, and when a shell coughed they hardly turned their heads. All four of the 1916 class talked of the past not the future — and so the ascetic discipline which trained them for death was carried on.)
From *Calligrammes* by Apollinaire

Preface
(found, unfinished, among Owen's papers)

This book is not about heroes. English Poetry is not yet fit to speak of them.
Nor is it about deeds or lands, nor anything about glory, honour, dominion or power,

except War.
Above all, this book is not concerned with Poetry.
The subject of it is War, and the pity of War.
The Poetry is in the pity.
Yet these elegies are not to this generation,
*   This is in no sense consolatory.*
They may be to the next.
All the poet can do to-day is to warn.
That is why the true Poets must be truthful.
If I thought the letter of this book would last,
I might have used proper names; but if the spirit of it survives Prussia, — my ambition and those names will be content; for they will have achieved themselves fresher fields than Flanders.
From *Poems* by Wilfred Owen, published 1920
By permission, Harold Owen and Chatto & Windus, Ltd

Finished with the war
A Soldier's Declaration

(This statement was made to his commanding officer by Second-Lieutenant S.L. Sassoon, Military Cross, recommended for D.S.O., Third Battalion Royal Welch Fusiliers. . . .)

I am making this statement as an act of wilful defiance of military authority, because I believe that the war is being deliberately prolonged by those who have the power to end it.

I am a soldier, convinced that I am acting on behalf of soldiers. I believe that this war, upon which I entered as a war of defence and liberation, has now become a war of aggression and conquest. I believe that the purposes for which I and my fellow-soldiers entered upon this war should have been so clearly stated as to have made it impossible to change them, and that, had this been done, the objects which actuated us would now be attainable by negotiation.

I have seen and endured the sufferings of the troops, and I can no longer be a party to prolong these sufferings for ends which I believe to be evil and unjust.

I am not protesting against the conduct of the war, but against the political errors and insincerities for which the fighting men are being sacrificed.

On behalf of those who are suffering now I make this protest against the deception which is being practised on them: also I believe that I may help to destroy the callous complacency with which the majority of those at home regard the continuation of agonies which they do not share, and which they have not sufficient imagination to realize.
From the *Bradford Pioneer*, 27th July 1917

Chapter 24

Introduction by J.M.Roberts

Bismarck is supposed once to have said that the most important fact of world politics in the 19th century was that the Americans and the British spoke the same language. Important as this may have been and be, many people in both countries have always been too ready to take for granted a 'special relationship'. In the early years of the First World War, this made it hard for the British to understand United States' policy. This Chapter is about the changes which that policy underwent down to the climax of entry into the war, and about some of the consequences which flowed from that event.

Hugh Brogan's article on **The American People and the War** describes the context of American policy-making. Their attitudes were among the factors which the President, Woodrow Wilson, had to take into account. They go a long way towards explaining the complicated and confusing appearance which American policy often presented to Europeans in these years. The President, too, was a complex, curious man. The leading authority on his life, his biographer, Arthur S.Link, contributes to this Chapter a study of **Wilson and the Ordeal of Neutrality**.

In the end, the entry of the United States to the war was determined by the German general staff. Once again in 1916, as in 1914, German foreign policy was subordinated to technical and strategic considerations. The adoption of the Schlieffen plan had made Great Britain's entry to a Franco-German war almost inevitable, as German military planning had recognized. Now, the adoption of the strategy of unrestricted war by U-boat—described by Wolfgang Steglich in **The Fatal Decision**—equally made the entry of the United States to the war inevitable. **Declaration of War**, the subject of an article by Robert H.Ferrell, came almost at once.

Ludendorff and his advisers had calculated that the U-boats would bring Great Britain to heel before the enormous manpower of the Americans could make itself felt in France. This calculation was wrong: the U-boats did not prove able to do the job given to them. Yet the Germans were right in thinking that the American armies would take a long time to reach the battlefield. That is why **The New Military Balance** which followed the American declaration of war (analysed in this Chapter by Correlli Barnett) is a more complicated matter than appears at first sight.

Nevertheless, the American entry to the war was decisive. It was also symbolic of the ending of an age. Four centuries of European world domination were coming to a close. The New World had entered the European ring to decide quarrels the Old could no longer settle for itself.

Blockade by submarine. A U-boat stops an Italian ship in the Mediterranean

The sentence of defeat for Germany— Wilson asks Congress to declare war

American soldiers, setting out to fight on the Western Front, look back at New York

Germany

1915 4th February: Germans announce that they will use submarines against all merchant shipping in war zones.
1st May: first American ship, *Gulflight,* sunk without warning.
7th May: Walther Schwieger in German submarine U20 sinks the *Lusitania.* 128 Americans are drowned. Wilson sends notes of protest.
6th June: the Kaiser insists that all passenger lines must be spared.
19th August: Germans sink British liner *Arabic.*
18th September: the new chief of naval staff, Holtzendorff, orders that U-boat commerce war should be carried out on 'cruiser' system.
1916 29th February: Holtzendorff gives permission for armed merchantships to be sunk.
4th March: Falkenhayn says he must use unrestricted submarine warfare to finish war by the end of 1916.
13th March: orders are given that both armed and unarmed merchantships are to be sunk.
15th March: Tirpitz resigns.
24th March: U-boat torpedoes French packet steamer *Sussex* with heavy loss of life.
18th April: Wilson threatens to break off diplomatic relations with Germany in protest about the sinking of the *Sussex.*
4th May: German government agrees to demands of USA that submarines should adhere to 'cruiser' rules of warfare, on condition that Great Britain abandons illegal methods of blockade.
29th August: Hindenburg and Ludendorff replace Falkenhayn.
6th October: U-boats are told to act on 'cruiser' rules.
12th December: the Central powers make a peace offer to the Allies.
End of December: Hindenburg and Ludendorff demand unrestricted submarine warfare.
1917 9th January: at Pless Bethmann Hollweg agrees to unrestricted submarine warfare.

United States

1914 4th August: Wilson says USA will stay neutral.
1915 House visits London to work for Anglo-American peace drive.
1916 18th January: US asks Allies to disarm their merchantships if Germany agrees to warn such ships before sinking them. Wilson has to abandon this plan.
22nd February: Grey and House sign Memorandum on Wilson's plan of mediation.
5th March: House returns to Washington to say that British and French wish for peace.
27th May: Wilson declares that USA will join a post-war league of nations, as part of plan for settlement of war.
7th November: Wilson is re-elected on peace programme.
18th December: Wilson asks belligerents to state terms on which they would be prepared to cease fighting.
1917 Mid-January: Wilson tries to persuade British and German governments to accept his mediation.
26th January: Great Britain tells Wilson it is prepared to accept his mediation.
31st January: Bernstorff informs USA of German decision to renew unrestricted submarine warfare on 1st February.
3rd February: Wilson informs Congress that he is breaking off diplomatic relations with Germany.
25th February: three Americans lose their lives when the Germans sink *Laconia.*
1st March: Zimmermann telegram is published in the American press.
2nd April: Wilson asks Congress to declare war.
6th April: USA enters war.
June: 1st Division of the American Expeditionary Force lands in France.

Elsewhere

1916 At the battles of Verdun and the Somme, French, British, and Germans all sustain appalling losses.
June: Brusilov's Offensive gives Russia victory over Austria-Hungary.
27th August: Rumania declares war on Austria-Hungary.
6th December: Rumanian capital, Bucharest, occupied by Central powers.
1917 March: revolution starts in Russia. Tsar Nicholas II is forced to abdicate.
April and May: French army under Nivelle is repulsed by the Germans.
1918 21st March: Germans launch first of a series of offensives on Western Front. These last until July.
18th July: the French launch attack on Villers-Cotterêt. The tide starts to turn against the Germans.

The Fatal Decision

For two-and-a-half years the Kaiser and his chancellor, Bethmann Hollweg, held out against the demand of the generals and admirals for unrestricted submarine warfare. Then at Pless, in January 1917, they succumbed, in a 'world-shattering decision', to the arguments of Hindenburg and Ludendorff

At long last, on 9th January 1917, Bethmann Hollweg, the German chancellor, at a conference at GHQ, Pless in Upper Silesia, signified his concurrence with the resolution in favour of unrestricted submarine warfare, that is he agreed to the torpedoing of enemy and neutral merchant and passenger ships without warning. His feelings were similar to those which had burdened him during the crisis of July 1914. For him the Pless decision was a leap in the dark, like the action of Austria-Hungary against Serbia in July 1914. On that occasion he realized that any attempt to overthrow Serbia might well lead to a European war. Now he was tormented by anxiety lest the reckless use of the U-boats result in war with the United States. And on both occasions his fears were justified.

In 1914 it was the growing consolidation of the Triple Entente, the increasing strength of Russia, and the critical situation in the Balkans which drove the German government to approve and guarantee the Austro-Hungarian attack on Serbia regardless of the risk of a European war. In 1917 the German government was impelled by the hopelessness of the land war to

agree to unrestricted submarine warfare and thereby to run the risk of a conflict with the USA. In 1917, as in 1914, Bethmann Hollweg yielded to the military demands through a mixture of fatalism and a hope that the general situation might be changed by violent action. Bethmann Hollweg's two shattering decisions resembled each other in that each was based on a collapse of political leadership and an excessive regard for the military standpoint.

The arguments about U-boat warfare among the military and political leaders of the German empire had begun as far back as late 1914. The first impulse was given by the unsatisfactory progress of the naval war. At enormous cost a German battle fleet was built up in sharp rivalry with Great Britain (Vol. 2, p. 170). On the outbreak of war, however, any large-scale naval enterprise was discouraged by the government, which needed to maintain the German fleet intact as a political instrument. It was not until 1916 that the naval commanders ventured to engage the Royal Navy, and the battle of Jutland (Vol. 4, p. 543) showed that Germany had not enough naval power to defeat the

A U-boat puts out to sea, festooned with garlands, the tribute of the German people's faith in its destructive power. Almost all the press and the people believed, like the high command, that unrestricted submarine warfare could bring Great Britain to her knees

British fleet in a battle on the high seas. The pretensions of the German naval leaders were badly injured because of the limited effectiveness of the fleet since 1914, and Germany was driven more and more to rely on submarine warfare against British seaborne commerce. The aim was to destroy the economic life and supply lines of Great Britain and thus force it to sue for peace. But this strategical switch was by no means due solely to the German navy's ambition to play some part in the war. It was forced on the naval leaders by the grim fact that in a few months Great Britain had won complete command of the world's seas and was trying to cut off Germany's overseas imports by a distant blockade. It seemed essential not to accept this gigantic British success meekly but to find some counterstroke in reply. In the first months of the war German U-boats had destroyed several large British warships by underwater torpedo attacks, and these brilliant successes led to an over-estimation of the U-boat weapon, which in fact was still comparatively undeveloped. The chief of the naval staff, Admiral von Pohl, pressed for a blockade of the British coasts as early as the beginning of November 1914. And a little later Admiral von Tirpitz, state secretary of the imperial navy office, gave an interview to Karl von Wiegand, a representative of the American press, in which he drew the world's attention to the possibility of a German blockade of Great Britain by submarines. Among the German people an impression grew that the U-boats were an infallible weapon in the war with Great Britain. The result was a violent public agitation concerning U-boats.

Commercial warfare by U-boat actually began as far back as February 1915 and was consistently carried on in various forms for two years, until January 1917. During this period the German government had time and again to justify the employment of a novel method of warfare in face of the vehement complaints of the European neutrals and, especially, of the United States. Yielding to such opposition, it set its face, until 9th January 1917, against the unrestricted use of the U-boat weapon demanded by the naval authorities. But at the same time, in internal debates, it repeatedly asserted that its negative attitude was not due to consideration for international law but was purely for military and political reasons. When, in January 1917, the ruthless exploitation of U-boat warfare was finally decided upon, Bethmann Hollweg expressly declared that he had never opposed it on principle, but had always been governed by the general situation and the respective strengths of U-boat weapons. In the various deliberations it was the Kaiser Wilhelm II alone

who expressed humanitarian scruples. For him the drowning of innocent passengers was 'a frightful thought'.

As the U-boat was a new weapon, there were in 1914 no international rules regarding its use in commercial warfare. The German government should have striven to obtain international recognition for the new weapon, for both the present and any future war. But instead, the Germans admitted the illegality of U-boat commerce war from the first by describing it as a reprisal measure against the illegal methods adopted by the British in their commercial blockade. For Great Britain, like Germany, had been forced by the advance of weapon technique to break the traditional international rules dealing with blockades. Because of the danger to its naval forces it could not carry on a close blockade of the German coasts—hitherto the only permissible method—but had to engage in a distant blockade directed at neutral as well as German ports. For this purpose the British declared the whole of the North Sea to be a war zone and prescribed for neutral shipping fixed navigational routes which could be supervised by British naval vessels. Moreover, Great Britain extended the regulations about war contraband and the confiscation of cargoes in neutral vessels. Liable to seizure were not only goods useful for the arming and supply of enemy forces, but all foodstuffs and raw materials intended for the Central powers. It was immaterial whether the cargoes were being carried direct to enemy ports or through neutral countries.

The new British contraband regulations initiated an economic and hunger blockade which was aimed at the enemy's civilian population. The German reprisal measure, commercial war by U-boat, was similarly directed against the civilian population. It might therefore be considered as merely a similar measure, by way of reprisal. But in fact there was one great difference. The British blockade was merely a confiscation of material goods, but the German submarine attacks endangered the lives of crews and passengers. When an underwater torpedo was fired without warning, it was impossible to take any steps to save the lives of those on board. And if the ship was attacked from the surface the crew and passengers taking to the lifeboats were exposed to the perils of wind and wave on the open seas, for the U-boat was in no position to pick them up and bring them to a place of safety.

The most difficult thing to justify was the effect of commercial war by U-boat on the neutrals, in whose case there was, of course, no question of reprisal. Instead, the German government demanded that the neutrals submit to submarine warfare as they had submitted to the British block-

ade of the North Sea. But there was only partial justification for this demand. True, neutral shipping used the prescribed routes through the English Channel and submitted to examination of cargoes in British ports. Nevertheless, the European neutrals, in spite of the British blockade, had delivered large food cargoes to Germany down to 1916. On the German side there was no desire to suppress neutral shipping by submarine warfare, but only to drive it out of certain sea areas. In the proclamation of 4th February 1915, which initiated submarine warfare, the waters

Bethmann Hollweg, who struggled in vain against the demands of the high command

around Great Britain and Ireland, including the whole of the English Channel, were declared a war zone. Every enemy merchant ship encountered in the war zone would be destroyed. Neutral ships were advised to avoid it, as attacks on enemy ships might, in the uncertainties of naval warfare, well affect neutral ships also. It was hoped that this warning might frighten neutral shipping off trade with Great Britain. Admiral von Pohl wanted to emphasize this warning by ordering all ships within the war zone to be sunk without distinction, a step which meant unrestricted submarine warfare. He actually wanted a few neutral ships to be sunk without warning at the outset of the U-boat operations so that there should be general uncertainty and neutral trade with Great Britain stopped as soon as possible. In subsequent deliberations the deterrent effect on neutral shipping was an important factor.

At the beginning of 1915, and again at the beginning of 1916, such intimidation seemed especially necessary, for Germany at those times was far from possessing enough U-boats to carry on a successful economic war with Great Britain. In February 1915 there were only twenty-one U-boats available for watching the shipping lanes to Great Britain. As the voyage to the war zone, the return journey, and the overhaul afterwards, took a considerable time, there were never more than three or four boats operating at any one time on the coasts of Great Britain. Obviously there were not enough of them to inflict any considerable damage to Great Britain's trade by direct action. Thus it was very important to keep neutral ships, and as many enemy ships as possible out of the war zone. But the Germans had no success. Even before the announced U-boat commerce war started on 18th February, very firmly worded notes of protest reached Berlin from the neutral maritime powers affected. Most serious of all, the American government held the German government strictly accountable for all measures that might involve the destruction of any merchant vessel belonging to the United States or for the death of any American subject. The war situation of the Central powers in February 1915 was much too strained to risk complications with powerful neutral states. The chancellor therefore persuaded the Kaiser to order the U-boats to spare neutral ships, especially those belonging to the United States or Italy. The U-boat commerce war began four days late, on 22nd February 1915, in this modified form. In March 1915, out of 5,000 vessels entering and leaving British ports only twenty-one were sunk. Neutral shipping soon resumed trade with Great Britain.

The Lusitania incident

In spite of precautions taken during the period of restricted submarine warfare, a grave incident occurred on 7th May 1915, when a German U-boat sank the British liner *Lusitania* with an underwater torpedo (Vol. 4, p. 521). Among the drowned were 128 American citizens. The sinking of the *Lusitania* aroused intense indignation in the United States, and a sharp exchange of notes between the American and German governments ensued. President Wilson had no desire to precipitate an armed conflict with Germany by his *Lusitania* notes, but he feared that a continuation of the U-boat war would one day leave him no other choice. He tried repeatedly to persuade Great Britain to allow food imports into Germany through neutral countries. At the same time he took a firm stand against the contempt for humane principles shown in the kind of warfare used by the U-boats. The first *Lusitania* note of the American government on 15th May 1915 denied the legality in international law of any form of U-boat commerce war, inasmuch as in neither an underwater nor a surface attack could the safety of passengers and crew be guaranteed. In the third *Lusitania* note of 23rd July 1915 Wilson conceded that submarines were a novelty in naval warfare and that no provision could have been made for them in the international regula-

Arming at sea — a U-boat takes ammunition on board. From May 1915 U-boats were fitted with deck guns as well as with torpedoes, and surfaced before attacking an enemy ship

Imperial War Museum

tions. At the same time it was admitted that the German submarine operations of the last two months had complied with the customs of war and had demonstrated the possibility of eliminating the chief causes of offence. This remarkable concession on the part of the Americans was based on the fact that since May 1915 the U-boats had been fitted with deck guns and, owing to the uncertainty of hitting the target with torpedoes, had carried on the commerce war in 'cruiser' style, according to the rules laid down for the taking of prizes. The U-boat came to the surface when attacking a ship and before sinking it allowed the persons on board to take to the boats. All enemy vessels were sunk without exception, but neutral ships were sunk only when they were carrying contraband.

Although this was the actual method of operation during the *Lusitania* crisis, the German naval authorities obstinately opposed any restriction being placed on submarine warfare and especially any attempt to confine U-boats to the rules of 'cruiser' warfare. They maintained that such methods were an intolerable danger to the submarine and its crew. They named as the chief dangers attempts of the merchant ships to ram the submarine, concealed guns on the ships, the use of a neutral flag by British ships, and attacks by enemy warships during the necessarily lengthy searches. The German government was not informed by the navy that in the period May-July 1915 eighty-six per cent of the merchant vessels that were sunk were dealt with according to the cruiser warfare rules, and that from February to July 1915 250 merchant ships carrying a neutral flag were examined and only on three occasions was any misuse of the flag dis-

covered. By its policy of secrecy the navy apparently wanted to avoid being permanently restricted to 'cruiser' warfare and losing for ever the chance of unrestricted submarine warfare. On 6th June 1915 the Kaiser ordered that all large passenger liners, whether enemy or neutral, must be spared. Nevertheless, on 19th August, the British liner, *Arabic*, was sunk without warning, two more American citizens losing their lives. The Kaiser then ordered that no passenger liner was to be sunk until it had been warned and the passengers and crew given a chance to escape. During the arguments about U-boat methods in the summer of 1915 Tirpitz, in order to put pressure on the Kaiser, twice offered his resignation. His offers were abruptly refused. Yet the Kaiser changed his chief of naval staff at the beginning of September. Vice-Admiral Bachmann, a Tirpitz adherent who had held the office since February 1915, was replaced by Admiral von Holtzendorff, who was more amenable to the political views of the chancellor. On 18th September 1915 Holtzendorff gave orders that the U-boat commerce war on the west coast of Great Britain and in the Channel should be carried out on the 'cruiser' system. The naval commanders were not ready for this step and brought the U-boat war around Great Britain to a standstill. Thus ended the first phase of the U-boat war. The *Arabic* case was settled on 6th October by German compliance. The German government did not defend the action of the U-boat commander, which infringed the order of 6th June. The *Lusitania* case remained unsettled. The German government refused to admit that the U-boat attack on the *Lusitania* was contrary to international law, for if it did so future unrestricted submarine warfare would be impossible.

In 1915 several U-boats, large and small, were sent to the Austro-Hungarian naval base of Pola, and also to Constantinople. These carried on trade war in the Mediterranean and the Black Sea with great success, limiting their actions to the 'cruiser' rules. They restricted the flow of supplies to the Anglo-French forces in the Dardanelles and Salonika. But at the beginning of 1916 U-boat activities were severely handicapped by the progressive arming of the enemy's merchant vessels. The U-boat flotilla at Pola therefore asked the naval staff for permission to sink any armed merchant ship without warning. Holtzendorff granted the request, but with the proviso that passenger ships should continue to be exempt. At the same time he re-opened the trade war around Great Britain by issuing the same orders. A new phase in the submarine war was begun on 29th February 1916 and was termed 'intensified' U-boat war.

The high-ranking officers of the German navy looked on the new measures as a mere transitional phase. Since the beginning of the year the prospects for unrestricted submarine war had considerably improved, for General von Falkenhayn, chief of the army general staff, was now expressly demanding it. Since the autumn of 1914 the German armies, in co-operation with those of Austria-Hungary, Turkey, and Bulgaria, had created firm front lines on enemy territory; they had driven the Russians far back to the east, and by the occupation of Serbia had opened the way to Constantinople. Falkenhayn was at the peak of his military successes. In February 1916 he intended to deliver an all-out offensive on the Western Front, starting with a holding attack on Verdun. In the summer and autumn of 1915 he had firmly advised against the ruthless use of the U-boat weapon because he thought that a break with the United States might produce unfavourable reactions from the European neutrals and in particular might make Bulgarian assistance in the campaign against Serbia doubtful. In 1916, on the other hand, when the Balkan situation had been stabilized, such considerations were no longer valid. He believed that unrestricted submarine warfare directed against Great Britain would help his offensive on the Western Front. The U-boat action was timed to start in the middle of March. Almost the whole of the German press advocated ruthless use of the U-boats. The alliance between Falkenhayn and the navy on this point put Bethmann Hollweg in a very difficult position, and he spent the first weeks of the New Year in a very worried state. He feared that the adoption of un-restricted submarine warfare 'might result in condemnation by the whole civilized world and a sort of crusade against Germany'.

The Charleville conference

In the decisive conference with the Kaiser on 4th March 1916 at GHQ, Charleville, Falkenhayn declared that, in view of the dwindling resistance of the German allies and the German civil population, the war must be brought to an end before the year was out. The only means of achieving this was by unrestricted submarine warfare. On his part Bethmann Hollweg argued that Germany could stand another winter campaign. He would rather have a compromise peace than risk prolonging the war indefinitely by challenging America. In his opinion there were still insufficient U-boats. In the middle of March 1916 there were only fourteen large submarines capable of carrying on a commerce war in British waters.

On 4th March 1916 the Kaiser, unable to make up his mind, postponed his final decision until the beginning of April and then indefinitely. Nevertheless, with the agreement of the chancellor, a further tightening of the U-boat blockade was ordered on 13th March 1916. In the war zone both armed and unarmed merchant ships were to be destroyed without warning. Outside the war zone the previous orders remained in force. Tirpitz, who had not been called to the Charleville conference, reported sick to the Kaiser in protest and on 15th March he agreed to resign. One of Bethmann Hollweg's chief opponents had left the scene.

Whereas the instruction for the sinking of armed merchant ships was made public, the new order of 13th March was kept secret. Its effects, however, were viewed by the neutrals with growing alarm. Washington suspected that Germany had already started unrestricted submarine warfare. A new incident soon gave rise to another German-American crisis. On 24th March 1916 two Americans were injured when the cross-Channel passenger steamer, *Sussex,* was torpedoed without warning. In the erroneous belief that American citizens had lost their lives in the sinking President Wilson sent a note on 18th April threatening to break off diplomatic relations with Germany if it did not abandon its current methods of submarine warfare. Under pressure from this ultimatum the Kaiser gave orders, at Bethmann Hollweg's request, cancelling the tightened-up rules for submarine warfare in the combat zone around Great Britain. The rules of the 'cruiser' system were to be observed until further notice. The commanding officers on the naval front declared that such a procedure was un-

Cynical German cartoon protesting against the outcry over the drowning of passengers – a 'blind' American passenger on an 'unarmed' merchant ship

workable, because of the danger to the U-boats, and they brought the submarine war in British waters to a complete standstill. In the Mediterranean the U-boats continued the campaign according to the new rules.

At the end of April 1916, when the reply to the American note had to be drafted, Falkenhayn again tried to persuade the Kaiser to agree to unrestricted submarine warfare. He asserted that he would have to forego action against Verdun if the U-boat war was suspended. Bethmann Hollweg indignantly rejected such an alternative and after a bitter dispute he once again convinced the Kaiser. In a note dated 4th May 1916 the German government agreed to the demands of the American government and informed it that the German naval forces had been instructed to observe the canons of international law with regard to the stopping, searching, and destruction of merchant vessels. At the same time it expressed its expectation that the United States would now induce the British government to abandon as soon as possible such of its methods of waging naval war as were contrary to international law. The German government reserved its complete freedom to alter its decision if this were not done. Wilson at once protested against the German claim to make respect for the rights of American citizens on the high seas dependent on the behaviour of the British government. Responsibility in such matters was individual not joint, absolute not relative. The two opposing standpoints were thus definitely laid down. If Germany again intensified the submarine war, it was to be expected that the

United States would promptly enter the war.

It was but a few months after the settlement of the *Sussex* case that the problem of unrestricted submarine warfare once again became acute. During the summer of 1916 the war situation was completely transformed. The Central powers, who had held the initiative for a whole year, were now forced into defensive battles lasting for months by the persistent offensive of the Russians in Volhynia and eastern Galicia and of the British and French on the Somme (Vol. 5, p. 562), which could only be withstood by huge efforts and losses. Falkenhayn had to break off the battle for Verdun, which was bleeding not only France but also Germany to death. His prestige was shattered, and when Rumania

'This is how your money can fight—turn it into U-boats.' An appeal for war loans. In the background is a sinking enemy ship

entered the war against the Central powers on 27th August 1916 he was replaced by Hindenburg and Ludendorff. Hindenburg, who was the most popular of the German military leaders, became chief of the general staff. Bethmann Hollweg had worked for Hindenburg's appointment to this post during the critical summer months of 1916 because he thought that a moderate peace could be made acceptable to the German people, so misled by exaggerated hopes, only if it were covered by the name of Hindenburg. In other words, Bethmann Hollweg hoped to use the great authority of the field marshal in his efforts towards a peace of understanding. But Hindenburg's authority was fatal to Bethmann Hollweg's policy. Hindenburg and Ludendorff were advocates of unrestricted

submarine warfare. After they had been summoned to take up the highest posts in the army they pleaded for a temporary postponement of this war measure only with respect to the difficult military situation. For at the moment great danger threatened from Rumania, and sufficient troops had to be made available as security against the European neutrals, who might regard unrestricted submarine warfare as a challenge. By the end of December 1916 the Rumanian army was defeated and in the following months military deployments against European neutrals could be initiated.

Bethmann Hollweg had previously been able to stifle the arguments of Falkenhayn and the naval authorities in favour of unrestricted submarine warfare because the war situation in the spring of 1916 did not make such a risky measure absolutely essential. By the summer, however, the war was threatening to become one of attrition of man power and exhaustion of resources. Germany would not be strong enough in 1917 to undertake a large-scale offensive with the land forces available. A weapon that might well win the war was offered by the U-boats.

In these circumstances Bethmann Hollweg, in the latter part of 1916, tried to avoid the necessity of unrestricted submarine warfare by bringing about an early peace of compromise. President Wilson was working for the same end, because he wanted to keep America out of the war. On 12th December 1916 the Central powers made a peace offer to the Allies. On the 21st President Wilson invited the belligerents to state their war aims and announced his willingness to take part in the discussions. Hindenburg and Ludendorff had notified their concurrence with the peace offer of the Central powers, but as soon as the first negative reports began to arrive from the camp of the Allies they demanded, at the end of December 1916, speedy and energetic action at sea.

The prospects for unrestricted submarine warfare at the beginning of 1917 were much better than they had been a year before. Germany now had 105 U-boats, of which 46 large and 23 small vessels were available for the campaign in British waters. In view of the bad world harvests of 1916 unrestricted submarine warfare, if started before the chief overseas transport season began in early February, would foreseeably have a grave effect on Great Britain's grain supplies. Since 6th October 1916 the U-boats had carried on the commerce war in British waters on the 'cruiser' rules. Total sinkings were reckoned at 400,000 tons a month (in actual fact the figure was round about 325,000). By the removal of restrictions one expected an increase to 600,000 tons. The navy esti-

mated that such a figure, enhanced by the consideration that neutral shipping would be frightened away, would in five months reduce the trade with Great Britain by thirty-nine per cent. This would force Great Britain to sue for peace. About the results of an American intervention in the war there was wide difference of opinion. The army thought that any great increase in the supply of American war material to the Allies was impossible, nor did it expect the arrival in Europe of large numbers of American troops. The politicians, however, thought that the American entry would encourage the Allied nations to hold out, would put large financial resources at their disposal, and would bring many American volunteers to join the Allies in Europe.

On the question of U-boat warfare Hindenburg and Ludendorff found their views supported by the vast majority of the German people. The largest party in the Reichstag, the Centre Party, passed a resolution on 7th October 1916 saying that the decision of the chancellor regarding submarine warfare must be based on the views of the supreme army command. As the Conservatives and National Liberals were in any case outright champions of unrestricted submarine warfare, Bethmann Hollweg knew that if he refused to make use of the U-boat weapon in opposition to Hindenburg and Ludendorff he could no longer count on a majority in the Reichstag. The feeling of the people was summed up by Bethmann Hollweg in his memoirs: 'No nation will stand for not winning a war when it is convinced that it can win.' He himself, in spite of his constant resistance to unrestricted submarine warfare, seems at times to have wondered whether, after all, the use of this extreme weapon might not achieve a turn for the better.

For the moment Bethmann Hollweg left the problem unsolved. When on 9th January 1917 he went to Pless to discuss the ever more pressing problem, he found the naval staff and the supreme army command united against him and they had already won over the Kaiser to their side. Hindenburg and Ludendorff saw no possibility of bringing the war to a victorious end unless the U-boats were used without restrictions. They declared themselves ready to shoulder all responsibility for any results caused by this war measure. The chief of the naval staff guaranteed that he could force Great Britain to its knees before the next harvest. Once again Bethmann Hollweg produced all his objections, but after the failure of the Central powers' peace move all hopes for a peace of understanding seemed to have vanished. Bethmann Hollweg could no longer maintain his opposition to the demands of the military and he told the Kaiser that he could not recommend him to oppose the vote of his military advisers. He felt he must refrain from offering his resignation, so as not to expose the inner dissensions in the German leadership to all the world. Until the last moment, however, he continued to doubt the wisdom of the decision of 9th January 1917. When towards the end of the month the prospects for a successful outcome of Wilson's peace efforts seemed more favourable, he tried to secure a postponement of unrestricted submarine warfare, but the naval staff assured him that most of the U-boats had already been despatched.

The beginning of unrestricted submarine warfare on 1st February 1917 was at first countered by Wilson with the rupture of diplomatic relations, whereby he hoped to bring Germany to its senses. The political tension between the two countries was increased at the beginning of March by the publication of a German offer of alliance to Mexico (intercepted by the British intelligence service) should the United States enter the war because of the submarine war. The sinking of seven American merchant ships by U-boats by 21st March finally obliged Wilson to summon Congress, which on 4th and 6th April approved a declaration of war.

At first the figures of sinkings by the U-boats surpassed the forecasts and expectations of the German naval authorities, reaching its maximum in April 1917. But when in the course of the summer merchant ships sailing for Great Britain were assembled in convoys and protected by destroyers the number of successes dwindled. Nevertheless, unrestricted submarine warfare brought Great Britain difficulties which led the British government to begin to take an interest in political solutions. But on the whole the strong urge towards peace that was expected from the U-boat menace failed to materialize. Looking back, it is clear that the German military leaders and politicians regarded the unrestricted submarine warfare as a failure. For from March 1917 onwards the Central powers were relieved of a great burden by the Russian Revolution. Russia dropped out of the war in the winter of 1917-18, and negotiations for a general peace of understanding might have been possible had not the Allies been encouraged to hold on by the prospect of American armed assistance. But the principal effect of unrestricted submarine warfare was on America itself, for it caused the abandonment of America's policy of isolation and its entry into world politics. *(Translation)*

'Shelling a merchantman' by H.R.Butler. This U-boat has warned the crew before firing, and they are escaping in lifeboats

Wilson and the Ordeal of Neutrality

President Wilson had almost undisputed control of the foreign affairs of the greatest of the neutral powers, and America's actions would vitally affect the major powers of Europe and the outcome of the war. Could America stay neutral?

Opposite page: President Wilson holding up a baseball at a World Series match, 1915. He 'played a part in the fate of nations incomparably more direct and personal than any other man'. Although he was an intellectual and an idealist, in this vital period Wilson understood and shared the attitudes of the majority of his fellow-countrymen

Different views of Wilson's conduct. Below: The British view, from a Punch *cartoon. 'Hail Columba! President Wilson (to American Eagle): "Gee! What a dove I've made of you!"' Bottom: A German view. Big Chief Old Serpent letting out a war-cry. The Germans felt that Wilson was threatening Berlin*

Punch

Kladderadatsch

The outbreak of war in Europe in August 1914 came, in its suddenness, to President Wilson like a bolt of lightning out of a clear sky. To be sure, Wilson had not been unaware of the possibility of a conflagration, for his confidential adviser and some-time agent, Colonel Edward M.House, writing from Berlin in May 1914, had warned that Europe was a powder keg about to explode. However, House's talks with German and British leaders had raised the tantalizing possibility of an Anglo-American-German entente under Wilson's auspices. No one in Washington (or in European capitals, for that matter) saw that the fuse was burning rapidly after the murder of the heir to the Austrian and Hungarian thrones and his young wife by a Serbian nationalist in Sarajevo on 28th June 1914. Moreover, when the great European powers went over the brink in late July and early August, Wilson was mired in controversy with Congress and in deep despair over the fatal illness of his wife. He could only wait in fascinated horror as Sir Edward Grey, the British foreign minister, wept as he told the American ambassador in London, Walter Page, about the British ultimatum to Germany, and King George exclaimed, 'My God, Mr Page, what else could we do?' One American well expressed what was surely Wilson's reaction when he wrote: 'The horror of it all kept me awake for weeks, nor has the awfulness of it all deserted me, but at first it seemed a horrid dream.'

But Armageddon *had* come. Wilson, as head of the greatest neutral power, whose interests would be vitally affected by belligerent measures, had perforce to work out his policies towards the warring powers.

Throughout the long months of American neutrality, from August 1914 to April 1917, Wilson, whatever his own predispositions, had to work within limits imposed by American public opinion. That opinion was so divided in its preferences for various belligerents during the first months of the war that any policy for the United States other than a strict neutrality would have been inconceivable. Wilson remarked to the German ambassador, Count Johann von Bernstorff, that 'we definitely have to be neutral, since otherwise our mixed populations would wage war on each other'. More important still, in spite of the attachments of various national and ethnic minorities, and of all the efforts of British, French, and German propagandists in the United States, the predominant American public

opinion was consistently neutral before 1917. But Americans, even though they clung doggedly to their traditional isolationism and refused to believe that their vital interests were sufficiently involved in the outcome of the war to justify voluntary intervention, were none the less jealous of their sovereignty and international prestige. In other words, they would tolerate only a certain amount of provocation, and no more. To an extraordinary degree Wilson understood and shared the attitudes of the majority of his fellow-countrymen. Both expediency and conviction dictated policies that were agreeable to the great majority of Americans.

Although Wilson had strong emotional attachments to the Allies, particularly Great Britain, he profoundly admired German contributions to modern civilization. As a sophisticated student of modern history, he well understood that the causes of the war were complex and never imputed exclusive responsibility to either side. He was able to detach emotions from decisions and policies and, self-consciously, to make decisions on the basis of what he considered to be the best interests of America and Europe.

Wilson exercised greater personal control over foreign policy than any other chief of state among the great powers of the world. Constitutionally, as President he was sovereign in the conduct of foreign relations, subject only to the Senate's veto on treaties. Weak Presidents have abdicated their responsibilities to strong secretaries of state or congressional leaders. But Wilson was a 'strong' President. He believed that the people had invested their sovereignty in foreign affairs in him. He not only refused to delegate this responsibility, but insisted upon conducting foreign relations himself. Because he used his full constitutional powers to execute policies that the great majority desired, Wilson not only held the conduct of foreign affairs in his own hands, but was irresistible while doing so. 'It seems no exaggeration,' Churchill later wrote, 'to pronounce that the action of the United States with its repercussions on the history of the world depended, during the awful period of Armageddon, upon the workings of this man's mind and spirit to the exclusion of almost every other factor; and that he played a part in the fate of nations incomparably more direct and personal than any other man.'

Wilson's whole world came tumbling down in the first week of August 1914. Ellen Axson Wilson, his beloved wife since 1885, died on 6th August. Great Britain,

which he loved, and Germany, which he admired, were already beginning to tear at each other's throats. Near hysteria reigned in Wall Street as a consequence of the disruption of international trade and exchange.

With his customary iron self-control, the President moved confidently and serenely to meet emergencies and establish American neutrality. The formalities were observed easily enough. Wilson proclaimed official neutrality on 4th August and, two weeks later, admonished his fellow-countrymen to be 'impartial in thought as well as in action'.

However, being neutral in the midst of a great war was easier said than done. For example, should the American government permit its citizens to sell vital raw materials and munitions to the Allies when British cruisers prevented the Germans from having access to such supplies? More difficult still, should the government permit American bankers to lend money, which the secretary of state, William Jennings Bryan, called the 'worst of all contrabands', to the belligerents?

Having decided upon a policy of strict neutrality, Wilson, helped by Bryan and the counselor of the State Department, Robert Lansing, proceeded as systematically and as impartially as possible to be neutral in every circumstance. Hence he permitted the Allies to purchase as much contraband as they pleased, for to have denied them access to American markets and the benefits that flowed from dominant seapower would have been not only un-neutral, but tantamount to undeclared war. For the same reason he permitted American bankers to lend money both to the Allied and German governments.

Wilson followed the rush of the German army through Belgium into northern France and was obviously relieved when the French and British were able to establish a secure defensive line by early autumn. At this point, at any rate, Germany seemed to threaten neither America's vital interests nor her neutral rights. Wilson's main problem in late 1914 was defending American trading rights against British seapower, or, to put the matter more realistically, coming to terms with the British maritime system.

Acting as neutrals always have during wartime, Wilson wanted to keep the channels of commerce to all of Europe open as widely as possible to American ships and goods. Acting as dominant seapowers always have, the British set about to cut off the flow of life-giving supplies from the United States to Germany and Austria-Hungary. Consequently, dispatches about these matters passed frequently between Washington and London, not only during the first months of the war, but as late as

1916. There was much talk of 'freedom of the seas' on the one side and of legitimate belligerent rights on the other. Actually, what sounded like the rhetoric of developing crisis masked the fact that there was substantial goodwill and accommodation on both sides. For their part, the British instituted maritime measures that were not only largely legitimate, but also were based upon precedents established by the United States government itself during the American Civil War of 1861-65. For his part, Wilson, understanding these facts, rejected demands of highly partisan German Americans and American economic interests with a large stake in free trade with Germany for measures to break the British blockade or prevent the Anglo-American trade in contraband.

Having passed through troubles that might have burgeoned into serious Anglo-American crisis, Wilson, at the end of 1914, could view the general state of American relations with the belligerents with some equanimity. There seemed to be no chance of serious conflict with Germany: there were simply no points of contact between the two nations. By Wilson's reckoning, the war would end either in stalemate or, more likely, in an Allied victory. He told a reporter for the *New York Times,* in an off-the-record interview on 14th December 1914, that he hoped ardently for a peace of reconciliation based upon negotiation. But, Wilson added, he did not think that it would 'greatly hurt' the interests of the United States if the Allies won a decisive victory and dictated the settlement.

Between the cruiser and the submarine

The German decision, announced on 4th February 1915, to use an untried weapon, the submarine, in a war against merchant shipping in the English Channel and a broad zone around the British Isles, created an entirely new situation, fraught with peril for the United States. Actually, at this time, the German navy did not possess enough submarines to prosecute an effective campaign, even against Allied merchant ships. But the Germans had compounded the blunder of acting prematurely, largely in bluff, by adding that *neutral* ships might be torpedoed because of the Allied use of neutral flags. It was only the first of a series of blunders by the German admiralty and the high command that would drive the United States into the war.

President Wilson replied to Berlin on 10th February with a stern warning that the United States would hold the German government to a 'strict accountability' and probably go to war if German submarines indiscriminately and illegally attacked American vessels on the high seas.

As it turned out, the gravest German

blunder was to provide the British and French governments with a good excuse for doing what they had already planned to do—severely to tighten their blockade measures. Now they need fear no serious American reprisal. Invoking the ancient right of reprisal, the London and Paris authorities announced on 1st March that, in retaliation against the illegal and ruthless German submarine campaign, they would stop *all* commerce of whatever character to the Central powers, even commerce through neutral ports.

Wilson and Bryan worked hard to arrange an Anglo-American agreement that would provide some protection for American shipping against the cruisers and submarines. Their efforts foundered upon the shoals of the German refusal to give up the submarine campaign except at the price of virtual abandonment by the British of an effective blockade. Wilson was in fact now helpless; he could only acquiesce in the new Anglo-French blockade so long as the sword of the submarine hung over his head.

The President waited in uncertainty all through the early spring of 1915 to see what the Germans would do. There were several attacks against American ships that might have set off a crisis. However, the submarine issue was brought to a head suddenly and dramatically when *U20,* Kapitänleutnant Walther Schwieger, without warning torpedoed the pride of the Cunard Line, the unarmed *Lusitania,* in the Irish Sea on 7th May 1915, killing 128 American citizens among many others.

It was impossible for Wilson to temporize, so violent was the reaction in the United States. Yet what could he do? It was evident after the first shock that a majority of Americans wanted their President to be firm and yet avoid war if possible. This, actually, was Wilson's own intention. In three notes between May and early July, Wilson eloquently appealed to the imperial German government to abandon what was obviously a campaign of sheer terror against *unarmed Allied passenger ships.* In the last note he warned that he would probably break diplomatic relations if the Germans did not abandon that campaign. To each of Wilson's pleas, the German foreign office replied by truculently refusing to admit the illegality of the destruction of *Lusitania.* The impasse was broken by a second incident that came hard on the heels of the *Lusitania* affair—the torpedoing without warning of the White Star liner, *Arabic,* outward bound from Liverpool, on 19th August. Only when they saw that Wilson was on the brink did the Germans yield and promise not to sink unarmed Allied passenger liners without warning. Indeed, Wilson's firmness, and the lack of enough submarines to prosecute

*Bottom: An election truck decorated
with Wilson's claim for the trust of his
country. In 1916 a wave of neutralist
feeling swept the USA and persuaded
Wilson to stand as a 'peace' candidate*

a decisive underseas campaign, paid even larger dividends in the form of guarantees that the German navy would sink American ships only after making full provision for the safety of human life, and that compensation would be made for all ships and cargoes captured or destroyed.

The subsequent German-American *détente* (encouraged by a temporary abandonment of the submarine campaign in general) set off demands in the United States, primarily by southern cotton producers in deep depression on account of the closing of their central European markets, for action against the total Allied blockade as firm as that taken against the German submarine campaign. Bryan had resigned in the middle of the *Lusitania* crisis, because he feared that Wilson's notes might lead the Germans to declare war against the United States. The new secretary of state, Robert Lansing, did prepare a formidable indictment of the British maritime measure, and Wilson permitted it to go to London on 5th November. But the President had no intention of enforcing the note's demands until German-American differences were clarified.

On the face of it, American relations with Great Britain and Germany had reached

a state of tolerable equilibrium by the end of 1915. The Germans had quietly abandoned their submarine campaign in the North Atlantic, hence there were no incidents in that area to exacerbate German-American relations. For their part, the British had gone to extraordinary (and successful) lengths to support American cotton prices and to come to terms with other American producers who had been hard hit by the Allied blockade. But Wilson and his two principal diplomatic advisers, Colonel House and Lansing, were not reassured as they contemplated potential dangers in the months immediately ahead. The Allies were beginning to arm not only passenger liners but ordinary merchantmen as well, and, apparently, were ordering these ships to attack submarines upon sight. Second, reports from Berlin made it unmistakably clear that there had been only a respite in the submarine campaign, and that the Germans were preparing to use the arming of Allied ships as an excuse for an all-out campaign. So far *ad hoc* solutions had sufficed to preserve the peace, but it now seemed that events might develop which would remove all options. For example, a really ruthless submarine campaign might drive the United States,

willy-nilly, into war, without any other purpose than sheer defence of national rights.

Wilson and House pondered long about the situation in the hope of gaining some initiative and of giving some purpose to American belligerency if it had to come. Sir Edward Grey had said only two months before that his government might be willing to consider a negotiated settlement if the United States would promise to join a post-war league of nations and guarantee to help maintain future peace. Seizing the seeming opportunity offered by Grey's suggestion, Wilson sent House to London in late December 1915 with instructions to work for Anglo-American agreement to co-operate in a drive for peace under Wilson's auspices. If that *démarche* should fail on account of German obduracy, Wilson said, the United States would probably enter the war on the Allied side.

While House was in London opening negotiations, Lansing and Wilson launched their own campaign to get the United States off the submarine hook. The secretary of state, on 18th January 1916, urged the Allies to disarm their merchantmen if the Germans would agree to warn such vessels and evacuate their crews before

sinking them. Lansing added that his government was contemplating treating armed merchantmen as warships, which would mean that they could not engage in commerce at American ports. The Germans, gleefully agreeing with the secretary of state, announced that submarines would sink all armed merchantmen without warning after 28th February.

Reaction in London to what was called Lansing's *modus vivendi* was so violent that it threatened to wreck House's negotiations. Wilson thereupon hastily withdrew the *modus vivendi*. This action in turn set off a panic in Congress that the United States would go to war to protect the right of citizens to travel on armed ships. Wilson beat back a congressional resolution warning Americans against travelling on armed ships, but he made it clear that only lightly-armed merchantmen would be permitted to use American ports, and, more important, that he did not intend to make a great issue with the German government over armed ships in any event.

There was considerable relief both on Capitol Hill and in Whitehall. In London, Sir Edward Grey and House initialled, on 22nd February 1916, what is known as the House-Grey Memorandum embodying Wilson's plan of mediation.

Colonel House returned to Washington on 5th March in high excitement to tell the President that the British and French were eager to move as rapidly as possible for peace under Wilson's aegis. While Wilson and House were in the midst of planning for the great venture, a German submarine torpedoed a French packet steamer, *Sussex*, in the English Channel on 24th March with heavy loss of life. Reports of ruthless attacks against unarmed merchantmen followed in rapid succession.

After much backing and filling, and mainly in order to pave the way for his mediation, Wilson sent an ultimatum to Berlin on 18th April warning that he would break relations with Germany if she did not agree hereafter to require her submarine commanders to observe the rules of visit and search before sinking all unarmed ships, whether passenger liners or merchantmen. The German admiralty lacked enough U-boats to justify the risk of war with the United States and European neutrals like Holland and Denmark. Consequently, the imperial chancellor, Theobald von Bethmann Hollweg, won the Kaiser's support for submission to Wilson's demand. However, while yielding the Germans reserved the 'right' to resume freedom of decision on the use of submarines if the American government failed to compel the Allies to respect international law in the conduct of their blockade.

The happy settlement of the *Sussex* crisis, coupled with intimations that the

Germans were eager for peace talks, spurred Wilson to action to put the House-Grey Memorandum into operation. His first public move was to announce, in an address in Washington on 27th May, that the United States was prepared to abandon its traditional isolationism and join a post-war league of nations. Privately, through Colonel House, he exerted heavy pressure on Grey to put the memorandum's machinery into motion by signalling his government's readiness for Wilson's mediation. Grey responded evasively at first; but Wilson would not be diverted, and then Grey had to tell him frankly that neither the British nor the French governments would consent to peace talks at this time or in the foreseeable future.

Grey's refusal to execute the House-Grey Memorandum, a crushing blow to the President's hopes for an early peace in itself, combined with other developments to cause Wilson to effect what would turn out to be an almost radical change in his policies towards the European belligerents.

First, the British government not only refused to relax its controls over American commerce, but, on the contrary, intensified its maritime and economic warfare in the spring and summer of 1916. In retrospect, the new British measures (including search and seizure of American mail on neutral ships and publication in the United States of a 'blacklist' of American firms still doing business with the Central powers) seem trivial when compared with policies in which the Washington administration had already acquiesced. However, Wilson and a majority of Americans resented the new measures as direct affronts to their national sovereignty. Second, the British army's severe repression of the Easter Rising in Dublin in April (Vol. 5, p. 596) not only inflamed Irish Americans, but also caused a great diminution in Great Britain's moral standing throughout the United States. Finally, the German-American *détente* following the *Sussex* crisis sent a wave of neutralism across the country, one so strong that it engulfed the Democratic national convention that re-nominated Wilson for the presidency.

These developments, of course, had their most important impact upon the man in the White House. They convinced him that the American people did not want to go to war over the alleged right of Americans to travel and work on belligerent ships. They forced Wilson to stand as the 'peace' candidate and to accuse his Republican opponent, Charles Evans Hughes, of wanting war. More important, they caused a very considerable hardening of Wilson's attitudes against the Allies, particularly the British. By the early autumn, Wilson believed that the Allies were fighting for victory and spoils, not for a just peace.

Wilson could do nothing, of course, while the presidential campaign was in progress. However, once the voters, on 7th November 1916, invested him with their sovereignty for another four years, Wilson was free to act. And action of some kind seemed to be imperative, for it was growing increasingly evident that both sides were preparing to use desperate measures to break the stalemate that was consuming human life and resources at a prodigious rate. For the British, this would mean further intensification of economic warfare; for the Germans, it would mean revoking the *Sussex* pledge and launching a wholesale campaign against maritime commerce. The only way to peace and safety, Wilson concluded, was to bring the war to an end through his independent mediation.

Diverted briefly by domestic developments and Germany's own offer to negotiate, Wilson launched his peace bolt on 18th December 1916 by asking the belligerents to state the terms upon which they would be willing to end the fighting. The British and French were stunned and furious. But they were helpless to resist, so dependent had they become upon American credit and supplies for continuation of their war efforts. Then Lansing intervened. Committed emotionally to the Allied cause, he set out to sabotage the President's peace move by encouraging the British and French governments to state such terms as could be won only by a decisive military victory. The Germans, who very much wanted Wilson to force the Allies to the peace table but did not want him meddling once the conference had begun, returned an evasive reply.

Wilson was undisturbed. In mid-January 1917 he launched the second and decisive move in his campaign for peace — high-level, direct, and secret negotiations with the British and German governments to obtain their consent to his mediation. While waiting for their replies, the President went before the Senate on 22nd January to tell the world what kind of settlement he had in mind and the American people would support by membership in a league of nations. The peace to be made, Wilson said, had to be a peace of reconciliation, a 'peace without victory', for a victor's peace would leave 'a sting, a resentment, a bitter memory upon which terms of peace would rest, not permanently, but only as upon quicksand'.

For reasons that are still obscure, the new British cabinet headed by David Lloyd George sent word on 26th January to Wilson that it was prepared to accept the President's mediation. The Austro-Hungarians were desperately eager for peace. But on 31st January Wilson was informed of the German decision to adopt unrestricted submarine warfare.

The American People and the War

In this great democracy the opinion of its people was of vital importance. How was it that a peace-loving, isolationist people of 1914 could in 1917 willingly embark on a crusade to keep the world 'free for democracy'

Few hours in history have been so full of real and self-conscious drama as that on 2nd April 1917 when President Woodrow Wilson came before the United States Congress, sitting in joint session, to recommend the declaration of war on Germany. The hall of the House of Representatives, where the scene took place, overflowed with listeners. Immediately below the rostrum sat the members of the cabinet, the justices of the supreme court, the senators, and the representatives. The galleries were packed with distinguished visitors, as well as with the diplomats, wives, and reporters who always throng to great official occasions in Washington. All present knew what was coming, knew that this was to be far and away the most momentous occasion of its kind since Wilson revived George Washington's practice of presenting his most important messages to Congress in person. 'As the President proceeded in his address,' reports an eyewitness, 'the tension of suppressed excitement grew until it burst all bounds . . . As the President recommended the declaration of war, applause, which seemed universal, rolled through the whole assembly from floor to gallery. The audience rose to cheer when Chief Justice White waved his hands in the air as he, in effect, led the expression of unanimous approval.' The central figure was almost alone in resisting the tide of enthusiasm. Later, in deep distress, he remarked to his secretary that 'my message today was a message of death for our young men. How strange it seems to applaud that'. Few others were capable of such Lincolnian melancholy at such a moment, or of counting the cost of the decision that Congress promptly took, by an overwhelming majority, ▷ 660

American delegation bound for the International Women's Peace Conference at The Hague, 1915. They were given a tumultuous send-off by their peace-loving countrymen. The flag was presented to them by New York's mayor

to follow the President's recommendation.

The rest of the country, it is true, did not respond with all the fervour of the capital. It flooded Congress with messages of support (and some of dissent), but recruiting was slow. The political strength of pacifism, which had been widespread and highly vocal up to the last minute, was broken, but pacifist sentiment persisted. However, opinion in general accepted the idea that the United States, under attack from German intrigue and German submarines, had no choice but to fight; and welcomed the President's declaration that the war was to be one 'to make the world safe for democracy'. One of Wilson's two bitterest political opponents, former President Theodore Roosevelt, spoke for the American people when he hailed the war message as 'a great state paper'; and the other, Senator Henry Cabot Lodge, Sr, echoed that message when he declared, 'What we want most of all by this victory which we shall help to win is to secure the world's peace, broad-based on freedom and democracy'. In this fashion the American people made the cause of the embattled French and British their own.

Only America at peace!

Very different had been the national consensus three years earlier, when news of Europe's collapse into war crossed the Atlantic. A peace-loving, optimistic, passionately democratic but not very well-informed people had been horrified by the dreadful tidings. One intelligent and representative lady (a congressman's wife) wrote: 'I feel as if some black-winged monster had come between us and the sun, breathing poison over all the lovely green things upon the earth that should be praising God and magnifying him forever.' Newspapers were immediately filled with news of a war which the *New York Times* characterized as the bloodiest ever fought on earth, and 'the least justified of all wars since man emerged from barbarism'. But such reactions were not, of course, confined to the United States. The essentially American note was struck by the *Chicago Herald,* which said that 'Peace-loving citizens of this country will now rise up and tender a hearty vote of thanks to Columbus for having discovered America', by the *Wabash Plain Dealer,* which 'never appreciated so keenly as now the foresight exercised by our forefathers in emigrating from Europe', and, above all, by the President, in 1914 as in 1917 the most eloquent spokesman for his fellow-citizens: 'Look abroad upon the troubled world. Only America at peace! Among all the great powers of the world, only America saving her power for her own people. . . . Do you not think it likely that the world will some time turn to America and say: "You

were right and we were wrong . . ."?' Neutrality instantly became the cherished wish and policy of the American government and people. Wilson, or so he said, 'looked upon the war as a distant event, terrible and tragic, but one which did not concern us closely in the political sense'. No European leader could say the same. America had reason to congratulate itself.

The horror mounted, so did the self-congratulation. A note of doubt, it is true, crept in early, as the struggle for mastery of the Atlantic raged, and it became clear that America could not automatically depend on safety from the European turmoil. But the election of 1916, which was won by Wilson and the Democrats with the slogan 'He kept us out of the war', was sufficient evidence of the nation's sentiments. Almost till the last minute, it thought it could stay out of the war; before and after that minute, it wanted to.

So clear is all this, and so solid were the reasons for continuing American neutrality; so immense were the obstacles between the United States and belligerent status, that it is still extremely difficult to understand how the plunge into war came about. American belligerency may have been right or wrong. It was certainly not inevitable. It was immensely important. Not only did it decide the outcome of the First World War; it clearly enounced, for the first time, what was to be the major theme of the 20th, the American, century — the coming of the United States into its heritage of power. Yet, given its true significance, the event seems more baffling than ever. The Americans of 1914 were isolationist as well as innocent. They did not want world power. The contrast with 1917 is so sharp, so enormous as to make all explanations seem inadequate.

The truth seems to be that the change was more apparent than real. As their rejection of the League of Nations was to show, the people of the United States remained isolationist at heart. In 1917 they simply failed to realize the full significance of what they were doing, for otherwise they would probably not have done it. Had they been told that American participation in the First World War was not inevitable, but that close and permanent American participation in the affairs of the modern world was, they would have been appalled. They wanted to believe the opposite. The nation had lived undisturbed by European conflicts for a century, and wanted to continue like that. Even most of those who whole-heartedly echoed the Wilsonian eloquence that spoke of a fight 'for a universal dominion of right by such a concert of free peoples as shall bring peace and safety to all nations and make the world itself at last free' would have denied that this involved a future commit-

Above: British cartoon showing the two faces of Wilson's policy of neutrality

American magazine illustrations. Above: New Year 1917 promises showers of Allied gold to America. Below: America impotent

ment of indefinite duration to meddle in the affairs of the Old World. By 'a world made safe for democracy' the American people on the whole understood a world in which they could safely be isolationist, one in which there would be no more alliances, no more wars or fears of wars, no more troubling intrusion of lesser breeds without the law on the peaceful preoccupations of the Land of the Free. This was to be a war to safeguard American interests and redeem American honour; a war to punish the aggressor; but, above all, a war to end wars.

To the end of his life Woodrow Wilson believed that American strength and American virtue could be successfully applied to make the dream come true. His countrymen soon abandoned this idea; but they did not substitute for it any perception that, as G.K.Chesterton remarked, 'the world cannot be made safe for democracy: it is a dangerous trade'. Instead, they fell back on the belief that the old principles were right, that the United States could and should keep itself to itself, shunning all overseas adventures. The great crusade had failed, like the turn-of-the-century imperialism which had preceded it. Now Americans would once more heed the solemn warnings of George Washington that 'Europe has a set of primary interests which to us have none or a very remote relation. Hence she must be engaged in frequent controversies, the causes of which are essentially foreign to our concerns. Hence, therefore, it must be unwise in us to implicate ourselves by artificial ties in the ordinary vicissitudes of her politics or the ordinary combinations and collisions of her friendships or enmities . . .' They would ponder the experience of their second President, John Adams, who, when minister at Paris, was told by a Swedish diplomat that 'I take it for granted, that you will have sense enough to see us in Europe cut each other's throats with a philosophical tranquillity'. They would follow the advice of their third President, Thomas Jefferson, who urged 'peace, commerce, and honest friendship with all nations, entangling alliances with none'.

The bubble of this pretty dream was to be pricked forever not long after the period with which this article is concerned. But it was intact, whatever the appearance to the contrary, throughout the war.

That war, in short, did not turn the Americans into proponents of *Realpolitik:* it launched them on one of the most high-minded enterprises in their history.

In 1914 the issues of the struggle had at first seemed, to the transatlantic onlookers, perfectly plain. The first weeks produced a storm of moral indignation, in which rational reflection was almost swamped. The storm did not, however, unite the nation. Not all Americans responded alike. The greater number, English-speaking when not of British descent, and sentimentally attached, thanks to French assistance during the War of Independence, to France, had no doubt that the blame all attached to Germany. The rape of Belgium was the chief justification for this feeling. Even today, when we cannot easily echo the virtuous protests at conduct (such as the bombing of Antwerp) which seemed unforgivable at the time, but which, we now recognize, was the logical result of modern war, it must be conceded that there was a wantonness about much of Germany's conduct which invited denunciation. It got it. On the other hand, the stories which inflamed American opinion to fever point, like that of mutilated Belgian children, some minus fingers, other minus hands, arriving as refugees in Wales, were simply false. It was no wonder that Americans of German descent or origin (6,400,000 of them) resented and vociferously repudiated the charges—without much effect. The fate of Belgium remained, throughout the war, one of the most potent stimulants of anti-German feeling.

Still, the German-Americans, vigorously assisted by the German embassy, did their best to throw the charge of sin on to the other side: and so the moralist attitude to the war was established.

Second thoughts, however, soon modified the indignation. For instance, a certain anxiety was felt in high places about the possible consequences of pro- and anti-German feeling for the domestic peace of the United States. The President issued an appeal for neutrality 'in thought as well as in act'; the Mayor of Cleveland, Ohio, a future secretary of war, was afraid that there might be war in the streets between the factions. He tells us: 'The Chief of Police smiled at my naïveté and said: "Mr Mayor, I will, of course, do what you suggest, but there will be no trouble here. Most of these people came from Europe to escape the very thing now going on there and their chief emotion will be thankfulness that they have escaped it and are not involved." ' The chief of police was right. All over the United States citizens gradually came to conclusions about the European powers like those expressed by the *Philadelphia Public Ledger* in September, 1914: 'All, in a mad stampede for armament, trade, and territory, have sown swords and guns, and nourished harvests of death-dealing crops.' Scepticism about the absolute righteousness of the Entente cause (especially as it was also that of Tsarist Russia from which many Americans, initially Poles, Jews, Ukrainians, had fled), though not faith in the cause of the Central powers, steadily strengthened as the months passed into years, and became one of the strongest props of Wilson's efforts to preserve neutrality and mediate a peace.

The ebbing of emotions solved few problems. The institution of a British blockade of Europe threatened to hamper American trade grievously, and immediately knocked the bottom out of the cotton market. Soon German submarines began to threaten neutral trade with Great Britain, and neutral lives embarked in British vessels. Most insidious of all, the Entente powers began to shop for armaments and munitions in America. Under the stimulus of their orders American trade revived: soon it was booming. And soon Great Britain and France, having exhausted their financial resources, sought to pay for American goods by raising loans in New York.

At first they had no success: the federal government discouraged such loans. William Jennings Bryan, the secretary of state, felt that they were unneutral. 'Money,' he said, 'is the worst of all contrabands because it commands everything else.' Unfortunately, if it was unneutral to supply Germany's enemies, it was unneutral not to. Perhaps, if America had refused to become the arsenal of the Entente, the chief result would have been a more rational strategy on the Western Front: Haig might not have been allowed to waste so much ammunition as he did in futile bombardment. At the time it was only clear that France and Great Britain, since their proposal was perfectly legal, would have a legitimate grievance if America refused to supply them. The prospective profits were tempting. America took the easy way. The ban was lifted, loans were negotiated, and trade with the Entente powers rose from $824,000,000 in 1914 to $3,214,000,000 in 1916. At the same time, because of the blockade, trade with the Central powers shrank from $169,000,000 in 1914 to $1,159,000 in 1916. In a Europe that was growing desperately short both of money and of materials, this amounted to an indispensable underwriting by the Americans of the Western cause. It is small wonder that the Germans grew increasingly indifferent to American feelings.

Yet, essentially, those feelings worked in the German interest. Any sort of peace concluded before April, 1917, would have been favourable to the Central powers, since the Entente had proved unable to dislodge them from their conquests. And Americans were overwhelmingly in favour of an early peace, especially as the price would have to be paid by others. Peace had been one of their pet causes for years before 1914. One industrialist-philanthropist, Andrew Carnegie, had set up a $10,000,000 Endowment for International Peace. In 1915 another, Henry Ford, sent a 'peace ship', filled with pacifists, to Europe, her mission being 'to get the boys out of the trenches by Christmas'. The German ambassador at Washington, Bernstorff, was so well aware of the usefulness of all this to his country that he worked unceasingly to preserve good relations between America and Germany, and encouraged Wilson's attempts to bring an early end to the conflict by mediation. His masters were not so wise. On 7th May 1915 one of their submarines sank the great English liner *Lusitania*: 128 Americans were among those drowned. Emphatic protests at this and similar sinkings eventually induced the Germans to hold their hand for a while,

Punch *cartoon—the ship of pacifists Ford sent to Europe. A U-boat shouts 'Welcome'*

but on 9th January 1917 they decided to resort to unrestricted submarine warfare. Wilson severed diplomatic relations. Then in March an intercepted cable, the famous Zimmermann Telegram, revealed that the Germans were embarking on an intrigue to draw Mexico into an attack on the United States in order to recover some of the vast areas lost during the 19th century. Roused to fury, America went to war in the following month.

There is nothing very remarkable about this list of challenges and responses; but it is worth pointing out that the reactions of the American people were, throughout, even more important than those of their government, which in fact they determined to a unique extent. In some respects the people were more extreme, going to the human heart of issues which the Administration tended to approach in legalities. After the sinking of the *Lusitania* some (Bryan among them) said that persons voluntarily sailing in British ships in submarine-infested waters had no one to blame but themselves if they were drowned. Wilson argued stiffly that the undoubted legal rights of the dead Americans had been wantonly infringed. Public opinion simply held that innocent women and children ought not to be drowned at sea

merely because their ship had small-arms ammunition in her cargo. 'The torpedo which sunk the *Lusitania*,' said the *Nation*, 'also sank Germany in the opinion of mankind.' For the first time interventionist sentiment developed—not, admittedly, on any great scale.

The pattern was repeated in all the subsequent crises. In every case Wilson may be said to have kept himself one step behind the nation, never taking an irretrievable step until it was demanded of him by the majority of Americans—never, that is, until America had actually entered the war. Only then did his Messianic instincts begin to get the better of his judgement.

It is easy to see now that the war could not be waged without action by the United States, and that the United States, without really intending to do so, early involved itself and its interests on the Allied side. It follows from this that Wilson early lost his most important freedom, the freedom to stay out, even though for most of the period of neutrality America consciously decided to put up with the inconveniences of being a bystander in the immense struggle. By the winter of 1916-17, at the latest, the decision as to whether America would go to war or not rested with Berlin. Germany took the decision for unrestricted submarine warfare, and hence for war with America (no pre-nuclear great power would tamely submit to be bullied) on the calculation that it could beat the Entente before American strength became effective. The calculation proved mistaken. It all seems almost inevitable.

In 1916, however, it seemed that another possibility existed. The Germans, it is true, had made themselves hopelessly unpopular in the previous year by their brutality. They were therefore on their best behaviour. On the other hand, the British were, and had been from the beginning, flouting the rights of property that were only a little less sacred than the right to live. Resentment could never be so fierce over the impounding of ships and goods as it was over the loss of life, even when there was all too much reason to suspect that Entente governments of wishing to sabotage American efforts to mediate. But Great Britain made itself odious to the 3,400,000 Irish-Americans by its bloody repression of the Easter Rising in Dublin (Vol. 5, p. 596). In view of the extravagant series of German blunders it is inconceivable that America would ever have fought on the side of the Central powers; but it might very well have deserted the cause of the Entente. After all, in November 1916, the President, while saying that relations with Great Britain 'were more strained than with Germany', prodded the Federal Reserve Board into issuing a statement that, in effect, put a stop—for the time being—

to Entente efforts to borrow money in New York. The Western cause could not have endured many more such blows. Yet, so far as public opinion in America was concerned, the President would not have been much blamed for launching them. Scepticism about the Franco-British cause had reached such a pitch that when at length the United States did go to war, one editor explained that one side (the Entente) was a gang of thieves, the other a gang of murderers. 'On the whole, we prefer the thieves, but only as the lesser of two evils.' The Americans went to war convinced that what high purpose and idealism there was in it they brought with them.

The American crusade

Nothing, in fact, is more striking than the identity of outlook which united the moralizing President and the people. The historian may think that the United States was drawn into the war just because it existed. The laws of geography proved stronger than the will of man, and America was drawn into the First World War as it had been drawn into the Napoleonic Wars, reluctantly but inevitably (though it must yet again be emphasized that involvement did not necessarily mean fighting). However, once it had in fact become a belligerent, it was bound to change the nature of the struggle. Not only was the United States fresh, strong, and rich. It was, or thought itself to be, a uniquely successful political society. Its commitment to democracy was more than a century old, and was still fervent. In Wilson this commitment found its perfect spokesman, for he utterly shared it. It was an elemental belief which made it possible (indeed, psychologically necessary) for Wilson, in all good faith, to propose a crusade to America, and for the Americans to respond. It is true that not all of them responded with maximum eagerness, and that the temperature perceptibly cooled when it emerged that a conscript army was to be sent across the Atlantic; but the prevailing tendency was a belief that an American war *must* be for some loftier purpose than the mere defence of territorial integrity and national honour. There was quite enough enthusiasm to fill the sails of Wilsonian idealism, with incalculable results, not merely for the course of the war and the nature of the peace, but for the future of the world. In April 1917 the Americans decisively threw their wealth, power, and energy into a quest for a peaceful, free, and democratic world order. It is a quest that seems little nearer success today than it was fifty years ago; but its continuing popularity makes it still possible to hope that it will one day succeed, and still impossible to regret the crisis which led the people of the United States to make their great decision.

Declaration of War

It was the German decision to begin unrestricted submarine warfare which lay at the basis of America's entry into the war. But a 'Bathing Beauty Scandal' and a strange telegram to the Mexican government also had their part to play....

It was Lloyd George who once remarked that Europe slithered into war in 1914, and this description, graphically accurate, applies equally well to the entrance of the United States into the World War in 1917. Prior to these separate if similar *dénouements,* neither the Europeans nor the Americans quite knew what they were doing. As late as January 1917, within weeks of the fateful date of the declaration of war on 6th April, President Woodrow Wilson was asking the belligerents for a peace without victory and hoping to achieve it through his efforts at mediation, while the United States remained outside the war as a neutral power. But then came a series of unexpected military, diplomatic, and political changes, none of them American in origin. Before long, Wilson, to use the description of Senator Henry Cabot Lodge, was 'in the grip of events'. On 6th April 1917 some of the election posters of November 1916 were still up on the billboards, and Americans could ponder the Democratic Party slogans which had helped re-elect the President: 'He Kept Us Out of War'; and 'War in the East, Peace in the West, Thank God for Wilson'. They were not, however, angry with Wilson, for they too had reacted to unforeseen events.

What were these events of early 1917 which moved the President and people? It is easy now to see that, given what had gone before, in January 1917 it would take only a few more blows from the German government to make America abandon her neu-

trality. Given that government's almost complete lack of understanding of the sensitivities of the American government and people, the wonder is that neutrality lasted as long as it did, that German blunders did not come sooner. It is also curious to observe, in retrospect, that Wilson and the American people believed in January 1917 that they still possessed freedom of manoeuvre. The President early that month told his confidant Colonel House that 'There will be no war'.

On 19th January 1917 the German government thoughtfully told Ambassador Johann von Bernstorff about the decision to resume unrestricted submarine warfare on 1st February but Bernstorff was to inform the American government, and duly did so, only on 31st January, at 4 pm. It was a crude beginning, this eight hours' notice. Bernstorff had done his best to prevent this stupidity, this tactic of loosing the submarines, which he knew would drive the Americans into war. It was not only the trans-Atlantic munitions trade, or the export of American food (harvests had been poor in 1916), that the Germans were seeking to prevent; they wanted to strangle British economic life by cutting off all imports. They did not have to use so thorough a submarine blockade, which would inevitably affront the Americans, Bernstorff thought. He had cabled his views,

Wild enthusiasm and waving flags on Broadway—America has entered the war

but the German leaders paid no attention.

Bernstorff meanwhile had lowered his stock with the American government and public, and with his own government (he deeply offended the Kaiser), by allowing a peccadillo to get into public print. On a vacation in the Adirondacks with a lady who often entertained him, he posed in a bathing suit for a photograph, with his arms intimately encircling two ladies similarly attired. At the very time when he needed whatever personal influence and dignity he could muster, this photograph

Below: The text of Wilson's declaration of war. Bottom: Bernstorff, the ladies' man – a diplomat discomfited by scandal

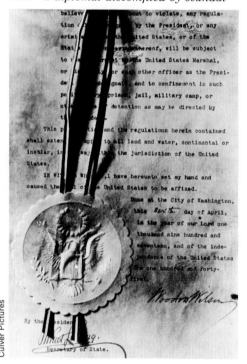

found its way into the hands of the Russian ambassador who passed it to the newspapers. Americans snickered at the Bathing Beauty Scandal. Bernstorff was a generally competent diplomat to whom both the American and German governments should have listened. Instead this 'good German' found himself ignored on public matters and laughed at over private ones. 'I am not surprised,' he said upon the break of diplomatic relations when he received his passports. 'My government will not be surprised either. The people in Berlin knew what was bound to happen if they took the action they have taken. There was nothing else left for the United States to do.' In despair he told a press conference afterwards that he was through with politics.

After the formal break, two events followed which together pushed the country into war. The first was a clear-cut case of a German submarine sinking a passenger vessel with American citizens aboard. Wilson on 3rd February, when he informed Congress that he was breaking relations, had added that 'I refuse to believe that it is the intention of the German authorities to do in fact what they have warned us they will feel at liberty to do. . . . Only actual overt acts on their part can make me believe it even now'. For two weeks after resumption of unrestricted submarine warfare no incident occurred, no open violation of what Americans liked to believe was one of their principal neutral rights. There was no paralysis of shipping during the period, as American tonnage clearing United States ports dropped only from 1,019,396 in January to 847,786 in February. The day the fatal vessel, the 18,000-ton British liner *Laconia*, sailed from New York harbour, sixty-six ships of all nationalities were in the roadstead, loaded or loading for ports in the zone of war. Wilson spoke again to Congress on 26th February, reporting that 'The overt act which I have ventured to hope the German commanders would in fact avoid has not occurred'. That very moment, however, news of the sinking of the *Laconia* the day before was being flashed to Washington. It was whispered around the House chamber before the President finished his speech, and printed in the country's newspapers the next day. Three Americans, including two women, had lost their lives. The deaths of the women were not pretty to contemplate: a torpedoing at night, a lifeboat half stove-in as it swung down over the careening hull, this fragile craft itself slowly sinking while it wallowed off into the darkness, Mrs Albert H. Hoy and her daughter Elizabeth standing waist deep in icy water throughout the long night.

This was interpreted as an open challenge, by the German government which

authorized it, and by the American government and people who had brought themselves into a frame of mind to oppose it.

The Zimmermann telegram

The second precipitating event came almost immediately when American newspapers on 1st March published the Zimmermann telegram. The *Laconia* disaster had proved that the Germans held no regard for international law and human rights. The Zimmermann telegram showed that they were guilty not merely of legal and moral turpitude but were enemies of the United States, willing to endanger the nation's very existence. In the annals of international stupidity during the 20th century, or any other century, this famous telegram hardly has an equal. It was a German proposal of an alliance to the government of Mexico (an alliance which was possibly to include the Japanese government as well). The Mexicans were to attack the United States during the hostilities now deemed imminent, in exchange for which the Germans promised a return of the 'lost territories' of the Mexican War of 1846-48: Texas, New Mexico, Arizona. The genesis of the proposal is now quite clear. The Americans had been giving Mexico much trouble in the past few years, even to the extent of sending in a punitive military expedition in 1916 under command of General Pershing. The Mexican regime of General Venustiano ('Don Venus') Carranza began to take interest in Mexican-German co-operation, and Don Venus in November made a suggestion, going so far as to offer submarine bases. An assistant in the German foreign office, one Kemnitz, turned the proposal into a project for an alliance. It was so preposterous a project that the German foreign secretary, Zimmermann, should have forgotten it. Instead he picked it up as a great idea.

Zimmermann sent his telegram to Mexico by several means, one of which was through the American embassy in Berlin and thence from Washington to Mexico City by Western Union. Ambassador Gerard transmitted this German message, in its original German code, as part of an arrangement which Colonel House had made, with Wilson's permission, for cable transmission of German messages pertaining to mediation. Ambassador Bernstorff had promised to use the arrangement only for peaceful purposes, but Zimmermann was not put off by that engagement.

The British government intercepted and decoded all three of Zimmermann's transmissions. Under the leadership of Admiral Sir William Reginald Hall, the Admiralty early in the war had set up a code and cipher-cracking operation, which triumphed with the deciphering of Zimmermann's idiotic telegram. Not wishing to

Culver Pictures

Culver Pictures

show his knowledge of the German code, Hall at first was in a quandary about publishing, but ingenuity triumphed. One of his agents in Mexico City procured from the Mexican telegraph office a copy of the still-encoded telegram which Bernstorff had obtained from the American State Department and relayed from Washington. It contained certain small differences from the other intercepts, and upon publication the impression prevailed that someone had stolen or sold a decoded copy of the telegram, getting it from the German legation in Mexico City. The Germans reassured Hall that they were without suspicion by engaging in a lively inquiry with Eckhardt, the German minister in Mexico City, asking how many copies of the decode Eckhardt had made and who had handled them, using of course the same code which Hall had cracked. Hall found it amusing to read that Eckhardt tried to pass the blame off on to Bernstorff in Washington.

No denial

Even after the cat was out of the bag, the telegram published in every American newspaper, it was still possible for Zimmermann in Berlin to quiet the uproar, or at the very least to make the Americans disclose how they obtained the telegram, by baldly denying that he had sent it. President Wilson himself, the author in 1918 of 'open diplomacy', once in a confidential conversation with Colonel House said, admittedly for House's ears only (and, as it turned out, for House's diary), that a man was justified in lying for two purposes, to protect the honour of a lady and to preserve secrets of state. Had Zimmermann but known it, he could have cited the President in support of a diplomatic denial. Secretary Lansing in Washington was certain that Zimmermann would lie his way out, and was incredulous to learn that the German foreign secretary almost at once admitted authorship of the telegram in a burst of truthfulness as naïve as the composition which inspired it.

What could the American government do after the publication of the telegram on 1st March? If Wilson does not go to war now, Theodore Roosevelt wrote to Lodge, 'I shall skin him alive'. The Prussian Invasion Plot, as the newspapers labelled the telegram, was transparently clear. Newspapers in the hitherto isolationist Middle West acknowledged the end of neutrality. The Chicago *Tribune* warned its readers to realize now, 'without delay, that Germany recognizes us an enemy', and that the country no longer could hope to keep out of 'active participation in the present conflict'. The Cleveland *Plain Dealer* said there was 'neither virtue nor dignity' in refusing to fight now. The Oshkosh (Wisconsin) *Northwestern,* an authentic voice from the Middle West, said that the telegram had turned pacifists, critics, and carpers into patriots overnight. Zimmermann, as Mrs Tuchman has written, 'shot an arrow in the air and brought down neutrality like a dead duck'.

The rest was anticlimax. The first Russian Revolution of March 1917 forced the abdication of the Tsar and the proclamation of a republic, and removed an embarrassing despotism from the ranks of the Allies, making it easier to say that the Allies were Democracy fighting the Central powers who represented Autocracy. About the same time, U-boats sank four American ships. The presidential decision to arm merchant ships, taken in mid-March, constituting a sort of armed neutrality, had no discernible effect on German policy. The President called a special session of Congress. On the evening of 2nd April 1917, Wilson went before both Houses, duly assembled in the Capitol building in Washington, and as the lights gleamed in the crowded chamber he asked his countrymen for what they were ready to give him. Many Senators had brought small American flags to the House chamber where the President spoke, and during the speech they clapped their hands and waved their flags.

British postcard. For Great Britain, America's declaration promised men—and hope

" We are coming, brothers, coming, A hundred thousand strong !"

I WANT YOU
FOR U.S. ARMY

NEAREST RECRUITING STATION

Left: Recruiting poster. Above: On another poster a drowned mother and her child, the supposed victims of a U-boat, appeal for recruits to avenge her

Above: Appeal for the war loan. Below: Tank Corps recruiting poster. At first the Americans tried to equip military units before sending them to France

Imperial War Museum

Lords Gallery

Huntingdon Hartford

The Western Front, April 1917/Correlli Barnett

The New Military Balance

America's entry into the war was greeted by the Allies with almost hysterical relief. Russia was undergoing revolution, German submarines threatened Great Britain's power to stay in the war, and the French army had been demoralized. Yet the immediate military help which America could bring was much less than was generally realized. What she brought was hope

On 6th April 1917 the United States entered the First World War. At the beginning of June General John J. Pershing, the commander-in-chief of the American Expeditionary Force arrived in England for a four-day visit, and then went on to France to began organizing his command. His reception by the British and French was warm to the point of hysteria: the King welcomed him, the crowds cheered and threw roses. The illustrated magazine *The London Graphic* caught the mood and the style of the time by surrounding a photograph of Pershing and his officers with a tabernacle in classical style, in which a luscious symbolic figure of a woman held a laurel wreath over Pershing's head; the caption read: 'Now is the winter of our discontent made glorious summer by this sun of (New) York.' (In fact, Pershing had been born in Missouri.)

The hopes, the great expectations, that were aroused in the British and French peoples by American entry into the war were understandable. The spring and early summer of 1917 saw Allied fortunes at their lowest ebb. The year 1916 had ended with apparently nothing to show for colossal losses but small territorial gains on the Somme and the preservation of Verdun. The expulsion of the Germans from French soil seemed as difficult and as far off as ever. The very real and heavy damage done to German power by the Allied offensives in the late summer and autumn of 1916 was hidden from view.

The third year of the war now unfolded for the Allies a prospect of catastrophe. On 1st February 1917 the Germans began unrestricted submarine warfare. The results of the first three months fully justified German calculations that before the end of the year Great Britain would be unable to prosecute the war because of lack of shipping to transport food, raw materials, and troops: the tonnage sunk rose from 470,000 in February to 837,000 in April. Admiral Jellicoe, the British first sea lord, believed that unless an answer to the submarine could be found — and in his estimation, none was in sight — the war was certainly lost. In March revolution exploded in Tsarist Russia and the Tsar Nicholas II abdicated. Although the Russian army had never fulfilled the hopes of 1914 that it would prove an irresistible steam-roller, it had nevertheless heavily engaged Germany's Austrian ally and brought her to the point of exhaustion, and had also drawn German resources away from the Western Front. In 1916 General Brusilov's Offensive (Vol. 5, p. 577) had inflicted a smashing defeat in the east on the Central powers. Now that Russia was paralysed by revolution, no man could say what help, if any, she would bring.

Finally, at the end of April and the beginning of May 1917, the French army, under a new commander-in-chief, General Robert Nivelle, was crushingly, appallingly, repulsed in a general offensive on the Western Front which Nivelle had promised would lead to a swift breakthrough and a rapid, and victorious, end to the war. In the aftermath of this shattering disappointment, all the accumulated war-weariness and exhaustion of the French nation exploded in widespread army mutinies and civil disorders. It was no wonder that the Allied leaders and peoples alike greeted the belligerency of the richest, most industrially powerful nation in the world, with all its unblooded manpower, with somewhat hysterical relief. America brought on to the Allied side a population of 93,400,000 and a steel production of 45,060,607 tons. The human resources went far to make up for the 180 million Russians now perhaps lost to the Allied cause. The industrial power was overwhelming; American steel production alone was nearly three times as great as that of Germany and Austria together. However, all this was only *potential*. How long would it be before American resources, human and industrial, were translated into vast, superbly-equipped armies on the Western Front able to crush down the exhausted and outmatched Germans? In view of the German submarine successes and the manifest unsteadiness of the French army and nation, would there even *be* a Western Front by the time the Americans had deployed their power?

Whatever its enormous long-term importance in 20th-century history, the American entry into the First World War in April 1917 in fact was in itself of far smaller strategic significance at the time than the cheering British and French crowds supposed — or than American national myth claims. There was no progressive transformation of the war — no massive rescue operation. On the other hand, it is certain that without America, the Allies would have lost the war. The clue to this apparent paradox lies in that American help *before* her entry into the war was more vital than many recognize; and American help *after* her entry less vital, at least for some fifteen months.

The German and Austrian war effort was

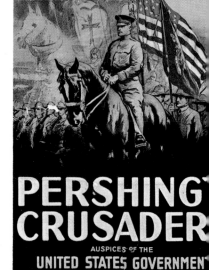

PERSHING
CRUSADER
AUSPICES OF THE
UNITED STATES GOVERNMENT
-THE FIRST OFFICIAL AMERICAN WAR PICTURE
TAKEN BY U.S. SIGNAL CORPS AND NAVY PHOTOGRAPHERS

*1 Medal awarded to American mothers whose sons were serving in the army. 2 Italian print – 'Five million American citizens become soldiers to defend the world's freedom'. 3 American view of her fighting sons – crusaders keeping the world free for democracy. 4 'Our boys' in action: Doughboy Shooting in Street Combat, painted by H.Dunn. It took a long while to mobilize the doughboys (infantry). **Opposite page:** A British tank, on Fifth Avenue, helping to campaign for funds for the American war effort – the 'Liberty loan'*

Crusading for democracy: with high hopes and a small army

entirely based on their own industries and technological skill. By the spring of 1915, after a temporary shortage of munitions, Germany had converted her vast chemical industry and her varied and highly modern engineering industries to the production of explosives, propellants, fuses, shells, ammunition, and weapons. Her machine-tool industry – the most modern and inventive in the world except for that of America – had no difficulty in equipping new munitions plants.

Great Britain and France, in sharp contrast, found when they tackled the problem of a massive expansion of war production that their industrial resources were largely out-of-date in equipment and techniques – and that they even lacked completely a whole range of the most modern kinds of industries. Thus, Great Britain and France before the war had been almost entirely dependent on Germany for chemical products, such as dyes, drugs, and photographic processing materials. It was plant that made dyes and drugs that could also easily make explosives. Great Britain had to create a chemical industry from scratch, based on seized German patents. While it was being built up, there was a bottleneck at the very base of shell manufacture – the propellant and the explosive.

British manufacturing industry was still largely mid-Victorian in its types of product, its methods of production, its skills and techniques. Mass-production plant, with lines of automatic or semi-automatic machines, producing all kinds of precision light-engineering work, was hardly known. Before 1914 Great Britain was dependent mostly on Germany, partly on America, for almost all the sophisticated products of the second phase of the industrial revolution – ball-bearings, magnetoes, sparking plugs, cameras, optical goods.

Great Britain therefore lacked both the general and the particular industries to sustain a modern war. Nor could her machine-tool industry equip the vast new factories that had to be created. Machine-tools were – and are – the basic industry of modern technological growth; they are the machines which make machines. The British machine-tool industry was also essentially mid-Victorian; it was small-scale, it made a limited range of tools to order by almost craft methods in small workshops. For the 'modern' kind of automatic or semi-automatic machine for a production-line, it contented itself in peacetime by acting as a distribution agent for American and German imports.

France was in no better case. Thus, American resources and know-how were, from the end of 1914, absolutely essential to the survival of the Allies. It was to America – and to a lesser extent to Sweden and Switzerland – that they looked to supply the specialized sophisticated products that they had imported from Germany. It was on American industry that Great Britain especially depended for shells and other munitions during 1915 and 1916, while Great Britain was still painfully creating her chemical and munitions industries. Even in 1915 a third of all shells issued to the British army were made in North America. In 1916 the debut of the mass British armies in battle was only made possible by shells from America and Canada. As the history of the ministry of munitions expressed it: 'During the early part of 1915, in fact, overseas contractors assumed a place of utmost importance, since upon them the War Office was forced to depend for the bulk of the shell supplies required for the 1916 campaign.'

The Allies were just as dependent on America for their longer-term needs in constructing their own munitions industries. The essential basis of the whole vast programme of national munitions factories, on which Lloyd George's fame as minister of munitions hangs, was the American machine-tool and the American methods and organization it made possible. In 1916, when Great Britain's new war industries were at last getting into full production, *The Times* wrote: 'One of the new factories has grown up on a spot which last November was green fields. Now there are 25 acres covered with buildings packed with machinery. Most of the machines are of American make, and some are marvels of ingenuity.'

The extent of Allied dependence on American technology, and also of their purchases (at the cost of their accumulated overseas investments) is illustrated by the increase in production of certain American industries *before* America began her own war-production programme. Between 1914 and 1917, American exports of iron, steel, and their products to Europe rose four-fold, American explosives production grew ten times between 1913 and 1917. Bernard Baruch, chairman of the US war industries board, wrote: 'Cincinnati is the greatest machine tool manufacturing center in the world. In 1913 the total value of the annual product of the United States was about $50,000,000. During the war period preceding our entrance, our productive capacity was more than doubled, but the expansion took place largely in the output of small and medium-sized machines — machines for the production of shells, rifles, fuses etc.'

It is therefore beyond question that without access to American resources, Great Britain and France would have lacked the material to sustain the war while their own industries were being created, and could not have created the industries at all. This indeed was acknowledged by the

*Above left: 'This destroyer is needed to sink Hun submarines' reads the sign on the right. The destroyer was built in seventeen days. **Above right:** The American commanders of the army and the navy, General Pershing (on the left) and Admiral Sims (on the right)*

*Above: The first American prisoners to fall into German hands. **Below:** Loading a troopship for France. As the soldiers, fresh recruits for slaughter, tramp across the dock, girls in Red Cross uniform give each a last gift from the American people and wish them good luck*

British history of the ministry of munitions: 'Great Britain was practically dependent upon the United States of America for material for propellant manufacture, for a large proportion of her explosives material. She depended to a considerable extent upon the United States for shell steel and other steel . . . for machine tools.'

Thus America had proved a decisive influence on the course of the First World War long before her own entry into it.

However, by April 1917 the creation of the Allied — especially the British — war industries had been largely completed. Great Britain was now able to supply munitions freely to France and Italy. There was no longer so desperate or so large a need for American shells or machine-tools. The American declaration of war was therefore largely irrelevant and unimportant where Allied war production was concerned. Indeed, the flow of help was reversed once the American armies began to build up in France; it was France and Great Britain who largely equipped the American armies, as they were formed in France. The Americans made the capital mistake of deciding to produce their own designs of artillery pieces and aircraft, instead of adopting French or British designs for which many of their own factories were already producing ammunition or parts. The inevitable teething troubles of new designs were such that the American army received American guns just about in time to fire a salute in celebration of the armistice in November 1918. Not only this, but acute shortage of shipping space made it evidently more sensible to fill ships with men rather than guns, and then equip the men in Europe. So in the event the AEF was given French 75's for its field artillery, French 155-mm guns and howitzers for its medium artillery, and mostly British mortars. The British also supplied machine-guns, steel helmets, and even uniforms. The air component of the United States was equipped with French aircraft.

Obviously the prime fact about American *belligerency,* as opposed to mere industrial availability, was that United States armed forces would henceforth take part in the war. This indeed was the hope that inspired the civilian cheers, when the 1st Division, AEF, landed in France at the end of June 1917. These were the healthy men, from a nation twice as numerous as the British, or the French, who would take over the weight of the fighting from the tired, battle-shaken survivors of three terrible campaigns. Unfortunately, the American declaration of war was by no means followed by a breakneck expansion of the army and its swift deployment in France, such as the British had achieved in 1914-15. The 1st Division was not followed by the 2nd until September; by 31st October 1917

the AEF numbered only 6,064 officers and 80,969 men. Lloyd George has pointed out in his memoirs the poorness of the American performance compared with the British in creating an army: '. . . at the end of six months (after the outbreak of war) the British Expeditionary Force on the Western Front numbered 354,750. The First American Division was put into a quiet sector of the French front on 21st October 1917 — nearly seven months after the severance of diplomatic relations with Germany. The tide of American forces in France . . . mounted only in dribbling fashion during these early months. By the end of October it was 87,000; by the end of November, 126,000; and at the beginning of 1918, 175,000. That was nine months after the entry of America into the war. At that stage in our own war effort we had already thrown 659,104 into the various war theatres.'

Thus the United States exerted no military effect at all on the critical year of 1917, when Russia subsided more and more from the war, when Pétain strove to quell the mutinies in the French army and keep it together until such time as the Americans should arrive in force, when the Italians suffered a catastrophic defeat at Caporetto, when the *only* Allied army still capable of an offensive — the British — slogged doggedly forward towards Passchendaele. And, the Germans hoped and expected, 1917 was to be the decisive and final year of the war. For it was their calculation that the American army, as a great force, would never arrive because the U-boats would have destroyed the shipping that might have carried it across the Atlantic; if in fact the war itself had not been ended by the U-boat blockade before the Americans were ready to cross. In 1917 the Americans provided hope, little else to the Allies.

The Americans are not to be entirely blamed for the extreme slowness of their military mobilization. The peacetime American army had been even smaller than the British, and far less prepared for modern war. Whereas the British had at least trained and prepared an expeditionary force of six divisions for a European campaign, and completed all the staff studies about organization and methods necessary for subsequent expansion, the Americans started absolutely from scratch in every way. For example, the size, organization, and ancillary services of the basic infantry division had to be worked out and decided upon, as well as of corps and armies. In peacetime the United States army had numbered 190,000 officers and men spread in small detachments across the face of America and her own overseas dependencies. The very size of America posed its own problems, for before troops

could go aboard the troopships, they had to be concentrated and accommodated near the eastern seaboard. This meant a vast programme of camp construction, on top of other programmes for training camps and training facilities. In France itself port facilities had to be enormously extended, and lines of communication built up from the ports allotted to the Americans to their designated sector in the right-centre of the Allied line, in the Argonne. This entailed major construction work to increase the carrying capacity of the rail links. Colossal supply depots had to be constructed and filled in France. The British had found that supporting an army in another country over twenty-two miles of sea involved enormous rearward services; America had to make war across 3,000 miles of sea. The major bottleneck however was shipping, both for troops and cargoes. The United States mercantile

Industry steps up production for America's participation in the war — war workers making steel helmets for doughboys

Culver Pictures

marine had nothing like enough ships available to move the American army across the Atlantic.

Finally, there was a fundamental difference of views between Pershing on the one hand and Haig and Pétain on the other about the employment of American troops. Haig and Pétain at the beginning of 1918 were keenly aware that their armies were seriously under strength and without hope of adequate national reinforcements. They wanted American infantry to fill out their own divisions; they wanted help quickly. Pershing on the other hand (and his government) was resolved to build up a completely independent, self-contained American army in France, with its own divisions, corps, and armies. He was not prepared to see Americans swallowed up in Allied formations; he was prepared to wait, for months if need be, until all the artillery and supply services, the higher headquarters and staffs, necessary for an independent force were organized, trained, and equipped. Thus it was that when on 21st March 1918, the Germans launched the first and greatest of a series of titanic offensives on the Western Front, there was only one American division actually in the overstretched and outnumbered Allied line and three divisions in training areas.

The rate of the American build-up in France had been crucial to the calculations of the German high command in deciding on great offensives in the west in the spring of 1918. By November, 1917, when the German decision was taken, unrestricted U-boat warfare had failed in its object of knocking Great Britain out of

Big guns under construction. But the army only received the new American guns just before the armistice in November 1918

the war; it had been beaten by the convoy system. Therefore, the Germans had to reckon on the entry into battle, sooner or later, of a mass and entirely fresh American army: certain defeat for Germany and her allies. Therefore, the war must be decided before that mass army arrived. Ludendorff told his colleagues: 'Our general situation requires that we should strike at the earliest moment, if possible at the end of February or beginning of March, before the Americans can throw strong forces into the scale.' In other words, since Russia had finally been knocked out of the war by the Treaty of Brest-Litovsk, the bulk of German strength could be concentrated on France and Great Britain before they could be rescued by their second great ally.

The crisis on the Western Front lasted from 21st March to 18th July, as the German onslaughts fell successively on different parts on the Allied front. Twice the British faced real danger of being driven into the Channel; once there was an acute risk of the French and British being separated; three times the French front was temporarily smashed and the French capital exposed again to possible occupation. In this largest, most violent, and

most decisive campaign of the war, the American army played little part. Some units took part in the defence of the Amiens sector after 28th March; the 1st Division carried out a spirited counterattack at Cantigny, near Montdidier, on 28th May; in June the 2nd Division helped the French block the German drive across the Marne, and launched a successful counterattack which led to the recapture of Belleau Wood; units of the 3rd and 42nd Divisions fought defensively in the sector of Château-Thierry. These were very welcome, but hardly decisive contributions to a campaign against 192 German divisions.

What was far more important—indeed decisive—in terms of the issue of the war was the effect of the German offensive on the speed of the American build-up. A week after the Germans attacked on the Somme, on 28th March 1918, Pershing abandoned his somewhat deliberate and pedantic attempt to create an independent American army before entering the conflict, and offered Pétain as a temporary expedient all the troops he had, to use as Pétain wished. So the individual American units saw action under French or British corps and army command, not American. This immediate gesture was one sign of the American realization that the French and British might not last long enough to be rescued; that there was a need for desperate haste in getting American troops over to France and into battle. At the same time, Pershing still remained anxious that his Allies should not rob him of his own independent army by the feeding of Americans into their own divisions. It was only after long arguments between the Allied and American governments and commands, that it was finally agreed, at the beginning of June, that shipping space should be saved by bringing over men—infantry mostly—instead of complete divisions with all their space-occupying equipment. 170,000 combat troops were to come in June and 140,000 in July out of some 250,000 men ready to be transported in each of the two months. New divisions would be formed and equipped in France. These shipments of men were made possible by the British mercantile marine, made available as part of the bargain by the British government by cutting down British imports.

Whereas in March 84,000 Americans had crossed the Atlantic, 118,500 crossed in April, 246,000 in May, 278,800 in June, and 306,703 in July—nearly half of them in British ships. These figures, far higher than the German command had thought possible, spelt defeat for Germany.

On 15th-17th July the last phase of the great German 1918 offensive petered out in failure. On 18th July the French launched a surprise attack, led by massed tanks, from the Forest of Villers-Cotterêts.

The attacking troops included two American divisions, each with a strength of 27,000 men, three times as large as a French or German division. The French attack marked the turn of the campaign; from then to the end of the war the Germans were to fight on the defensive.

It was now—and at very long last—that the American military presence in the war proved decisive. The great battles of March to July 1918, which the Allies had won virtually without American help, had left the British, French, and German armies all exhausted, with scant reserves and little hope of reinforcement from the homeland. For the original combatants of the war nothing remained but to break up divisions—to see their armies gradually decrease. A German battalion now numbered on average 660 men. The German gamble on victory had failed: neither the German army nor the German people (hungry, miserable, and despairing after years of blockade) had any further hopes to clutch at. In August, when the British offensive on the Somme (some American units took part), confirmed that the Allies now possessed the initiative, and confirmed also that the morale and discipline of the German army was beginning to disintegrate, there were nearly 1,500,000 Americans in France. The only German reservoir of fresh manpower lay in the 300,000 youths of the 1919 class called up in June. Whereas Allied leaders were planning for a campaign in 1919, whose principal weight was to be borne by a hundred American divisions, for Germany's leaders another year of battle was absolutely unthinkable.

Thus it was that even in the last months of the war, it was the American military *potential,* advertised by their limited offensives at St Mihiel and in the Argonne, rather than the actual fighting achievements of American troops, that affected the outcome of the Great War in 1918. In point of fact, the brunt of the fighting from July to November 1918 was borne by the tired but still dogged British, who took 188,700 prisoners as against 196,000 taken by the French, Belgians, and Americans together.

The American role in the First World War was therefore decisive: decisive industrially between 1914 and 1917, decisive in terms of military potential from midsummer 1918 onwards. It illustrated two facts of enormous importance to the future balance of power in Europe: that Germany was militarily the equal of the British and French empires together; and that Great Britain, the 19th-century 'work-shop of the world', was no longer a first-rank industrial and technological power, no longer able to defend herself and her empire out of her own resources.

Revolution in Russia
Chapter 25

Introduction by J.M.Roberts

1917 brought two great changes: the United States entered the war and Russia began to leave it. Before Russia finally made peace in the following year she had suffered two changes of regime, a German invasion of remarkable depth and success, and the beginning of a civil war. Not surprisingly many observers thought her well on the way to national disintegration. The first step towards this had been the **Overthrow of the Tsar,** which David Floyd describes. Its preparation and its consequences are the subject of this chapter.

Of the three great European imperial dynasties, Russia's was the first to collapse because, whatever was said and believed about the corrupting effects of German sympathies and German gold, her government and people could no longer bear the harsh impact of two and a half years of fighting. On this topic we have asked for the collaboration of Soviet historians and one of them, Alexander Grunt, provides an article on **Russia at War** which describes the cumulative effect of defeat, privation, and suffering. They had imposed from the start enormous burdens on an overwhelmingly peasant society still only beginning to experience real industrial growth in 1914. After the last, glorious moment of success in the Brusilov Offensive, there came further defeats. As Geoffrey A.Hosking shows in **Rasputin and the 'Dark Forces',** the regime could no longer escape responsibility in the eyes of the people for what was going wrong. The result was the revolution in March. It was much less a great offensive rising than the sudden collapse of a facade long since worm-eaten.

Russian politics in the summer which followed were essentially about the issue of peace or war. To Russia's allies, the moral and ideological advantage they won by the disappearance of a despot from their ranks was more than outweighed by the danger of Russia leaving the war altogether. She had saved her allies by making impossible the concentration of German effort on one front. Now this threat loomed up again. As a result, the precarious political health of the Provisional Government whose career is described in **Kerensky's Summer** by George Katkov was of great interest both to the Allies and the Central powers.

The ordinary Russian soldier saw things very differently. To him, only two things really mattered. The first was peace. The other was land. Those who fought in Petrograd for control of the crumbling state apparatus had to take this longing into account if they were to succeed. The Bolsheviks found it much easier to do so than most of their opponents. In large measure, this was because they were led by a political tactician of genius, Lenin.

German cartoon: 'Russia'. Nicholas II with his enraged peasants at his heels

The Tsarina's 'holy man', whose amazing sexual excesses had political repercussions

'Workers of all countries unite'. Workers demonstrate in Petrograd, May 1917

Russia

1914 1st August: Germany declares war on Russia.
1st August: the Duma meets to consider the way the war is being conducted.
22nd August: six parties in the Duma form the

6th September: the Tsar assumes supreme command of the armed forces.
8th September: programme of moderate reform backed by Progressive Bloc is put before council of ministers.
15th September: Goremykin informs cabinet that Tsar has rejected proposal of ministers to resign so that ministry enjoying public confidence can be appointed.
16th September: the Tsar prorogues the Duma.

1916 15th February: the Duma meets. Goremykin is replaced by Stürmer.
September: new wave of strikes gathers momentum and continues throughout October.
30th December: Rasputin is murdered by Yusupov.

1917 19th February: Khabalov is appointed by Tsar to maintain order in Petrograd.
27th February: the Duma meets.
7th March: Tsar leaves Petrograd for army GHQ.
8th March: crowds start to demonstrate against the regime in Petrograd. Workers go on strike. Disorder spreads throughout 9th and 10th March.
11th March: soldiers sent against the crowds defect and join them. Tsar prorogues Duma.
12th March: Duma forms a committee to replace the Tsarist government. The Petrograd Soviet of Workers and Soldiers' Deputies is formed.
13th March: Soviet news sheet *Izvestya* calls on people to take affairs into their own hands.
15th March: Milyukov explains to the crowds the formation of the Provisional Government. Tsar abdicates. 'Order No. 1' of the Soviet puts armed forces in Petrograd under its own command. The Provisional Government forbids the use of force against rioting peasants.
May: units of Petrograd garrison demand the dismissal of Milyukov and Guchkov. Kornilov resigns his command of forces in Petrograd, and Milyukov and Guchkov resign from the government. Kerensky initiates coalition government.
26th June: soldiers refuse to take offensive at their officers' commands and many of them desert. Kornilov demands that the offensive be called off, and is appointed supreme commander-in-chief.
16th July: Bolsheviks organize armed demonstration of sailors and Red Guards. Troops are sent hastily from the front to suppress it.
20th July: Lvov and Kadet ministers resign.
3rd August: Kerensky resigns. Party leaders give him a free hand to form the government.
August: Kerensky holds Moscow State Conference to settle differences between Kornilov and the soviets. It fails.
8th September: Kerensky promises to put Kornilov's demands before the cabinet. Lvov misleads him about Kornilov's intentions, and he denounces Kornilov's 'plot' to overturn the government.
9th September: cavalry corps sent by Kornilov to Petrograd to maintain order is thrown into confusion by news of Kornilov's mutiny.
2nd November: pre-parliament refuses to give Kerensky powers to deal with the Bolsheviks.
7th November: Kerensky flees the Bolsheviks. The ministers of the provisional government are arrested by the Bolsheviks.
(All Russian dates are given in the new – western – style)

The Eastern Front

1914 26th August: battle of Tannenberg starts. Russia is resoundingly defeated by Germany.
5th September: Germans attack the Russians who suffer severe losses in the ensuing battle of the Masurian lakes.
3rd September: Russians take Lemberg. After the battle of Lemberg (8th-12th September) they force Austrians to leave Galicia.

1915 2nd May: Austro-German offensive in Galicia defeats and demoralizes the Russians.
1st July: Austro-German offensive against Russia starts. By the end of September Russia loses Poland, Lithuania, Courland, and a million men.

1916 Brusilov Offensive starts. The Russians fail to exploit their success and lose a million men.

1917 1st July: Brusilov starts offensive in Galicia.
18th July: battle of East Galicia opens. Germans and Austrians drive Russians back.
3rd September: the Germans attack and take Riga.

Russia at War

A Soviet historian shows how the Tsarist government failed to grapple with the immense problems posed by the war, and how the ground was being prepared for the revolution

For Russia 1st August 1914 was the last day of peace. At about seven o'clock in the evening of that day the car of the German ambassador, Count Pourtales, drew up outside the building of the Russian ministry of foreign affairs on Palace Square in St Petersburg. The ambassador entered the building, where he was received by S.D. Sazonov, the minister of foreign affairs, to whom he handed a statement to the effect that Germany considered herself in a state of war with Russia. A day later Germany declared war on France. At dawn on 5th August the British ambassador in St Petersburg, Sir George Buchanan, received a telegram from his government which

read: 'War with Germany—take action.'

It had turned out to be impossible to resolve the tangle of conflicting interests, which had emerged at many different points of the globe, without resorting to war; and so began the most painful and bloody war of any that mankind had known. For the majority of people with little interest in politics the war came as a surprise. After all, what could the illiterate Russian peasant or factory worker know of the actual plans and aims of his own or of other governments? On the face of it one thing was clear: the German Kaiser had attacked Russia, and Russia must be defended. And it never occurred to those who were closer

Nicholas II, 'Autocrat of all the Russias', holds up an icon to be venerated by his troops. But under the strain of the war the traditional veneration for the Tsar was to melt away

to the centre of affairs and understood what was happening to try and explain the real significance of events to the ordinary people. At a ceremonial session of the State Duma everybody, from the monarchists to the representatives of the liberals and of the petit-bourgeois *Trudoviki* (who inclined towards the Socialist Revolutionaries and had until then been in opposition to the government), declared their full support for its actions, thus demonstrating the 'patriotic unity' of the Tsar with the people and of the people with the Tsar. The war suited them, because it promised the acquisition of new territories, markets for their goods, sources of raw materials, and huge profits. The sober voice of a Social Democratic deputy, who protested in the name of the working people against the fratricidal slaughter, was drowned in the general chorus of loyal speeches. The Social Democrats' refusal to vote for the military budget did not alter the situation. It was passed by an overwhelming majority. That is why in the first days of the war the country was swept by a wave of patriotic demonstrations in which the ordinary people also took part.

Only in time and after much suffering did the millions of ordinary people come to feel and understand how utterly unnecessary and senseless was the bloody slaughter into which they had been led by their rulers, that it was not for their native land but for the achievement of entirely selfish ends.

Meanwhile, the news from the front brought little consolation. An attempt by the Russian armies to drive deep into East Prussia ended in failure. They were forced to retreat, having lost 20,000 men dead and 60,000 prisoners. The situation was somewhat better on the south-western section of the front. The Russians had taken Galicia and thus threatened German Silesia, where a considerable part of German industry was concentrated. But they did not succeed in inflicting a final defeat on the Austro-Hungarian army. Towards the end of the year the exhausted troops on both sides went over to the defence. The front also became stabilized in the west, where the Germans had failed to inflict a decisive defeat on France. Hopes of a quick victory on one side or the other turned out to be illusory. All the warring countries found themselves faced with the necessity of waging a long and exhausting war which would require gigantic efforts of every kind.

Russia had entered the war without suffi-

cient preparation. Though a great power, with a population of over 150,000,000 and inexhaustible natural resources, she lagged considerably behind the foremost countries of western Europe in terms of economic and political development. The basic reason for this backwardness was the fact that the country's economic and political system had retained features handed down from the feudal past. The preservation of the inequitable form of land ownership was the principal economic survival of this nature. About 300,000 square miles of land belonged to 30,000 landowners. And a similar area of land was divided among 10,000,000 peasant holdings.

Survivals from the days of serfdom in the agrarian system acted as a brake on the development not only of agriculture but of industry as well. On the eve of the war, in 1913, Russia produced less than 4,000,000 tons of coal, and 9,000,000 tons of oil. Russia continued to be an agrarian country: eighty-six per cent of the total population of the empire was employed on the land, and agricultural output accounted for sixty per cent of the total national product.

The strain of war

Russia had remained an autocratic monarchy. The establishment of the State Duma, which the Tsar had been forced to accept during the first Russian revolution of 1905-07 (Vol. 1, p. 78) had turned out to be only the semblance of a parliament. Even the bourgeoisie, let alone the working people in the population, were debarred from taking part in 'high politics'. The real power in the state was in the hands of the monarchy, which represented primarily the interests of the small and politically conservative class of courtiers and landowners. Civil rights were practically non-existent. All this naturally acted as a brake on the country's advancement and had a negative effect on all aspects of its life. The industrial bourgeoisie, though they disliked the situation in which they found themselves and could not come to terms with the 'extremes' of reactionary policy, still lacked the resolution to enter into open battle with the monarchy, fearing a violent upheaval by the masses, who had already demonstrated their strength in the first Russian revolution. The activity of the bourgeois parties did not go farther than modest parliamentary opposition in the Duma.

The first months of war had already shown that the Russian economy was not capable of satisfying the demands placed on it by the war. It was immediately affected by the call-up into the army which in the course of the war snatched 15,000,000 able-bodied men out of industry and agriculture. The stocks of arms and ammuni-

tion in the war department's stores were quickly used up, and industry could not make good the losses. Attempts on the part of the government to introduce controls over the economy and to mobilize industry for war production brought no substantial results and served in the end only to speed the collapse of the economic structure.

The exhaustion and gradual running down of the economy soon became apparent. Businesses were closed down one after the other. In 1915 alone 573 factories and mills stopped work. Only half the total number of plants were operating throughout the war. Production began to drop in the most important branches of the economy. By 1916 36 of the 151 blast-furnaces which the Russian iron and steel industry had at the beginning of the war had been shut down. The whole of the output of the iron and steel industry went to meet war needs, and this had a disastrous effect on those branches of industry which were not connected with the war. The country began to experience a fuel crisis, and a considerable proportion of the country's industrial plants came to a standstill through lack of fuel.

Transport, that most important element in the economy, was in a state of paralysis. At the beginning of 1916 there were 150,000 truck-loads of goods waiting to be moved on the railways. Five hundred and seventy-five railway stations were no longer capable of handling any goods at all. In the port at Archangel, through which communications were maintained with the Allies, the crates of goods literally sank into the ground under the weight of the fresh deliveries of various kinds of machinery and equipment piled on top of them. As a result of the disorganization of transport, there were food shortages in the towns of central Russia as early as 1915, while at the same time thousands of tons of grain, meat, and butter were rotting away at railway stations in Siberia. Following the February Revolution the former chairman of the council of ministers, B.V.Stürmer, said in his evidence before the special commission of investigation: 'There were so many trucks blocking the lines that we had to tip some of them down the embankments to move the ones that arrived later.'

The country's financial system was also disorganized. The conduct of the war involved enormous expenditure, which the normal pre-war budget was quite unable to cover. Increased taxes and the launching of domestic loans did not make up for the losses. The government had to resort to foreign loans and to increasing the circulation of paper money without adequate gold backing. This soon led to a fall in the value of the rouble, the disorganization of the whole financial system, and to an exceptional rise in the cost of living.

The war also had a very bad effect on agriculture. Large-scale mobilization left the countryside without man-power, while the requisitioning of horses deprived it of draught animals. Even before the war the manufacture of agricultural machinery had not been a very flourishing branch of industry. Now it came to a complete standstill, as did the production of chemical fertilizers. The result of all this was a sharp fall in the output of every kind of agricultural produce. The threat of famine hung over the country.

Rumblings of discontent

As is always the case, it was not the propertied classes but the labouring sections of the population who felt the burden and the deprivations of war soonest and most harshly.

As early as December 1914 prices of manufactured goods had risen by twenty-five per cent compared with 1913, while prices of consumer goods were up by eleven per cent. In 1915 prices of manufactured goods rose by 145 per cent and food prices rose by 122 per cent. Wage increases lagged far behind the catastrophic rise in the cost of living. Between 1914 and 1916 the working man's earnings rose on the average by 100 per cent, while prices of foodstuffs and consumer goods increased by from 300 per cent to 500 per cent.

Millions of ordinary people were bound sooner or later to ask themselves the purpose of all their suffering, the end to which they were sacrificing their lives and their health. They saw, and they knew from their own experience, that the war would bring them nothing but misfortune and privation. The first burst of patriotic excitement quickly passed, to be replaced among the masses of the people by a smouldering discontent with the war and the whole policy of Tsarism. This elemental discontent and ferment among the masses sought an outlet, and it could not fail ultimately to take the form of open revolt against the existing order. The police prepared alarming reports about the growth of the strike movement, which had practically ceased in the first months of the war. A particularly serious wave of strikes swept the country in June 1915, when 80,000 workers downed tools. A strike of textile workers in Kostroma in the same month ended in a bloody clash with the police. In August the blood of the working people was again flowing, when troops fired at a demonstration of textile workers in Ivanovo-Voznesensk. These repressive actions on the part of the authorities evoked indignation among the workers in many towns throughout the country. In September 200,000 working people were on strike.

The Russian revolutionary movement, which had gained great experience in the

ВСЕ ДЛЯ ВОЙНЫ!

ПОДПИСЫВАЙТЕСЬ НА 5½%

ЕННЫЙ ЗАЕМЪ.

SAVE THE WOMEN OF RUSSIA

OU PASS BY THIS PICTURE WITHOUT SENDING HELP TO
EORGINA BUCHANAN, RUSSIAN EMBASSY, CHESHAM PLACE, S.W.1.

struggle against Tsarism during the years 1905-07, began once again, after a brief lull, to gather strength and to become a major factor in public life.

The growth of anti-war feeling was further encouraged by Russia's experiences in the war itself. Russian troops ended the campaign of 1914 in a state of extreme exhaustion. They had suffered great losses. The army had lost half a million men, and the situation with regard to the supply of arms and ammunition was bad. Reinforcements arriving at the fronts remained in their transports because there were no rifles to arm them with. The situation was just as bad when it came to providing the army with uniforms and food. 'We go about in ragged uniforms, and without boots. I have to go practically barefoot, just in my socks,' one soldier wrote home. 'Our infantry is so poor, they march in home-made boots', wrote another. This sort of thing could not fail to have its effect on the army's fighting qualities. Cases of desertion became more frequent; there was a sharp increase in the number of soldiers who deliberately inflicted wounds on themselves so as to avoid military service; and on every side could be heard comments on the futility of the war in which Russia's foolish rulers had involved the country.

Meanwhile, having failed to achieve a victory in the 1914 campaign, the German high command decided to concentrate its efforts on the Russian front, to inflict a defeat on Russia, put her out of the war, and then turn all its forces against Great Britain and France. In the first days of May 1915 German and Austrian troops succeeded in making a breach in the Russian front in Galicia, forced the Russians to withdraw from Galicia and Poland, and seized part of Russian territory. Altogether in the summer campaign of 1915 the Germans achieved several major successes, while the Russians suffered enormous losses, which now totalled, since the beginning of the war, no less than 3,400,000 men. Of these 300,000 were killed and 1,500,000 officers and men were taken prisoner.

Patriotic alarm

These defeats at the front brought about a sudden change in the relations between the bourgeois circles, for which the State Duma provided a platform, and the ruling group at the top. Hopes that the monarchy would be able to organize a victorious war, put an end to revolutionary ferment and, finally, involve the bourgeoisie in the business of governing the country were not borne out. 'Patriotic enthusiasm' gave way to 'patriotic alarm'.

The military machine turned out to be incapable of carrying out the tasks which faced it. Ominous signs of popular revolt became ever more evident. Efforts on the part of bourgeois circles to put their relations with the authorities on a proper business-like footing met with no success.

As they acquired a steadily increasing importance in the country's economy, the Russian bourgeoisie tried to find a place for themselves at the centre of the country's administration and to influence policy in the way they wanted it to go. In the first days of June 1915 a conference was held in Petrograd, as St Petersburg was now called in deference to anti-German feelings, of representatives of trade and industry to consider questions connected with the adaptation of industry to wartime needs. The conference decided to set up war industry committees which were to become one of the political centres of the bourgeoisie, in the same way as had the unions of the *zemstvos* and town councils which had been set up in the summer of 1914. From the very beginning these unions tried to interfere in the business of running the country's economy, but all their efforts were brought to nothing by the government, and were limited to rendering help to the sick and wounded. The leader of the central war industry committee was the energetic and determined A.I.Guchkov, the recognized leader of the upper bourgeoisie and one of the organizers of the Octobrist Party (the party of rich bourgeoisie and landowners formed in October 1905 which supported the Tsardom).

One of the principal demands put forward by the bourgeois community at the Petrograd conference was that the State Duma should be called into session. Since the beginning of the war the Duma had met on only two occasions – in August 1914, in connection with the outbreak of war, and in February 1915, for the formal approval of the budget. This did not suit the bourgeoisie in the least, because it regarded the Duma as the one institution able to exert pressure on the government.

'The State Duma,' said P.N.Milyukov, leader of the Kadet Party (Constitutional Democrats), at one of its meetings, 'is the only organizational centre of the national mind and will, the only institution which is capable of standing up to the bureaucracy.'

Insistent demands that the Duma should be summoned went along with a further demand that the government itself should be re-formed. The liberal bourgeoisie, in the form of the Kadet Party, was not prepared at that time to announce as part of its programme the demand for a 'responsible ministry', since it considered it possible to make do with changes in the membership of the council of ministers. After all, to enter into open battle with the authorities would have meant appealing to the masses and giving rein to the forces of revolution, which the bourgeoisie feared

no less than reaction. The frequent introduction of new people into the cabinet, 'to ensure the correct organization of the home front, the maintenance of internal peace in the country, and close collaboration between the government and the public', was put forward as a condition for summoning the Duma and one that would ensure that it worked effectively.

Defeats at the front and the growth of bourgeois opposition forced Nicholas II to make certain concessions. A group of people was formed within the council of ministers itself who considered it necessary to pay more attention to 'public opinion' and to adopt a more moderate policy towards the 'public'. It became ever more clear that the council of ministers could not, in its original composition, meet the Duma without coming into sharp conflict with it.

N.A.Maklakov, the minister for internal affairs, was the first to be dismissed. He was succeeded by Prince N.V.Shcherbatov, a member of the State Council, whom the liberal press described as 'a conservative in the European sense of the word', who respected the law and was opposed to any 'extremes'. However restrained were the opinions of the new minister, the departure of Maklakov gave great satisfaction to the middle classes who considered him, together with the war minister V.A.Sukhomlinov, one of the men principally responsible for all the troubles and misfortunes besetting Russia. Sukhomlinov, who had been in charge of the war department since 1909, was next to go after Maklakov. He was replaced by General A.A.Polivanov.

The campaign against Sukhomlinov had begun in the spring of 1915 when Russian troops were swept out of Galicia. His opponents dug up everything they could find against the minister: his compromising marriage with the wife of a Kiev landowner, Butovich, his close relations with a very doubtful character called Altschuller, and his connexion with the German spy Myasoyedov, who was hanged in the winter of 1915. The word 'treachery' was heard ever more frequently in connection with the war minister. One way or another Sukhomlinov had to be got rid of. As for Polivanov, it would have been difficult to think of a better sop to throw to the Duma.

Even when he had been assistant to the war minister, from 1908 to 1912, Polivanov had won popularity for himself in the Duma through his ability to get along with the bourgeoisie, and had earned the reputation of being a 'leftist' in bureaucratic circles. The Tsar had no special liking for the man, but force of circumstances obliged him to agree to his appointment.

Two others to be dismissed were I.G. Shcheglovitov, the minister of justice, and V.K.Sabler, chief procurator of the Holy Synod (head of the church council). The former was replaced by A.A.Khvostov and the latter by A.D.Samarin, both completely conservative in their views but lacking the regard of the empress Alexandra Fedorovna and Rasputin, which was in itself an excellent recommendation in the eyes of the bourgeoisie. These appointments were the only changes which were made in the composition of the government on the eve of the new session of the Duma. The council of ministers was still headed by the very elderly I.L.Goremykin, who had long since earned himself the reputation of being an extreme reactionary and a persecutor of any kind of liberalism. The danger of a conflict between the 're-formed' government and the bourgeoisie had not been removed. This was fully confirmed by the events which followed.

The Duma meets again
It was on 1st August 1915, the first anniversary of the outbreak of war, that the State Duma met again. And, while the right-wing groups, representing the landowners, continued as before to give the government their unconditional support, the bourgeois section of the Duma made no attempt to conceal its dissatisfaction. The bourgeoisie was not interested in bringing about a radical change in the policy of the Tsarist regime. Their only concern was to introduce into the government people enjoying the unquestioned confidence of the middle classes, and able to represent their interests in it. A substantial majority of the factions in the Duma united around the slogan of 'a ministry of confidence'. The liberal Moscow newspaper *Morning Russia* even published a commentary under the heading

'A Cabinet of Defence' in which it gave the possible composition of a government which would suit the bourgeoisie. M.V. Rodzyanko, the Octobrist and chairman of the Duma, was named as premier, another Octobrist, A.I.Guchkov, was named as minister for internal affairs, and the Kadet P.N.Milyukov was named as minister for foreign affairs.

On 22nd August negotiations between the leaders of the factions in the Duma concluded, with the signature of a formal agreement among them. In this way a 'Progressive Bloc' came into being in the Duma—an organization which was fated to become the political centre of the whole bourgeois opposition. Many of the twenty-five members of its bureau—P.N.Milyukov, A.I.Shingarev, N.V.Nekrasov, V.N.Lvov, I.V.Godnev, and others later became members of the Provisional Government. Six of the factions in the Duma, from the Kadets to the 'progressive' nationalists—236 of the 442 deputies—entered the Bloc. Those who remained outside it were, on the right, the extreme right wing and the nationalists, and, on the left, the Social Democrats and the Mensheviks, and the Socialist Revolutionaries. The Socialist Revolutionaries, though they did not formally enter the Bloc, always voted with it and supported its policies.

As for the Bloc's programme, its central point was the demand for the formation of a 'government of confidence'. The remaining points in it were very modest: changes in the personnel of local administration, a partial amnesty for religious and political offences, some initial steps towards removing the restrictions placed on Jews, the revival of trade-union activities, and so forth. There was nothing in it likely to undermine the power of the Tsar. The programme was not aimed at bringing about a breach with Tsarism, but at achieving agreement with it on the basis of liberal reforms and the organization of a victorious war with Germany. The central idea in the minds of the leaders of the Bloc was to bring about such a state of affairs in the country as would exclude the very possibility of a revolutionary outburst, which appeared to them as equivalent to utter chaos and anarchy. But even this

Victims of the war — Russian soldiers taken prisoner with their weapons near Lwów. 1,500,000 officers and men were taken prisoner during the terrible summer campaign of 1915. Heavy losses, added to hardships at home, increased the bitter resentment of the Russian people at the war and the foolish rulers who had involved them in it

extremely modest programme was too much for the monarchy. The formation in the Duma of a stable majority in opposition would put an end to any possibility of manoeuvring between the extreme flanks of the bourgeois landowning parties as the ruling group at the top had done since the first Russian revolution. Less than a month passed before the Tsar signed a decree dissolving the Duma. 'They brushed aside the hand that was offered them,' P.N.Milyukov recalled later. 'The conflict between the monarchy on the one hand and the representatives of the people and society on the other became an open breach.'

The leader of the opposition was obviously exaggerating when he said that what happened in September marked the end of efforts to find a compromise solution. Even before the final breach came about the bourgeoisie had more than once offered its hand to the government in the hope of arriving at a solution acceptable to both sides. But so far the monarchy had been quite unyielding. The sudden swing of policy away from partial concessions to reaction was not limited simply to the dissolution of the Duma. Before that Nicholas II had dismissed the Grand Duke Nikolay Nikolayevich from the post of supreme commander-in-chief and put himself in his place. It was quite clear that this change was in no way dictated by military considerations. Nicholas was not a military man and could be no more than a decorative figurehead. His assumption of the post of 'supremo' was unquestionably a political move, inspired by the Empress and Rasputin. Neither the objections of his ministers nor protests from members of the Tsar's family could make him alter his decision. The pro-German group led by the Empress Alexandra Fedorovna did its best to divert Nicholas's attention from domestic affairs, to put an end to the insignificant concessions being made to society, and to set course towards a separate peace with Germany.

This time it turned out to be not so difficult to deal with the bourgeois opposition. The concluding session of the Duma lasted just three minutes. The deputies listened in deathly silence to the words of the imperial decree pronouncing their dissolution, shouted a loyal 'hurrah', and dispersed without a single word of protest. They had too great a fear of the 'street', of any movement on the part of the masses, to embark on any open opposition to the whole system of government which had led the country to disaster.

Months passed. There were no signs of an end to the war, and the situation in the country became ever more tense. At the beginning of 1916 the strike movement flared up again on an even greater scale.

Every year the working people of Russia went on strike in memory of those who died in the 'Bloody Sunday' of 22nd January 1905. On this occasion the traditional January strike assumed enormous proportions. In Petrograd alone at least 100,000 people went on strike. Neither police arrests nor the use of the army to guard the largest factories brought the movement to an end. The ferment of revolution spread even into the army. The people of the villages, crushed by the excessive requisitions, also began to raise their voice. An enormous quantity of inflammatory material was piling up, ready to burst into flame at any moment. The landowners and farmers began to be haunted by the memory of the things that had happened to them in 1905.

Government of tumblers

The Tsar and his government were helpless in the face of the approaching catastrophe. They were unable to avert either the economic crisis or the advance of the revolutionary movement. In their search for a solution the Tsar and those close to him had recourse to the dismissal of persons holding major posts in the government, and this only threw into relief the crisis among the men at the top, who had lost the capacity to assess the situation in a realistic and sober manner.

I.L.Goremykin, the prime minister, that faithful defender of the foundations of the monarchy, was the first to lose his seat in the government. It was the same story as in the summer of 1915. There was no question of any real change of policy in the direction of 'liberalization' but only of giving the Duma an opportunity to work off its anger on those who were dismissed. Goremykin's place was taken by the sixty-eight-year-old B.V.Stürmer, whose political reputation left no doubt that there was no reason to expect any changes for the better. Moreover, Stürmer's pro-German sentiments were widely known, which made it seem not unreasonable to regard his appointment as evidence of the Tsar's desire to start negotiations for a separate peace with Germany. The news was received with unconcealed alarm by the French and British ambassadors. Sir George Buchanan wrote: 'Possessed of only a second-class mind, having no experience of statesmanship, concerned exclusively with his own personal interests, and distinguished by his capacity to flatter and his extreme ambition, he owed his new appointment to the fact that he was a friend of Rasputin and enjoyed the support of the crowd of intriguers around the empress.'

There is a vast literature in existence about Rasputin. Innumerable legends have grown up around the name of that semi-literate peasant from Tobolsk who became

the uncrowned ruler of Russia. Maybe not everything in them is true, but there can be no question about the tremendous influence which 'our friend', as the Tsarina called him, exerted on the country's policy. There can also be no doubt but that the emergence of Rasputin and all that Rasputin meant became possible only at a time when the whole system of autocracy was in decline and in a state of decomposition and decay.

Goremykin's replacement by Stürmer was not the end of the business. Sazonov, the minister for foreign affairs, and Polivanov, the war minister, were retired soon afterwards — both men with whom the bourgeoisie had had great hopes of collaborating. A real game of 'ministerial leap-frog' now began. Ministers were replaced one after the other. Two and a half years of war saw the removal of four prime ministers, six ministers of internal affairs, three war ministers, and three foreign ministers, among others. No wonder the council of ministers came to be known as the 'government of tumblers'.

The summer of 1916 appeared to bring some easing of the situation. There was some improvement in the way things were going at the front. Thanks to the energetic measures taken by General A.A.Brusilov, (Vol. 5, p. 577), the commander of the south-western front, Russian troops had not only succeeded in breaching the Austro-German front in the Lutsk region, but also in turning the break-through into a strategic advance which led to the rout of the Austro-Hungarian army. The advance on the south-western front forced the Germans to transfer dozens of reserve divisions to the east and halt their attacks on Verdun. The Austrians were obliged, in their turn, to bring their advance in Italy to a halt. But, in the absence of support from the other fronts, the Russian advance did not affect the outcome of the war. Towards the end of the summer the armies had reverted again to trench warfare.

The tension within the country also appeared to have relaxed. There was some reduction in the wave of strikes by the proletariat, which raised hopes that the revolutionary movement would be suppressed. It is true that a spontaneous uprising broke out in the south-eastern regions of the country — in Kazakhstan and Central Asia — among the local population, which had been reduced to a state of desperation, but the government did not at first attach serious importance to it. The bourgeois opposition also appeared to have quietened down. In any case the so-called 'voluntary' organizations set up to manage wartime supplies and industry, who had formed the core of bourgeois opposition, now worked hard to establish contact with government circles. ▷682

Left: A homeless beggar. Above: Barge-haulers on the banks of the Volga, unaffected by industrialization. The war increased the burden that fell on Russia's peasants, born to hard labour and deprivation

The Subjects of the Tsar

In 1914 Russian society and institutions still bore the stamp of her feudal past. The Tsar, supported by a highly privileged nobility and church, ruled absolutely over a huge people who were mostly primitive peasants. But industrialization was shaking the traditional structure of 'Holy Mother Russia'. To factory workers socialism promised power as the reward for organization. Those who had made money through industry wanted power to correspond with their wealth. And Russia's long-suffering peasants had been driven to the point of rebellion by their misery.

Right: Figure of 'Holy Mother Russia' on a Russian sticker protesting against German atrocities. Below: Workers and peasants — raw material of revolution. They are at a sale of boots in a provincial market

Herman Axelbank

Novosti

Novosti

Novosti

Left: The world of toil: a quarryman breaking stones. **Above:** The world of privilege: ministers of the imperial court in a procession commemorating the 300th anniversary of the Romanov dynasty, 1913

Above: Leader of the Holy Synod, the high council of the Russian Orthodox Church. The Tsardom and the church were linked. The first Tsars saw themselves as heirs of Orthodox Byzantium. **Right:** Music at a peasant fair. **Below:** Beginnings of industry: a carrying ramp at a gold mine

Disaster strikes

But all this was no more than a passing, and to a large extent illusory, period of calm. By the end of 1916 the catastrophic situation in which Russia found herself became fully apparent. Disaster struck every single branch of the economy. Industry, transport, finance, and agriculture were all in a state of complete collapse. One of the signs of the general economic disorganization was the severe food crisis which broke out in the autumn of 1916.

The grave economic situation, the severe shortage of foodstuffs, and the government's repressive measures led the workers to embark on a new wave of strikes on a larger scale than anything that had gone before.

In September 1916 the strike movement had not involved more than 50,000 working people. But in October 1916 nearly 200,000 people were on strike. No less than 1,542 strikes were recorded in the course of 1916, involving more than 1,000,000 workers— that is, roughly twice as many as in the previous year, 1915. The strikes assumed an ever larger scale and the strikers' demands became ever more insistent, with workers being drawn into the movement from the remoter districts as well as from the industrial centres. It was not, however, simply that the strike movement became a real mass movement, embracing the whole country; in the final months of 1916 it took on a clearly defined political colouring. What had been a struggle for the satisfaction of limited economic demands became a struggle against the existing system of monarchic rule, against the war and those who had brought it on the people.

The Bolshevik section of the Russian Social Democratic Party played a great part in giving this spontaneous movement an organized and purposeful character. The Bolshevik party had close links with the more advanced, most intelligent, and most active part of the working class, and it was in effect the only one of the socialist parties to have fought consistently and uncompromisingly against the war and against Tsarism. It regarded revolution and a complete break with the domestic and foreign policy of Tsarism as the only way to save the country from ruin.

But the party had to work in unbelievably difficult conditions. As far back as November 1914 the five Bolshevik deputies to the State Duma had been arrested and exiled to Siberia, and this meant the loss of a most important legal centre and platform from which the party could put forward its views. It therefore had to operate in conditions of complete secrecy. But despite all the difficulties and dangers besetting the Bolsheviks at every step, their revolutionary anti-war activity was not halted. It is sufficient to say that, from the beginning

General Sukhomlinov (left) a minister of war so corrupt that he was suspected of treason. He was tried and found guilty of having neglected the supply of munitions before the war

of the war and up to the February Revolution, local branches of the party put out more than 600 leaflets totalling around 2,000,000 copies. They were published in eighty towns and distributed throughout the country. In Petrograd, Moscow, Riga, Kharkov, and several other towns the Bolsheviks even succeeded in publishing illegal newspapers, and although these publications were usually soon shut down by the police, they did their job of educating the people and exposing the truth about the war. Bolshevik slogans became steadily more popular with the masses who were exhausted by the intolerable burden of war.

Despite the obstacles to communication put up by the censor, news of the tense situation at home, and of the growth of the revolutionary mood and revolutionary ferment got through to the front. Indignation grew in the army at the actions of the government and the Tsar in bringing the country to disaster. Instead of being an instrument for pacifying and suppressing the emancipation movement, the army

became a part of the revolutionary people, ready for an assault on a regime which had outlived its day.

'We shall be crushed'

The ruling and owning classes found themselves faced with an inexorably approaching revolutionary explosion. Both the supporters of the Tsarist system and the opposition-minded bourgeoisie started feverishly to look for a way out of the crisis. The state in which the ruling group at the top found themselves towards the end of 1916 can be described in one word— isolation. They were isolated even from those classes and social groups whose interests they had represented and defended for many long years. Even the landowners, that most conservative of all the classes in Russian society, backed away from the group of intriguers around the throne who were all heavily under the baleful influence of Rasputin. Significantly, even V.M.Purishkevich, one of the most violent reactionaries and an opponent of any kind of freedom, who hated the liberals hardly less than he did the revolutionaries, appealed publicly for the Tsar's attention to be drawn to the 'terrible reality' and for Russia to be 'rid of Rasputin and supporters of Rasputin, both big and small'. The landowners wanted to preserve the monarchy, but not in the person of the indecisive and weak-willed Nicholas II, who was surrounded by rogues and careerists and who 'decided' on policies at the dictation of his wife and the black-bearded 'monk' Rasputin. In such circumstances there remained only one thing for the intriguers at the court to do: to carry the policy of repression to the very extreme and at the same time to conclude a separate peace with Germany as quickly as possible and, with the help of their old friend 'Willy', Wilhelm II of Germany, to put an end once and for all to both the 'revolutionary infection' and the liberals. This is the path on which the clique at the court decided. From autumn 1916 efforts to get talks going with the German government were transferred to the realm of practical politics.

The possibility of such a solution to the situation in no way suited the Russian bourgeoisie, for it would only prevent them from achieving the objectives at which they were aiming in the war, and they feared the political consequences of such a step for the country's internal order. The class which dominated the country economically could not, and certainly did not want to, find itself cut off from the centre of power. On this issue the bourgeoisie had a large and very important account to settle with the monarchy, and to achieve this long-cherished aim they were ready to resort to anything—anything, that is, except an appeal to the masses.

Fear of the masses, the fear of revolution, pushed the bourgeois opposition into making sharp attacks on a government which was incapable of dealing with revolution. But that same fear forced them at the same time to refuse to enter into conflict with the government. They feared that harsh words spoken in the State Duma might serve as a spark to start the conflagration which would destroy the throne, the government, and the bourgeoisie itself. It was V.V. Shulgin, one of the leaders of the Progressive Bloc, who put the situation remarkably neatly when he said: 'The crowd is pushing us in the back. . . . We are being pushed and we have to move, though we resist as far as the strength lies in us, but all the same we must move. . . . If we stop moving we shall be crushed, the crowd will break through and rush for that thing which we are trying to preserve—to preserve, despite all our protests, complaints, and reproaches—and that thing is power.'

The hopelessness of the situation became more apparent every day. Nicholas remained deaf to appeals by members of the Duma and the more reasonable of his officials. Neither he nor the clique of maniacs grouped so tightly around him would retreat a single step from the reactionary course they had set in domestic affairs and insisted on working for the conclusion of a separate peace with Germany. But outside the palace, in the working-class districts, the tide of popular discontent was rising and was ready at any moment to reach the flood. It was in these conditions that the bourgeoisie, having lost faith in the possibility of 'persuading' the monarchy to make concessions, embarked on the preparation of a palace revolution. The idea of such a step had been broached some time previously. One evening in the autumn of 1915 when one of the usual attempts to come to an agreement with the government had failed, a member of the Bloc said 'I am relying on 23rd March'. More than one hundred years before, on 23rd March 1801, conspirators had murdered Paul I and enthroned a new emperor. This was the recollection of men who could not and would not fight the Tsarist regime together with and at the head of the people. But at that time it was just talk.

In the autumn of 1916, however, such a solution turned out to be the only one possible. Leaders of the Progressive Bloc and of the bourgeois voluntary organizations joined the circle of conspirators. Generals Krymov, Denikin, Ruzsky, and others were also drawn into the affair. According to A.I.Guchkov, one of the active participants in the plot, it was proposed to seize the imperial train between GHQ and Tsarskoye Selo with the help of reliable guards' units, to force Nicholas to abdicate, then with the same forces to arrest the government in Petrograd, and then to announce what had taken place. If the Tsar refused to sign the abdication, his 'physical removal' would have to be carried out, as Denikin wrote later. Those were the plans and the immediate future would show how practicable they were.

The murder of Rasputin

On the frosty night of 30th December one more event occurred which was an interesting and not insignificant page in the historical drama which unfolded towards the end of 1916. On that night Grigory Rasputin was murdered in Prince Felix Yusupov's private residence in Petrograd by a small group of conspirators, Yusupov himself, Grand Duke Dmitry Pavlovich, and the deputy V.M.Purishkevich. Although the direct participants in the murder were few, behind them stood a wide circle of men interested in the elimination of the all-powerful favourite of the imperial couple.

The idea of removing Rasputin and the Empress from affairs had been debated in aristocratic circles from the beginning of 1916, and towards the autumn of 1916 the idea began to assume its final form.

After Rasputin's murder the wife of the chairman of the Duma, Rodzyanko, wrote to Princess Yusupova: 'I am told that there are 106 persons under suspicion . . .' It was not, however, only the aristocracy, but members of the Duma too who were drawn into the conspiracy against the 'monk'. Quite apart from Purishkevich, a direct part was played in the preparations for the murder by V.A.Maklakov, a prominent member of the Kadet Party and brother of the former minister for internal affairs. It was he who gave the conspirators the potassium cynanide which they put in the food and into the madeira with which Rasputin was to be 'entertained'. It was he also who gave Felix Yusupov 'just in case' a rubber truncheon, which, incidentally, came in useful. A few days before the murder Purishkevich told his friend V.V.Shulgin about what was being planned. Other members of the Duma must also have known about it.

The drama which took place in the Yusupov mansion became public knowledge on the following day, when the body was hauled out of the Moyka into which it had been thrown. The Empress was beside herself and demanded severe punishment for the murderers. But Nicholas did not care to go very far, since it was found that members of the imperial household were involved in the affair. The Grand Duke Dmitry Pavlovich was exiled to Persia, Felix Yusupov was banished to his own estate in the Kursk *guberniya*, and Purishkevich, without any let or hindrance, got into his own hospital train and set off for the front. The Grand Duke Nikolay Mikhaylovich, who was also exiled as one of the people mixed up in the affair, wrote in his diary: 'Alexandra Fedorovna is triumphant, but I wonder if the wretched woman will remain in power very long.'

The murder of Rasputin, which was part of the general conspiracy against Nicholas II, was an attempt to save the monarchy in the 'old Russian way', and, as V.Shulgin very shrewdly pointed out, it was a 'profoundly monarchistic act'. But in itself it could change nothing and save nothing. The whole Rasputin affair had sunk roots deep into every part of the organism of the state. As though in reply to the murder, there followed a further series of reshuffles in the government. The position of chairman of the council of ministers was taken by the last premier of a Tsarist government, the weak-willed and decrepit Prince N.D.Golitsyn. The Romanov empire was rushing headlong downhill. It was the beginning of 1917, a year of revolution. *(Translation)*

Above: Water-tower destroyed by Russians retreating through Lithuania, 1915. **Left:** Wounded Russian soldiers carted into Lwów. The Tsar's ministers failed to equip his army for modern war

The Soldiers of the Tsar

Fifteen million peasants· were summoned to fight for the glory of the Tsar and Holy Mother Russia. The army showed in microcosm the weaknesses of Nicholas II's regime. The high command, responsible only to an ineffectual monarch, were negligent in organizing equipment and supplies. A rigid caste system separated the officers from the masses they commanded. As this unwieldy army was pushed back from Galicia (Austrian Poland) through Russian Poland and Lithuania, the peasants went hungry, the soldiers died in their thousands and the Tsar lost his throne

Below: Nicholas II with his staff. In 1915 Nicholas assumed supreme command of the forces — a symbolic assertion of autocracy irrelevant to the needs of his army. **Bottom:** German troops enter the blackened streets of a smoking Russian town. **Right:** After an attack — troops relax in a captured German trench

Novosti

Above left: *Grim conditions for the wounded. Russian officers visit a field hospital.* **Above:** *German gas attack on Russian trenches. German equipment and weapons were incomparably more sophisticated than those of the Russians.* **Left:** *French poster: 'On enemy territory Russian prisoners are dying of hunger'*

SUR LA TERRE ENNEMIE
LES PRISONNIERS RUSSES
MEURENT DE FAIM

Przemysl jest
wrenkach naszych
Miesiancu Maja złapanych 300000 Rusków
1000 Officerów.

Above: *Placard displayed by Germans to the Poles of Galicia: 'Przemysl is in our hands. We captured 1,000 Russian officers and 300,000 men in May.'* **Right:** *Bridge blown up by Russians in retreat.* **Below:** *Russian troops assembled to leave Czernowitz, the capital of Bukovina, which the Russians had to evacuate in July 1917*

'The Last Naval Hope of Russia. The Baltic Fleet preparing for Sea', painted by J.M.Price. But, like the army, the navy was disaffected. Sailors were to take a leading part in the later stages of the revolution

Rasputin and the 'Dark Forces'

While the foundations of the Russian state were being shaken by the war, a crisis was developing at the top—a crisis which was symbolized by and embodied in the career of one of the most extraordinary men ever to have swayed a nation's destinies

The Russia which entered the First World War in 1914 was a strange mixture of contradictions. The contemporary Western picture was of the 'steamroller', of the mass of Russian peasants, dragged from the ignorance and poverty of backward agrarian conditions to form the six million strong army which Russia was able to mobilize by the first winter of the war. These peasants were both Russia's strength and her fatal weakness.

Less known to the outside world was the new industrial and urban Russia which had grown fast in the last twenty or thirty years before the war, a Russia of coal, steel, and railways, of industrialists and financiers, of lawyers, doctors, and professors, and from 1905, of political parties, professional associations, and even trade unions. Tsarist Russia did not, as is often thought, 'decay' or 'decline': on the contrary, in its last years, it expanded and blossomed in a variety of conflicting forms which imposed an ultimately fatal strain on its structure.

The new Russia could find no place in traditional Tsarist society. Already in 1905 the peasants, urban workers, professional intelligentsia, and even part of the nobility, in uncertain alliance, had shaken the autocracy and compelled it to concede the establishment of a national parliament, the Duma (Vol. 1, p. 78). This body represented, however imperfectly, all classes of the nation, but gave the predominant voice to landowners and the wealthier urban elements. The aim of its establishment was to provide a forum in which the government could work with the more influential sections of Russian society to carry out the reforms which, during the 1905 revolution, were widely felt to be necessary. But as the revolution faded into the past the sense of urgency excited by this task weakened, and the old habits of autocracy reasserted themselves, strengthened by the fear of renewed social violence, by the memory of the Moscow barricades and of rural arson, lynchings, and murders. On the right wing of the Duma, and in the upper house, the State Council, strong groups emerged, on which the government came increasingly to rely

Far left: 'The Russian Royal Family'— the Tsar and Tsarina in the arms of their presiding evil genius—an irreverent Russian cartoon. Above left: Rasputin and his court followers—women found 'spiritual purification' through sexual intercourse with him. Left: 'The simple Russian peasant' with two other advisers of the Tsar

for its majority, groups who were concerned to emasculate or indefinitely delay reforms which they feared might open the flood-gates of revolution. This process led among the intelligentsia and on the left wing of the Duma to growing disillusionment with political action and to a helpless and even irresponsible bitterness.

It is against this background of political stagnation and embitterment that we must view the emergence of the figure who for many historians has exemplified the ultimate decadence of Tsarism. Grigory Rasputin was a peasant from the village of Pokrovskoye in western Siberia. To describe him as a monk or a priest would be misleading, for he had no connexion with any organized church: yet he had gained from his early years of lonely wandering round Russia, the Balkans, and the Middle East a certain faith in himself as a spiritual healer, and had evolved for himself a doctrine of redemption through sin which has deep roots in Russian, and especially sectarian Russian, religious thought. When he first appeared in St Petersburg in 1903, his sturdy, unkempt peasant figure and his independent teaching and manner won him adherents at court (where traditionally mystical religions had been sought as a panacea for insoluble social ills).

A simple Russian peasant

There were special reasons why he should have attracted the attention of the imperial couple. Their long awaited male heir, the Tsarevich Alexey, had inherited haemophilia, and Rasputin's powerful, soothing personality proved able to staunch the painful and dangerous internal bleeding which characterizes this disease. In this way he won the devotion of the Empress, whose concern for her son had made her a lonely and hysterical woman. But there was more to the attachment than this. In the years of disillusionment, especially from 1911 onwards, which followed the failure of government and Duma to work constructively together, both Emperor and Empress came to see in Rasputin a representative of the simple Russian peasant folk, from whom, they felt aggrievedly, the Duma and the bureaucracy had separated them. To Dedyulin, palace commandant, who once expressed doubts about Rasputin's character, Nicholas replied: 'He is just a good, religious, simple-minded Russian. When in trouble or assailed by doubts I like to have a talk with him, and invariably feel at peace with myself afterwards.' Rasputin took care to cultivate his peasant image, going so far as to take part at court banquets unwashed

The Tsarina and her son, Alexey. Rasputin owed his power over her — and in Russia — to his ability to soothe the pain haemophilia caused her beloved son

and plunging filthy hands into the soup tureen. Or he would talk to the imperial couple about the sufferings of the peasants and the measures which might be taken to alleviate them. In the uncertainty of the last years, the imperial couple liked to look on Rasputin as their link with the Russian people, and regarded the men of the Duma, the *zemstvos*, and the war-time voluntary organizations as selfish intriguers.

Rasputin was thus not only a symptom of the imperial couple's estrangement from the changing politics of contemporary Russia, he increased it. His arrogant behaviour in society, his religious unorthodoxy, and above all his overt sexual licence alienated many. Some of the national newspapers, in particular *Golos Moskvy (The Voice of Moscow)*, mouthpiece of Guchkov, leader of the moderate liberal Octobrist Party in the Duma, began to publish regular reports of Rasputin's movements, written in an insinuating tone, as well as the 'confessions' of women who had sought spiritual purification through sexual intercourse with him. Early in 1912 a leading article appeared in *Golos Moskvy*, in which Novoselov, a specialist on religious sects, denounced Rasputin as a member of the *Khlysty* (a sect which practised flagellation as a means of erotic stimulation and of communion with God). This issue of the paper was confiscated, but Guchkov raised the question of Rasputin in the Duma, and circulated copies of letters from Rasputin to the Empress, containing expressions which might be interpreted to indicate sexual intimacy between them. *Golos Moskvy* even issued, in its illustrated supplement, a short biography of Rasputin, which ended: 'Representing himself as a saint, this blackguard and erotomaniac practises unbelievable debauchery in the village of Pokrovskoye, together with local girls, or with ladies who

come to him for "instruction". Recently, Grigory Rasputin has settled in St Petersburg, where he has found himself powerful patrons and, more especially, patronesses. Here rumour has it that he has instituted the same "good works" as in his native village.'

This extract gives a good picture of the way in which liberal politicians vented their frustration through poisonous innuendo, extending even to the imperial family, and thus contributed to the atmosphere of suspicion and personal enmity in which politics were conducted in the last years of the empire.

Watchful unity

The outbreak of war restored temporary unity and a sense of common purpose. The Duma meekly accepted an indefinite prorogation, and the opposition parties declared their complete solidarity with the war effort. The *zemstvos* and town councils hastened to complement the government's war organization, first in the relief of the wounded and sick, and then increasingly in transport and supply. The government gave legal status to the body *(Zemgor)* which co-ordinated their work, and allocated treasury grants to it.

This unity and co-operation was, however, watchful and doubting. Russia's first major defeats, those of the spring and summer of 1915, when most of Poland and Galicia was lost, almost shattered it. Like all the combatant states, the Russian government had under-estimated the length and complexity of the war, with the result that, at an early stage, shortages of ammunition and supplies became apparent. *Zemgor* increasingly exceeded its functions in order to meet the most elementary needs of the army and the population. The civil and military branches of government were at loggerheads, and no supreme directing institution, except the Emperor, existed to co-ordinate their plans. The council of ministers, with its functions usurped on the one side by *Zemgor,* and on the other by the military command, felt powerless and isolated; at one of its meetings, Shcherbatov, minister of the interior, exclaimed with a sudden acute and anguished sense of reality: 'A government which has the confidence neither of the Emperor, nor of the army, nor of the towns, nor of the *zemstvos,* nor of the nobles, nor of the merchants, nor of the workers — not only cannot function, it cannot even exist! It's sheer absurdity. We're sitting here like a bunch of Don Quixotes!'

Some steps were taken to increase the effective co-operation of army, government, and society in the fields of industrial production and supplies. The unpopular war minister, Sukhomlinov, was replaced by Polivanov, who had worked

Prince Yusupov. 'What remained, therefore, to save the Tsar and Russia from that evil genius? . . . There is only one way — to destroy that criminal "holy man" '

with Guchkov and the Octobrists in the past over military questions. But the Duma parties wanted to go much farther and gain some ministerial posts for themselves at this time of national emergency. Milyukov, leader of the radical liberal Kadet (Constitutional Democratic) Party, and the most determined and subtle exponent of purely parliamentary forms of struggle, gathered a bloc of the moderate parties. In spite of the considerable political differences between them, they united, under the name of Progressive Bloc, on a programme of moderate reform and the demand for a ministry enjoying public confidence. On 8th September 1915 this programme came before the council of ministers, most of whom were agreed that the reform proposals were largely sensible. But the premier, Goremykin, aged and inert, though single-mindedly devoted to the autocratic ideal, was unwilling to meet members of the Bloc and insisted that the appointment of a future cabinet rested with the Emperor alone. Four ministers, led by Krivoshein, minister of agriculture, nevertheless consulted with leaders of the Bloc and as a result recommended the collective resignation of the cabinet to make way for a ministry enjoying public confidence. Goremykin reluctantly conveyed the proposal to the Emperor, who rejected it and ordered instead that the Duma be prorogued once more. Goremykin, relieved, reported the Emperor's decision to the cabinet on 15th September, remarking privately to the cabinet secretary: 'Let them abuse and slander me — I'm already old and have not long to live. But as long as I live, I shall fight for the inviolability of the Tsar's power. Russia's strength lies in autocracy alone. Without it there will be such chaos that everything will be lost.' The meeting was a stormy one: Polivanov and Krivoshein were embittered and little

The Tsar and his hated clique of advisers (Russian cartoon, 1916). Rasputin in particular made the Tsar the object of bitter personal enmities and contempt

short of offensive, while Sazonov, the temperamental foreign minister, refused to give Goremykin his hand at the end and staggered out shouting 'I refuse to shake hands with that senile idiot — *il est fou, ce vieillard!*'

The Emperor refused to receive petitions from the Duma or *Zemgor,* and with that any serious effort at conciliation between the monarchy and these social organizations came to an end. The Emperor had initiated plans of his own for meeting the crisis. Recognizing it correctly as a crisis of confidence between the monarchy and the various sections of his people, he attempted to solve it in the manner which background and upbringing suggested to him: by a re-affirmation of his autocratic power. On 6th September he announced that he was assuming personal supreme command of the armed forces. In this decision he was encouraged by his wife, who constantly urged him to be more authoritarian, and by Rasputin, whose views on government were identical with Goremykin's. But more than this, the traditions of autocratic imperial Russia, with which Nicholas was himself deeply imbued, had formed in his mind a paternalist vision of social cohesion, in which national unity was a matter of unquestioning obedience, of immaculate military reviews, of popular acclamations, and of religious ceremonies held in common (all of which he lovingly records in his diary and letters). Beside these things the demands of *zemstvo* organizations, political parties and recalcitrant ministers were no more than the tiresome intrigues of ambitious and petty troublemakers.

From August 1915, therefore, Nicholas asserted more consistently his personal rule. The situation, however, was much too complex for such a drastically simple solution, and the only result was that he

became more and more isolated from men with a sense of responsibility and reality, and fell more exclusively under the influence of his beloved and unhappy wife, of her 'saviour', Rasputin, and of the sycophants who were prepared to minister to their common delusions.

The Duma parties and the social organizations were helpless. On the one hand, they felt the monarch's policy was leading to certain military defeat and probably revolution; and on the other, they were afraid to raise their hands against the monarch for fear of precipitating a mass revolution which they felt they had no means to control. They therefore vacillated between half-hearted co-operation and incipient conspiracy. Russian politics again became a murky world of suspicion and plotting, made the more sinister by the dual threat of national defeat and social revolution.

'Dark forces'
This was the world in which the legend of the 'dark forces' was born. As a succession of incompetent or even shady ministers was appointed on the strength of Rasputin's advice, the idea gradually took form, and became widely accepted, that he and 'the German woman' (the Empress, who was by origin a minor German princess) formed the centre of a court clique which was opposed to the war and was even passing secrets to the Germans. Some of the Emperor's closest advisers had indeed in 1914 advised against involvement on the side of Great Britain and France in a war which would 'undermine the monarchical principle'. But there was (and still is) no evidence to support the view that treasonable relations existed with Germany, or even that any serious attempt was being made to conclude a separate peace with her. Nevertheless, the members of the Progressive Bloc and the voluntary organizations co-ordinated by *Zemgor* had little else to unite them in their indecision except a virulent nationalist propaganda combined with insinuations about the patriotism of the monarchy. Liberal politicians, and even some of the Grand Dukes, began to discuss openly the possibility of a palace coup in which the Empress would be exiled or immured in a monastery and Nicholas forced to abdicate. Hints circulated on the possibility of regicide if all should fail.

The most convinced monarchists were not prepared to envisage such steps. But, determined to save the country from the evil which they felt was spreading over it, they settled on Rasputin as the single ulcer poisoning the whole body politic. Prince Yusupov, a wealthy young nobleman, who initiated the conspiracy which was to result in Rasputin's murder, described his feelings thus: 'From childhood

Bust by Naoum Aronson of Rasputin, spiritual healer and debauchee, unkempt peasant and political intriguer — the strange adviser of a doomed imperial court

I had been accustomed to regard the imperial family as special people, not like ourselves. I grew up to hold them in reverence, as higher beings, surrounded by some intangible halo. For that reason, everything that was said and passed around, all the rumours blackening their name, deeply offended me, and I did not want to believe what I heard.

'The war began . . . In spite of the general patriotic uplift inspired by the war, many were pessimistic. An atmosphere of gloom hovered around Tsarskoye Selo. The Emperor and Empress, cut off from the world, isolated from their subjects, and surrounded by Rasputin's clique, decided matters of world-shaking importance. One came to feel dread for Russia's fate.

'. . . There was no hope that the Emperor and Empress would understand the whole truth about Rasputin and dismiss him. What way remained, therefore, to save the Tsar and Russia from that evil genius? Inevitably the thought would run through one's mind: there is only one way — to destroy that criminal "holy man".'

Yusupov found two principal accomplices, Grand Duke Dmitry Pavlovich and Purishkevich, a flamboyant, erratic, and deeply patriotic member of the extreme right, monarchist wing of the Duma. With the help of these two men, Yusupov invited Rasputin to his home on the night of 29th-30th December 1916 and murdered him.

This murder was a futile and macabre melodrama. It solved none of the real problems facing Russia, and only increased the brooding bitterness which divided the imperial couple from almost all the nation. By so demonstratively removing a symptom in the guise of curing a disease, it left the Tsarist autocracy in all its nakedness, an idol no longer capable of attracting devotion, and ready to be deserted by all at the first breath of revolt in March 1917.

Overthrow of the Tsar

After Rasputin's murder discontent with the monarchy gathered rapidly. Although he clung to his imagined authority Nicholas was powerless. Three months later, after a week of strikes and disturbances, and demands for bread, the end of autocracy and of the war, the Tsar was deposed

The murder of Rasputin did nothing to restore the fortunes of the monarchy or increase popular respect for the Tsar. If the removal of her 'friend' lessened the influence of the Tsarina on the nation's affairs, Nicholas showed no inclination to listen to the advice of the more liberal-minded of his ministers; on the contrary, he turned his back on both the government and the Duma and relied on his own imagined authority, exercised primarily through his minister of the interior, Protopopov, who dominated the administration.

Throughout January 1917 the storm of discontent gathered as the war continued to take its toll on the economy. Food shortages and a rapidly rising cost of living resulted in widespread unrest among the industrial workers, particularly in Petrograd and Moscow. There were as many strikes in the first six weeks of 1917 as in the whole of the previous year. But discontent with the monarchy and the conduct of affairs extended far beyond the working-class and the peasantry, into the ranks of the middle class, the progressive deputies to the Duma, the military leaders, and even the Grand Dukes themselves.

In January the Grand Duke Alexander wrote to Nicholas to persuade him to set up a government capable of inspiring confidence in the people. 'The Tsar alone cannot govern a country like Russia', he wrote. Rodzyanko, the chairman of the Duma, warned the Tsar on 20th January that 'very serious outbreaks' were to be expected. Russia wanted a change of government because, he said, 'there is not one honest man left in your entourage; all the decent people have either been dismissed or have left'. But such warnings had no effect on the obstinate and autocratic Tsar. His only reaction to the increasing threat of trouble in the capital was, on 19th February, to place the city under the command of General Khabalov, who was made directly responsible to the Tsar alone for

An enthusiastic welcome to the February Revolution. Soldiers at the front cheer at the news that the days of Tsardom are over. 'Nowhere in the country,' wrote Trotsky later, 'were there any popular groups, parties, institutions, or military units prepared to defend the old regime. Neither at the front nor in the rear was there to be found a brigade or a regiment ready to fight for Nicholas II'

Right: March 1917. Revolutionary newspapers handed out. Centre right: Funeral procession for 'Victims of the Revolution'. But only two hundred people died in the revolution. Bottom right: German cartoon. Tolstoy's ghost asks: 'People of Russia, are you happy now that you are freed? You are not free as long as you are the soldiers of England'

the maintenance of order. The Petrograd garrison was reinforced and equipped with artillery and machine guns. For the first fortnight of February an uneasy peace reigned in the capital; the police and the military appeared to have the situation in hand.

But Rodzyanko knew that the situation was deteriorating, and on 23rd February he told the Tsar he thought a revolution was possible. Nicholas brushed the warning aside and told Rodzyanko that, if the deputies did not watch their words, the Duma would be dissolved. It met, nevertheless, in the Tauride Palace on 27th February, and the government, expecting trouble during the session, stiffened the censorship, arrested all potential troublemakers and braced itself against the popular wrath. Tension in the capital rose. A week later, on 7th March, the Tsar decided to leave Petrograd for the army GHQ in Mogilev.

Next day disorders broke out in the capital which were to lead only a week later to the overthrow of the monarchy. Apparently without any central direction, and initially without any clear political aims, the workers of several large factories in Petrograd came out on strike. Their action was mainly a protest at the breakdown in food supplies, but the nervous reaction of the authorities soon turned industrial and economic unrest into political protest.

Troops were sent immediately to back up the police in the working-class districts of the city, with the result that next day, 9th March, the disturbances spread to the whole city, and protests against the continuation of the war were added to the demand for bread. The central Nevsky Prospect became a mass of marching people, some of whom were now shouting 'Down with the autocracy!'. By the third day, a Saturday, 10th March, a quarter of a million workers were on strike, the city's transport was at a standstill, and the authorities were desperate.

But for Nicholas the situation presented no problem. From the remoteness of Mogilev he cabled Khabalov: 'I order that the disorders in the capital shall be ended tomorrow; they are quite inadmissible at this grave moment of war with Germany and Austria'. But Khabalov, faced with the whole population in revolt, was no longer in a position to carry out his monarch's orders.

It was not that he had scruples about using force to suppress the revolt. The fact was that he could no longer be sure he had the necessary force at his disposal, and that what he had was rapidly slipping out of his control. The normally trustworthy and brutal Cossacks he had sent into action against the crowds had simply

L'Illustration

Novosti

Imperial War Museum

been lost among the demonstrators. The police had started to fire on the crowds, only to incense them still further and make them bolder in their resistance to brutality. The wave of arrests had continued, but the protest movement had no obvious outstanding leaders, and Khabalov could not arrest the whole population.

An affair of the capital

What ultimately decided the outcome of the revolt and the collapse of the regime, however, was the defection of the soldiery to the side of the revolution. It began with isolated cases of 'fraternization' between soldiers and demonstrators on the Sunday of 11th March and then spread like wildfire throughout the Petrograd garrison, so that by the Monday evening the whole force of 150,000 men had disintegrated. And when, in despair, Khabalov formed a special detachment of a thousand picked men and sent them into action, they too disappeared among the crowds. Whole regiments revolted, shot their officers, and threw in their lot with the working people, taking their weapons with them. On the Monday evening the workers seized the arsenal, where they found 40,000 rifles which were quickly distributed round the city.

The government was helpless. A decision to have Khabalov declare a state of siege was rendered ineffective by the fact that the authorities no longer controlled a printing press on which the declaration could be produced. The Duma was equally incapable of taking effective action. When Rodzyanko, its chairman, sent the Tsar a message saying that the fate of both the country and the monarchy was in the balance, and that urgent steps must be taken, Nicholas replied on 11th March with an order dissolving the Duma. Though it feared to defy the Tsar outright, the Duma remained in informal session and on 12th March elected a 'Provisional Committee' of twelve members, including representatives of the Progressive Bloc, with Alexander Kerensky, the Socialist Revolutionary, and Chkheidze, the Social Democrat. The Committee assumed the impossible task of 'restoring order'.

On the same day and in the same place — the Tauride Palace — another new body

Top left: Sentries stand guard over the bodies of men killed during the revolution. Centre left: The burned shell of a police building. The police, instruments of Tsarist repression, represented everything the revolutionaries wanted to destroy. Left: A baker tramples on his old shop sign, 'By appointment to the Tsar'. (Russian postcard, 1917.) Even the petit bourgeois climbed on the band-wagon of revolution

came into existence. It was the Petrograd Soviet (Council) of Workers' and Soldiers' Deputies, representing in a rough and ready way the interests of the rebelling factory workers, soldiers, and 'democratic and socialist parties and groups'. Such real power as could be said to exist in the capital — and in the country as a whole — was now vested in these two *ad hoc* bodies; the central government and the administration of the country had already collapsed. On the morning of Tuesday, 13th March, the Soviet issued a news sheet — *Izvestya* (News) — bearing a proclamation announcing its existence and calling on the people everywhere to take the conduct of affairs into their own hands. 'We shall fight to wipe out the old system completely and to summon a constituent assembly elected on the basis of universal, equal, secret, and direct suffrage.'

Rodzyanko kept the Tsar informed of the disastrous course events had taken, urging him first to institute reforms and then, when the situation worsened, to abdicate in the interests of the monarchy as an institution. Isolated and deprived of friends and supporters, Nicholas made his decision with surprising speed and lack of emotion. He left Mogilev to return to his capital on 13th March, but was diverted by the revolutionaries to Pskov. There, still in his royal train, on 15th March, he signed a document abdicating the throne in favour of his son Alexey and nominating his brother, the Grand Duke Michael, as regent. But before the two delegates from the Duma could reach Pskov Nicholas had changed his mind and finally handed them a document which said: 'We hereby transmit our succession to our brother, the Grand Duke Michael, and give him our blessing for his accession to the throne of the Russian empire'.

But, after some thought, Michael refused, and with that the Russian monarchy was at an end. It had been overthrown by the ordinary people of the capital with extraordinary little loss of life. Total casualties were estimated at less than 1,500, with less than 200 people killed. As Trotsky later pointed out, the revolution was almost exclusively an affair of the capital. 'The rest of the country simply followed its lead. Nowhere in the country were there any popular groups, parties, institutions, or military units prepared to defend the old regime. Neither at the front nor in the rear was there to be found a brigade or a regiment ready to fight for Nicholas II.'

The same day as Nicholas signed his act of abdication a Provisional Government was set up in Petrograd. But it had to share power with the Soviet, and the conflict between the two bodies was to occupy the next eight months of 1917.

Kerensky's Summer

The overthrow of the Tsar brought to power the ill-starred Provisional Government, and eventually Alexander Kerensky as its leader. Why did it fail? Did it deserve its failure?

On 15th March 1917 a large crowd of dishevelled soldiers, enthusiastic intellectuals and students, and glum-looking workers— a typical cross-section of the people who had been demonstrating in the streets of the capital since 8th March—milled around in the large Catherine Hall of the Tauride Palace in Petrograd. They knew that after the prorogation of the Duma by the Tsar on 11th March, a committee of its members had replaced the Tsarist government, which had ceased to exist after failing to control street rioting and the mutiny of a part of the Petrograd garrison.

The leader of the influential liberal Kadets (Constitutional Democrats), and of the parliamentary opposition to the autocratic regime, P.N.Milyukov, addressed the crowd, announcing that a Provisional Government had been set up and giving the names of its members. He was warmly applauded when he said that A.F.Kerensky (the head of the socialist, though non-Marxist, Labour faction of the Duma) had agreed to become minister of justice. Names of other ministers were greeted with surprise and disappointment in the crowd, and Milyukov was asked 'who appointed you?'. He answered that the Government had been appointed 'by the Revolution itself'. The crowd's suspicions were not allayed, and Milyukov was asked what was to become of the dynasty. When he disclosed the plan—which never materialized—to proclaim the infant Alexey Tsar under the regency of his uncle, indignant cries rose from the audience and Milyukov was at pains to point out the necessity of a gradual and orderly transition to a democratic regime. As soon as things were settled, he

Alexander Kerensky (left) takes a salute at a military parade. Kerensky, volatile and flexible, was for six months the dominant figure in Russian politics

said, the people would elect a Constituent Assembly by universal suffrage, and it would decide on the future of Russia. Democratic freedoms would be introduced immediately. This assurance restored the original delirious enthusiasm of the crowd and Milyukov was given an ovation and carried shoulder high from the hall.

Some eight months later, after a turbulent history in which the Provisional Government underwent at least four major reconstructions, only three of its original members remained in office. But the convocation of a Constituent Assembly, to secure a democratic regime for Russia, was still the aim of the government and the polling date was fixed for 28th November.

The footsteps of fate

Yet on 7th November 1917, on the eve of the elections to the Assembly, which could be expected to endorse its policy, the Provisional Government was reduced to a dozen distraught men, huddled in a room of the Winter Palace, with nothing but a group of cadet officers and a women's battalion to defend them from an assault of Red Guards and rebellious sailors led by Bolsheviks. As the approaching steps of the invaders rang through the endless corridors of the Winter Palace, the Provisional Government was asked whether the officer cadets should fight to prevent its falling into the hands of the rebels. The answer was that the Provisional Government would rather yield to force than have blood shed in its defence. And so the ministers were arrested and led off to prison in the Peter and Paul Fortress. The premier, Kerensky, was not among them; a few hours earlier he had left the capital to rally troops to fight the Bolshevik rebellion.

We may well ask what happened in these eight months to reduce the Provisional Government by the beginning of November to this sorry state of isolation and impotence. The Provisional Government was still vested with powers far exceeding those of the last Tsar; it still had under its orders a rudimentary administrative apparatus inherited from the old regime; Kerensky, the prime minister, was supreme commander of all Russian armed forces, at least in name. All political parties, except the monarchists and the Bolsheviks, were in some way represented in the government. And yet the people, whose will and aspirations the Provisional Government claimed to champion, made no move to support it in its hour of trial and Kerensky could not muster the few hundred soldiers needed to suppress the weak and poorly organized Bolshevik rising.

The government which was formed under the wavering and diffident leadership of Prince Lvov in March 1917, combined the highest executive power with full

*Above: The armband worn by the followers of Kornilov. **Right:** German cartoon, July 1917. Nicholas from his prison listens as Lloyd George, President Wilson of the United States, and Ribot, prime minister of France, exclaim: 'We never deal with an autocratic government, never.' Nicholas muses: 'Once these rascals were like brothers to me.' **Below:** Dutch drawing of Nicholas on his way to Siberia, where the Provisional Government sent him and his family in August 1917*

DE ROMANOFFS NAAR SIBERIË

legislative powers; and it soon arrogated to itself the right to interfere with the judiciary. Its claim that it was entitled to act as head of state, replacing the monarch and assuming all his prerogatives, soon brought it into conflict with Finland and other national minorities of the Russian empire.

This concentration of power, the government claimed, was necessary for introducing reforms—such as putting an end to national and religious discrimination—without which no democratic election to the Constituent Assembly was possible. In fact there was more to it than that: the collapse of the monarchy and the promise of every kind of democratic liberty brought about spontaneous changes and threatened a general landslide in the social and legal structures of the country. In order to stem and canalize this revolutionary flood the Provisional Government sought to give a legal form to what were then known as 'the conquests of the Revolution'. But the former revolutionary parties which surfaced from the underground after the Revolution now insisted on 'taking it farther' by destroying every vestige of the 'accursed past' in the shape of state and public institutions, all privileges and prerogatives, and social and army discipline. The popular appeal of these parties, known as the 'revolutionary democracy', was considerable; they dominated the soviets (councils) of workers', soldiers', and peasants' deputies, as well as the trade unions and other rapidly proliferating professional organizations; and they infiltrated the newly formed soldiers' and officers' committees of army units, both at the front and in the rear. Their demands went beyond what the Provisional Government could concede if it was to maintain the fighting capacity of the army and guarantee freedom of decision to the future Constituent Assembly.

It soon became obvious that a certain amount of coercion was necessary to prevent anarchy. For this, however, the Provisional Government lacked both the will and the means of enforcement. The Provisional Government admitted its reluctance to resort to force when, in mid-March, it received the first news of agrarian disorders in the countryside. The government instructed its commissars that force could not be used against looting and rioting peasants: agrarian anarchy was to be prevented by local land committees who were instructed to prepare for the nationalization of land and exhort the peasants to be patient and await the decision of the Constituent Assembly on land reform. Similarly, when told that a mob of soldiers, whose train had been delayed at a station for half an hour, had beaten the stationmaster to death, the Provisional Government ordered the railway authorities to explain to the soldiers that delays were

sometimes necessary to prevent collisions and loss of life to passengers. At the same time, the Provisional Government, though it had forbidden them, acquiesced in the unauthorized arrests of former Tsarist officials and army officers; some of them were kept for months in inhuman conditions in the naval fortress of Kronstadt in defiance of government orders.

Disorder in the army

Even if the government had been willing to use force in order to prevent 'revolutionary democracy' from interfering with its administration, it would have found itself without the proper means of doing so. One of the first actions of the Provisional Government had been to disband the police and gendarmerie—bodies which had been guilty of persecuting revolutionaries in the past. Local authorities were told to organize a 'people's militia' for the maintenance of order; but, lacking experience and training, this militia proved to be unequal to the task. There remained the army, but the Provisional Government was unlucky in its relations with the armed forces right from the beginning. In Petrograd, which had a garrison of just under 200,000, the Provisional Government pledged itself in its first proclamation not to transfer any of the units stationed in the capital. This was done to reassure those soldiers who had rebelled against the Tsar and had even killed some of their officers, and who were, therefore, afraid of possible reprisals if they were sent to the front.

The Provisional Government's control over the army was further weakened by the publication on 15th March of the notorious Order No. I of the Petrograd Soviet. This introduced elected soldiers' committees in all units and boldly stated that orders of the Duma Committee were only to be obeyed when they conformed to the instructions of the Petrograd Soviet. Although addressed only to the troops in the capital, Order No. I soon set the pattern for 'revolutionizing' other garrisons and front-line units. It also put the armed forces in the capital virtually under the command of the Soviet, strengthening it against the Provisional Government.

Nor was the Provisional Government successful in its efforts to control the army in the field or in establishing good working relations with the successive supreme commanders whom it appointed. The 'revolutionary democracy' suspected the army, which had played no part in the February Revolution, of a lukewarm attitude to it, and was bent on 'revolutionizing' the rank and file. These efforts, made on the eve of a general offensive agreed upon with the Allies, met with resistance both from GHQ and from officers at the front. A horde of propagandists from Petrograd and other

revolutionary centres in the rear descended on the troops at the front where they undermined discipline and relations between officers and men.

The first minister of war of the Provisional Government, Guchkov, did nothing to remedy this situation. He himself had fomented discontent and organized sedition against the Tsar before the Revolution, and now, on becoming minister of war, he started a purge of the officers' corps without consideration for the stability so necessary for an army in the field. Dismissed officers crowded GHQ, where they were joined by others who had lost their commands on the insistence of soldiers' committees infiltrated by Bolsheviks. They were resentful and bitter men looking for leadership in order to stop the process of 'deepening' the Revolution.

The Petrograd Soviet had issued at the end of March an appeal to all warring nations to conclude an early peace renouncing any aggressive war aims. The Provisional Government endorsed this in principle, at the same time assuring the Allies, through the minister of foreign affairs, Milyukov, that Russia would stand by its international obligations. Out of this hardly explicit discrepancy a conflict arose between Milyukov and Kerensky—who felt himself the representative of the Soviet attitude—and this led at the beginning of May to open demonstrations, some demanding and some opposing the resignation of the ministers of foreign affairs and war, Milyukov and Guchkov. Units of the Petrograd garrison took part in one of the demonstrations demanding their resignation. General Kornilov, whom the government had appointed commander-in-chief in Petrograd, had not authorized the demonstration and asked the government to support him and stop the Petrograd Soviet interfering with the troops under his command. Having failed to get satisfaction he resigned his post and returned to the army at the front. His departure coincided with the first ministerial crisis of the Provisional Government. Guchkov and Milyukov resigned, less as a concession to popular clamour than as a result of profound dissensions and divided loyalties inside the government itself. Party ties between Kadet and other liberal ministers proved less binding than the allegiance of some of them to the political masonic organization to which they belonged. Milyukov found himself 'betrayed' by his former deputy party chairman, Nekrasov, who like other Russian masons supported Kerensky in his conflict with Milyukov. His and Guchkov's departure opened the way to the entry of socialists into the cabinet and Kerensky emerged as the initiator of the first coalition government, in which he became minister of war. ▷ **698**

An inglorious story of vacillation, betrayal, and misunderstanding

Kerensky decided to instil into the army a new revolutionary spirit and a new faith in the justice of the cause for which it was fighting. The supreme commander, General Alexeyev, was dismissed without further ceremony and replaced by General Brusilov, known for his offensive in 1916 (Vol. 5, p. 577). Kerensky instituted government commissars attached to various headquarters of the army, who would assist officers in all political matters, including contacts with soldiers' committees, and keep the government informed of the state of the army. The main weapon in Kerensky's arsenal was direct contact with the soldiers at army delegates' conferences and meetings of army units. Mesmerizing them by his eloquence, he impressed on his listeners that they had now become the army of a new-born world. With the proclamation of a 'just peace without annexations or indemnities' by the Revolutionary Democracy of Russia the war, he said, had changed its purpose and had obtained a new historical significance. The soldiers had always readily sacrificed their lives under the knout wielded by the tyrannical, autocratic regime. With how much more enthusiasm would they do so now, Kerensky claimed, as free citizens of a liberated Russia which would lead the world towards a new and happier era. Kerensky's exhortations flattered the other ranks who greeted him with ovations. The officers naturally resented being accused of having used cruel methods in the past to force their men to fight for the unworthy cause of the Rasputin clique: but they were willing to put up with anything which might raise the morale of the army.

When, however, the order for the offensive was given on 26th June, Bolshevik propaganda, supported by a fraternization campaign cleverly carried on by the German high command, proved stronger than Kerensky's oratory; soldiers' committees units at company, regiment, or even divisional level discussed battle orders and questioned their commanders' decisions to take the offensive in a war which supposedly had no aggressive aim. After an initial success, mainly due to patriotic volunteer detachments, the offensive collapsed ignominiously through the defection of whole units. The entire 11th Army deserted the front, lynching its officers, disrupting communications, looting, raping, and burning down whole villages. General Kornilov, who had been transferred from Petrograd to the south-western front, demanded that the government should call off the offensive and reintroduce the death penalty at the front as an emergency measure. In this he was supported by the government commissars attached to the units under his command, in particular by Savinkov, a Socialist Revolutionary (like

Kerensky), and a former leading terrorist. In view of the desperate situation the Provisional Government not only met all Kornilov's demands but appointed him supreme commander-in-chief.

The need for a return to sanity in the army was forcefully impressed on the Provisional Government by the Bolshevik attempt to seize power on 16th July, which coincided with the German break-through in Galicia. The Bolsheviks organized a so-called 'spontaneous' peaceful, armed demonstration under the slogan 'All power to the soviets'. The Soviet and the Provisional Government, unable to rely on the capital's garrison, were faced with a rebellion of armed workers organized as Red Guards and Kronstadt sailors who had invaded the capital at the call of the Bolsheviks. The position of the Provisional Government, however, was quickly restored by the arrival of a few reliable troops from the front. But it had been a narrow escape, and the first coalition government never recovered from the shock.

The abortive Bolshevik coup sharpened the internal dissensions in the government between those who, like Prince Lvov and the Kadets, wanted to strengthen the authority of the government and those who, like Kerensky and the representatives of 'revolutionary democracy', sought to increase the government's popularity by initiating further revolutionary changes. On 20th July Prince Lvov and the Kadet ministers resigned, leaving Kerensky with the task of reconstructing the cabinet. After trying unsuccessfully for a whole fortnight to bridge the differences between the liberal and socialist camps, Kerensky himself resigned on 3rd August, leaving the country virtually without leadership. That same night his deputy, Nekrasov, summoned a memorable joint session of the cabinet and the party leaders in the Malachite Hall of the Winter Palace. After a torrent of speeches it was decided to accept and support a cabinet of Kerensky's choice. He was left free to define his programme, and the ministers were to be free of all control by their party committees and the Soviet.

Except for some changes of personnel, of which the departure of the 'defensist' Menshevik, Tsereteli, was the most important, the second coalition government differed little from the first. Premier Kerensky remained minister of war, but appointed Savinkov, the commissar at Kornilov's headquarters, to be his deputy in charge of the ministry. In practice, delicate political questions were dealt with by an unofficial 'inner cabinet', consisting of Kerensky, the minister of foreign affairs, Tereshchenko, and Nekrasov.

Kornilov himself, on accepting his appointment from a shaky and divided government, demanded that there should be no

Mansell

Novosti

Herman Axelbank

Herman Axelbank

Above left: June 1917: Demonstration of soldiers' wives demanding votes for women. *Above right:* Kerensky (centre) at the funeral of cossacks killed in the Petrograd riots, July 1917. They had been recalled from the front to deal with Bolshevik-organized armed workers and sailors. *Below:* Kornilov — determined to restore the fighting capacity of the army

Below: Kerensky. His hesitation won him the mistrust of both the officers' corps and the revolutionaries. *Left:* Delegates from the army in Petrograd. Some, the radicals, have torn the bands off their shoulders to show their scorn for authority. *Right:* July demonstration. The banner says: 'Down with the capitalist ministers. All power to the Soviets'

L'Illustration

The Duma in session before (inset) and after the revolution. The trappings of Tsardom, the portrait and the imperial coat of arms had been removed by April

interference with his choice of commanding officers and claimed that as supreme commander he would be responsible only to his conscience and to the nation as a whole. He then urged the government to take the measures which he claimed were indispensable for restoring order in the country and the fighting capacity of the army. These measures, including the death penalty for sedition in the rear, spelled a curtailment of democratic freedoms – for instance freedom of propaganda, which was one of the 'conquests of the revolution' – which were deemed essential by the soviets for free elections. Kerensky hesitated, in spite of pressure from Savinkov who mediated between him and the supreme commander. Kerensky hoped to overcome the split in public opinion between supporters of Kornilov and those of the soviets at a monster debating rally, the Moscow State Conference, in late August. The conference only showed the chasm, presaging the possibility of civil war.

The Kornilov affair

After the failure of the conference, Kerensky decided, without consulting his cabinet, to approach Kornilov through Savinkov, asking for his loyal co-operation in fighting anarchy. He agreed to meet Kornilov's demands. If the publication of the new laws embodying them caused an outbreak of civil disobedience in Petrograd, it was to be suppressed by troops which Kornilov was to send to the capital and put at the disposal of the Provisional Government. A cavalry army corps was concentrated at the approaches to Petrograd on 9th September. Kerensky had not yet, however, put Kornilov's demands before

the cabinet, despite Savinkov's urging. On 8th September he promised to do so that night, when the cabinet was to meet. Shortly before the meeting was due to start, Vladimir Lvov, a former member of the first two Provisional Government cabinets, an unbalanced, excitable, and totally irresponsible character, came to see Kerensky. Lvov had been acting as a self-appointed go-between posing both to Kerensky and Kornilov as a secret emissary of the other. From Lvov's confused and mendacious statement, Kerensky understood that Kornilov was now demanding the resignation of the government and the surrender of all power to him. The idea of a 'Kornilov ultimatum' henceforth dominated all Kerensky's actions at the helm of his foundering government, and was to be the major theme of everything he wrote during the next fifty years. When the cabinet met the same night, Kerensky denounced Kornilov's 'plot' and ultimatum and asked for a free hand to deal with the insubordination of the supreme commander. The ministers who had been given no information of the preceding developments, agreed, but, horrified by the new ordeal threatening Russia, handed in their resignations. Just before the meeting, Kerensky had been communicating with Kornilov by teleprinter, but failed to ascertain whether what he understood Lvov to have reported was correct: he feigned, however, to be in full agreement with Kornilov and promised to join him at GHQ the next day. Instead, after the cabinet meeting, he sent a curt informal telegram dismissing Kornilov from his post and summoning him to Petrograd. Indignantly Kornilov refused to submit and was backed by the overwhelming majority of his senior officers. The conflict had still not been made public and might have been settled, had not a proclamation of the Provisional Government denouncing Kornilov been released to the press prematurely. Kornilov appealed to the country, calling Kerensky's account a complete lie.

Neither Kornilov nor Kerensky disposed of sufficient forces to escalate their exchange of insults into a real trial of strength. The troops sent by Kornilov to Petrograd believed that they were going to support the Provisional Government and were shocked by the announcement of Kornilov's alleged mutiny: they refused to obey marching orders and broke up in confusion. Kerensky was not effectively in control of the capital's garrison; this and the Kronstadt sailors' detachments, ostensibly under the orders of the Soviet, were in fact controlled by the Bolsheviks.

The Kornilov affair petered out ingloriously. Kornilov called the whole thing off and allowed himself to be put under arrest. Kerensky appointed himself supreme com-

mander. A committee of lawyers set up to investigate the alleged mutiny was appalled by the double-crossing and the lack of dignity on all sides, but was unable to complete its work before the collapse of the Provisional Government.

Kerensky is right in referring to the Kornilov affair as the 'prelude to Bolshevism'. But the return of the Bolsheviks to active politics and their final victory in November were made possible not by Kornilov's pressure on the Provisional Government to strengthen its authority, nor by his military measures to back up that pressure, nor even by his angry gesture of insubordination on being suddenly without warning denounced as a mutineer. These actions of Kornilov, who was widely supported by public opinion outside Soviet circles – even by socialists, such as Plekhanov and Argunov – were all brought about by the indecision and procrastination of Kerensky and his closest friends in the cabinet. While conceding in secret negotiations the urgency of the measures demanded by Kornilov, Kerensky seems never to have wanted to implement them and was relieved when he could interpret V.Lvov's incoherent innuendoes as an insolent and arrogant ultimatum by Kornilov, which released him from the promise he had just made to Savinkov to comply with the supreme commander's demands. Kerensky has only himself to blame that both his contemporaries and historians have shown so little sympathy with his behaviour at that critical moment. For after it he was considered by the officers' corps and the Kadets as one who had provoked Kornilov to rise in open rebellion and by the 'revolutionary democracy' as one who had had secret dealings with counter-revolutionary conspirators. Not even the ties binding Nekrasov, Kerensky, and Tereshchenko survived the Kornilov episode, and Nekrasov had to leave the government.

Kerensky's assumption of the highest functions of the state could not restore his popularity nor strengthen his authority. His attempt at establishing a kind of pre-parliament, from appointed representatives of various party and public organizations, led to a final humiliation: when Kerensky demanded full powers from the pre-parliament to deal with the incipient Bolshevik rising, he was rebuffed and told by the representatives of 'revolutionary democracy' that the Bolsheviks could best be fought by the acceptance of a government programme of immediate revolutionary reforms – reforms of a kind which were supposed to be decided by the future Constituent Assembly. Two days after his defeat in the pre-parliament, Kerensky was in flight from the Bolsheviks and the members of his government were incarcerated in the Peter and Paul Fortress.